SAMUEL SMITH AND
THE POLITICS OF BUSINESS:
1752–1839

General Samuel Smith
painting by Rembrandt Peale, 1817

Samuel Smith and the Politics of Business: 1752–1839

John S. Pancake

The University of Alabama Press
University, Alabama

for Frances

6|17|82

087038

Preface

T HIS STUDY was originally inspired by the requirement for the
Ph. D. degree at the University of Virginia. It was continued intermit-
tently because Samuel Smith became a good friend, and one likes
to keep in touch. It was completed because no one else seemed inclined
to correct the misjudgments of the man and his motives. I suspect
that these misjudgments were partly due to the fact that while many
writers pointedly corrected Henry Adams's acidulous pronounce-
ments on Jefferson, Madison, and other major figures, they have
tended to accept uncritically his treatment of Samuel Smith.

A writer of biography sometimes is tempted to look about for
a villain to be the foil for his hero (and also to account for his failures).
Samuel Smith and his brother, Robert, have been cast as the "heavies"
long enough and it is time that they be allowed to play it straight.
I do not claim top billing for the General, and I have tried to avoid,
perhaps unsuccessfully, recasting anyone as a villain.

It is worth noting, in passing, that in the early republic men
had a kind of code of behavior that enabled them to engage in mortal
combat in political matters and still retain a certain civility toward
each other. Walter Lippman has recently written that "the American
Constitutional system. . . . assumes an unwritten code of good manners. . . . The central principle of that code is that political opponents
will never regard one another as enemies, that no differences will
be pressed until they are unreconcilable." Biographers, take note.

As with all historians, I am much in debt to others. Henry Adams
was the first historian to use the Samuel Smith papers extensively—and
almost the only one until the middle of the twentieth century. Frank
Cassell wrote a dissertation in 1968 on Samuel Smith's political career
which was very helpful, particularly in his exhaustive investigation

of manuscript collections. He has recently published *Merchant Congressman in the New Republic: Samuel Smith of Baltimore, 1752–1839,* (Madison, Wisc. 1971). The biographies of Dumas Malone, Merrill Peterson, and Irving Brant contributed many insights. The volumes by Bradford Perkins on Anglo-American relations are essential to an understanding of the background of the War of 1812.

Of the many people who contributed their time and talent only a few can be named: Bernard Mayo, Thomas Govan, and Edward Younger, who were "present at the creation." Joseph Hobson Harrison at Auburn University who read the final draft of the manuscript; John Cross and Larry Sutley, students—in the very best sense of the word—who performed all sorts of tasks, both scholarly and menial; the people at the Library of Congress, Alderman Library at the University of Virginia, the Washington and Lee Library, the Amelia Gayle Gorgas Library at the University of Alabama, the Ralph Draughon Library at Auburn University, and the staff of the Maryland Historical Society.

I wish to thank the University of Alabama Research Committee for its generous assistance.

Despite all this help I am sure that there are many mistakes and errors of judgment, and for these I assume unlimited liability.

Tuscaloosa, Alabama   JOHN PANCAKE
March, 1972

Contents

Baltimore in 1752

1

Young Man and Young Town

H IS NAME WAS SAMUEL SMITH and he was twenty years old. He stood on an Italian beach watching a December storm sweep out of the Adriatic and batter to pieces what was left of the brig *Carlisle*, 6000 miles out of Baltimore. The blundering of a native pilot had put the ship on a reef outside the harbor of Venice, and only the skill of her Captain Howard had prevented her from sinking. So the wreck itself was not the fault of young Samuel Smith. But the *Carlisle* flew the blue and white ensign of his father's firm of Smith and Buchanan, and John Smith had given his son his first independent assignment as the ship's supercargo.[1] As such he was responsible for the business management of the ship, and it was his decision to charter this voyage which had brought her to the scene of her disaster. This decision had been made, moreover, against the implied wishes of his father. It was not an auspicious beginning for a young merchant's career.

The voyage seemed to have gone badly from the beginning. The *Carlisle* had left Baltimore in the late spring of 1772 bound for Le Havre. After disposing of part of her cargo in the French port, the ship had proceeded to London. But sagging prices caused by a good wheat crop in England forced Smith to dispose of the remainder of her consignment at a loss.

Colonials like young Sam Smith, only two generations removed from the mother country, considered themselves Englishmen, but he found England strange to his American eyes. He could not get used to the casual Englishmen who refused to do business until ten o'clock in the morning, "and when they do see you, send you to a factor who in turn sends you to a banker." The young fellow may have been the recipient of some of that contempt which most Englishmen had for Americans.² Desertions began to plague the ship, and Sam took the new hands' clothes away from them until the ship put to sea. One of his slaves escaped, and he had trouble with the captain and the mate "quarreling over a barrel of beer." Yet he went about the business of seeking consignments with a mixture of stubbornness and aplomb which gave evidence of considerable maturity. He finally obtained a charter for the *Carlisle* with the Bristol firm of Mildred and Roberts to carry a cargo of lead to Venice.

John Smith had intended that his son should serve an apprenticeship in the office of one of his agents in England. But Sam had other ideas. Safe in the knowledge that mails containing possible parental disapproval would be months crossing the Atlantic, he remained aboard the *Carlisle* as supercargo.³ The opportunity to see the world was too good to miss and the opportunity for a European tour was infinitely more attractive than a clerk's stool. In the early fall of 1772, the *Carlisle* cleared Bristol for the Mediterranean; by mid-December, Sam Smith had a disaster on his hands in more ways than one. The storm which destroyed his ship also ended any hope of salvaging more than a fraction of her cargo. The fates had not dealt kindly with him, but he was to learn in the long career before him that, in the world of ships and shipping, a fair voyage seemed often the exception rather than the rule.

He paid off the crew and arranged for their passage back to England, but he refused to be discouraged by his misfortunes. Or perhaps it was the fascination of Christmas in Italy which led him to write his father that he "was obliged" to stay in Venice to dispose of the salvaged cargo and settle the details connected with the shipwreck. It took him more than a month.

If England was strange to young Sam, Venice was a broad education. "Honesty is entirely banished; the son will if possible cheat the father, and the father will tell you that the son is not to be trusted; women until they are married are coy and have little liberty; afterward they take every liberty and their husbands think nothing of it."⁴ The disappointing failure of his mission could not dampen his fascination with the wonders of the Old World. Beneath the sober, businesslike tones of his reports to his father was the keen pleasure the young man found in the holiday season. The stay in Venice only whetted his appetite and he decided on a tour of southern Europe.

After a few days' sojourn in Ancona, he went to Rome. A month, and another festival in the city of the Ceasars; then he continued to Leghorn, Genoa, and Marseilles. There followed a swing southward which included Barcelona, Gibraltar, Cadiz, and Lisbon. He finally reached London on December 20, 1773. Despite his having acted without his father's approval, Sam devoted much of his time to business. At each port he dispatched a letter home containing a careful description of harbor facilities, commercial firms, exports, and the wants of the inhabitants which could be supplied by his father's firm. He made a point of visiting the merchants of each port and establishing personal contact as a representative of Smith and Buchanan.[5] This fund of information not only laid the ground for his career as a merchant but gave him expert experience and knowledge that were to serve him well in his later role as a statesman.

When Sam opened his mail back in London, he found to his surprise that his industry and energy had earned him his father's approbation instead of the expected parental wrath. John Smith was proud of his son. He realized that not many young men could take off on a tour that covered half of Europe and a year-and-a-half's time and still pay attention to business. His highly commendatory letter informed the young man that he was to be a partner in the company on his return to America.[6]

Sam remained in London for nine months as the representative of Smith and Buchanan. By the end of the summer of 1774, he was ready to return to America. Whether it was the growing tension between England and her colonies or whether John Smith considered his son's apprenticeship to be at an end, the lad who had boarded the *Carlisle* as supercargo two years before returned as a partner in his father's firm in September, 1774. He was twenty-two years old, a slender, muscular young man of medium height. Blue eyes peered from beneath rather heavy brows, and a long, straight nose with slightly flaring nostrils surmounted a wide, mobile mouth and a solid chin. He was, in the eighteenth century word, a fine figure of a man.[7]

Sam's ancestry went back to an English family of considerable wealth who had moved to Ireland. The first Samuel Smith, however, was not possessed of business talent, nor was he inclined to take valuable time from "The Four Bottle Club" of Dublin for the drab business of managing his estate. He thought to solve this problem by taking in another man as his partner, the latter to manage the accounts while Sam enjoyed the proceeds in the company of congenial companions and the excitement of the gaming tables. His confidence in his partner received a rude jolt when the latter disappeared with a large portion of the estate. It was the best thing that could have happened to Samuel Smith. He collected the small portion of his wealth that remained and, leaving his wife and seven-year-old son John in Ireland, set out for the New World in 1729. He obtained permission from the proprietors of the colony of Pennsylvania to buy land in Lancaster County and then sent for his family.

Samuel Smith's enthusiasm and high spirits may have been responsible for his lack of success in the Old World, but he was made to order for the New. As a frontier fighter and a successful landholder, he soon became socially and politically prominent. Sam had the exact temperament for a country squire. Years later his grandson and namesake said of him: "More fond of gay company and Bottle Companions (the fashion of the day) than prudence justified . . . yet he was by no means an intemperate man." The failings which brought misfortune in Ireland he used to advantage in this new country. He was elected High Sheriff of Lancaster County in 1735 and soon proved his ability as a peace officer. Two years later he was elected a member of the Pennsylvania Assembly and held the office of justice of Lancaster County from 1740 until 1750. In that year he moved to Carlisle with his son John, who was married by this time, and there the two established a trading post. John's son, Samuel, named for his grandfather, was born in Carlisle in 1752, the eldest of eleven children.[8]

John Smith realized that, however successful he might be in his father's trading post, the big profits must lie at the seacoast. Philadelphia was the commercial center of the Middle Colonies, but recently the traders had been taking a shorter route from the west to the sea. The terminal point was the hamlet of Baltimore on the Chesapeake Bay. It consisted of eighteen buildings in the vicinity of Jones' Falls, north and east of where the city now stands. The first seagoing vessel had anchored in its harbor in 1750. Nine years later, John Smith moved to Baltimore. With his brother-in-law, William Buchanan, he formed a partnership and soon had a thousand-foot wharf extending out to the ship channel, the first in Baltimore and the only one the town had until 1782. The firm became the most prosperous in the early history of the city, and the white pennant with the blue "S" and "B" became a familiar sight in the ports of Europe and the Americas.[9]

The town grew and trade grew with it. Immigrants from England and Ireland swelled the population along with people from the frontier who found Baltimore more to their taste than the dangers from the French and Indians in western Pennsylvania, particularly after Braddock's defeat.[10] While Annapolis remained the chief tobacco port, Baltimore was developing as an outlet for wheat, flour, and lumber. Before the end of the century, it was to become the chief port for the rich Monocacy Valley and the agricultural region to the west.

An important factor in the development of the wheat trade was the increased demand in Europe for the sugar and molasses of the West Indies. To meet this demand, the West Indian planters brought in increasing numbers of slaves and so needed larger imports of food. Baltimore found there a ready market for flour and for barrel staves.[11]

Sam Smith was destined by inheritance and nature to be a merchant, and the counting house was his real school. To provide for a more formal education his family sent him to an academy at Little Elks and then, for two years, to a school in nearby Newark. He then returned to the recently established school in Baltimore, where he remained until he was fourteen. By that time he had acquired a fair knowledge of the Latin and Greek classics and little else, since the frequent changes had made his education sketchy—something he complained about in later years. After finishing his schooling, Sam joined his father's firm as a clerk.[12]

These were troublesome times and already the quarrel between the colonists and the mother country which was to end in revolution had broken out. Neither John Smith nor his partner took any part in the first disturbances, which came as a result of the restrictive commercial policy of George Grenville. The Acts of 1764, which tightened the existing Navigation Acts and levied additional duties on imports, had little effect upon the colony of Maryland or the port of Baltimore. Production and export were not greatly influenced since the acts were designed largely to prevent illicit trade in the Northern colonies. The Sugar Act, although it checked the West Indian trade, created little distress and occasioned almost no complaint.

The Stamp Act of 1765, which levied a tax on all legal documents, printed matter, and commercial bills, was more serious. It came at a time of general slump when prices of wheat and tobacco were low. The "Sons of Liberty" made their appearance in Baltimore in 1766 and acts of open violence swept the western counties. The firm of Smith and Buchanan, while it did not participate in any of the demonstrations, supported the brief non-importation agreement which existed until the Stamp Act was repealed. With its abolition, trade began to take a turn for the better. Wheat and tobacco prices rose and a profitable market for flour and lumber was found in Spain, Ireland, and Portugal.[13]

The next trade recession came as a direct result of the efforts of the Maryland "Association." In 1768 this organization instituted and enforced non-intercourse with England in retaliation against the taxation embodied in the Townshend Acts passed by Parliament. It seems probable that John Smith and his brother-in-law supported this organization at the outset, for it was launched in the name of all the inhabitants of Maryland as represented in the House of Delegates. But by 1770 non-intercourse, built as it was on the fragile base of public opinion, began to crack. The decisive external event for Baltimore was the abandonment of non-intercourse in Philadelphia. John Smith and William Buchanan were among the Baltimore merchants who petitioned for a convention to repeal the resolutions. The vote in the rest of Maryland for continuance did not change their minds. Baltimore began to trade, and the agreement that had outlived its economic if not its political usefulness broke down.[14]

It was after Sam had left America for his European journey that trouble between the colonies and the mother country began to revive. During his stay in England, young Smith was undoubtedly aware of the rising tension, but his correspondence with his father has virtually nothing to say on the subject. This was undoubtedly because his letters dealt with the business affairs of the company and as such were probably perused by his English business associates. A discussion of American grievances would have been embarrassing to all concerned. In Maryland, John Smith did not hesitate to declare the direction in which his feelings lay. The seriousness of the quarrel became apparent early in 1774 when Parliament, in retaliation against the Boston Tea Party, passed the Boston Port Bill closing the city's trade. Such action was especially alarming to American merchants. The remaining Intolerable Acts added fuel to the flames.

The day that Sam Smith disembarked in Baltimore, September 5, 1774, was the day that the First Continental Congress met in Philadelphia to decide upon measures to be taken against England. The result was the passage of non-importation, non-exportation, and non-consumption resolutions, and the establishment of the Continental Association to enforce them.[15] John Smith and his partner were signers of the Maryland Articles of Association and both were appointed to the committee of observation for Baltimore. The elder Smith also served on the Baltimore Committee of Correspondence, and he later was a member of the state convention which drew up Maryland's first constitution.[16] In October, 1774, Maryland patriots registered their protest to the Tea Act by burning the *Peggy Stewart* and her cargo of East India Company tea at Annapolis. Curtailment of shipping to England led to increased trade with the Spanish and French West Indies, all the more desirable because the routes were shorter and more profitable now that the war clouds were gathering. Goods imported by Smith and Buchanan now showed significant increases in gunlocks, saltpeter, drugs, and sulphur.[17]

As the tension between England and the colonies increased, Sam Smith joined with other young men in Baltimore in organizing the Baltimore Independent Cadets under command of Captain Mordecai Gist. There were sixty-one men in the company and they made a handsome sight in their uniforms of blue turned with buff and their black half-boots. Sam continued to work in his father's firm; for William Buchanan had retired, and Sam and his brother John were now full partners in the reorganized company of John Smith and Sons.[18]

In April, 1775, the guns of Lexington and Concord signaled the outbreak of hostilities. Sam Smith did not join the first wild rush of young hellions who followed the Indian fighter Michael Cresap to Boston in the spring of 1775. Being an orderly businessman, he waited to go when Maryland went. But the slack in business occasioned by increasing pressure from the British blockade and the stoppage of mails gave him more time to devote to the Independent Cadets. His diligence in assisting Captain Gist in the training of the company earned him a promotion to sergeant, then to company adjutant. In January, 1776, the company was incorporated into the regular Continental Army and attached to Colonel William Smallwood's regiment, later to become renowned as the famous First Maryland. Two additional companies were added to the Baltimore area; Gist received command of these troops and was promoted to Major. Sam was awarded the rank of Captain vacated by Gist.[19]

Captain Smith received his first orders to active duty in April, 1776. The Baltimore Council of Safety ordered him, with a detachment of ten men, to Annapolis to capture the royal governor, Robert Eden, who was suspected of giving military aid to the British. Sam arrived at the capital and reported to the State Council before proceeding with his mission. That august body, impatient at the show of initiative on the part of the subordinate organization, sent Captain Smith and his men back to Baltimore. Shortly afterward, Smith, Major Gist, and Samuel Purviance, head of the Baltimore committee, were summoned to Annapolis to answer charges of undue assumption of authority. Purviance was sharply reprimanded but the two officers were excused since they were acting under orders. The governor's departure went unmolested. It was Sam's first encounter with "chain of command" and the delicate situations which could arise from it.[20]

Six weeks later, Sam Smith marched with Smallwood's Marylanders when they were ordered to join the American army in New York. The town turned out to watch them go and, no doubt, the eyes of at least one young lady, "the beautiful and imperious" Miss Margaret Spear, followed the erect figure of Captain Smith. Whether or not she and the young captain had reached what was then called "an understanding," she was to play an important part in Sam Smith's military career. Already the men of the company were developing the martial air which caused Lt. Alexander Graydon to remark a year later: "There was none by whom an unofficer-like appearance and deportment could be less tolerated than by a city-bred Marylander, who at this time, was distinguished by the most fashionably cut coat, the most *macaroni* cocked hat, and the hottest blood in the union. . . ."[21]

2

The Hero of Fort Mifflin

WHEN THE FIRST MARYLAND REGIMENT joined the American army, it was attempting to block the advance of the British army on New York City. To cope with the tactics of the enemy, George Washington, the American commander in chief, occupied Long Island. General Howe, having taken Staten Island, landed his forces on Long Island and advanced on the American army with the intention of trapping it between his troops and a British naval force which would move up the East River to cut off any attempt by the Americans to retreat. Outnumbered nearly two to one, Washington established a defense perimeter in a strong position occupying Brooklyn Heights, with his right flank on Gowanus Bay. When Smallwood's Maryland troops reached New York late in August, 1776, they were assigned to this flank with two regiments of Delaware and Pennsylvania troops, all under the command of William Alexander, self-styled Lord Stirling.

The American left, commanded by General John Sullivan, was unprotected by any works and therefore less defensible than other parts of the American line. Nor had Sullivan made proper provision for scouting and reconnaissance. Howe took full advantage of this tactical defect. On August 27, while engaging the strongly fortified center and right with a token force, Howe himself led a flanking movement against the American left, which was taken completely by surprise. The British had no difficulty in rolling the American flank back upon the center.

Smith was with his company in line on the American right when the news of the collapse of the American left wing was received. A retreat was ordered and the right wing was withdrawing when the British appeared on the left. Smith wheeled his company to face the enemy and Lord Stirling promptly ordered the Maryland regiment to counterattack. He perceived that, unless a diversion was made, the main American army could not escape destruction. Sam Smith was one of the four hundred Marylanders who advanced against a force five times their number. Despite their inexperience, the regiment advanced with such determination that the British were almost driven from their position. Though men were dropping on all sides, Sam was miraculously untouched. The little force was finally overwhelmed by superior numbers and Lord Stirling was captured. Sam extricated the remnants of his company and began to withdraw northward toward a new position which the American army had established under cover of the Maryland charge. The regiment left 250 casualties on the field.[1]

Between the American lines and Smith's little force lay Gowanus Marsh, a tangle of mud and undergrowth into which Smith led his men. His progress was checked when he came upon a creek which was too deep to ford. He and his sergeant swam the creek, collected logs and planks, and ferried those who could not swim to the other side. Smith finally found his regiment in a redoubt on the right of the American line, which had been set up at Fort Putnam near the East River. Smith was ordered to take up a position as outpost to this redoubt. The army remained inactive for two days, the British having delayed in following up their victory. Only a northeast wind prevented the British fleet from moving up the East River and blocking the army's escape.

On the night of the 29th, one of Captain Smith's outposts reported that the vicinity immediately in front and to the left of his position was empty of both British and American forces. A scouting party soon confirmed the fact that the American army had evacuated its position. Thinking that he had been left with a token force to cover the retreat, Smith withdrew his company to the main redoubt. He barely reached the spot when Colonel Ware, battalion commander in the Maryland regiment, appeared and informed him that the rest of the regiment was in New York and that he was to proceed to the embarkation point at Fulton's Ferry at once. General Washington, by commandeering every boat, scow, and canoe in the vicinity, had slipped his army across the East River under cover of darkness and bad weather. Smith and his men were the last to embark with the commander in chief and his staff. They barely escaped a troop of British cavalry that arrived soon after they pulled away from the Long Island shore.[2]

Smith rejoined Smallwood's regiment in Manhattan. As Washington began his retreat from the city, he placed the Maryland troops in the rearguard. A mix-up of orders prevented the regiment from participating in the battle of Harlem Heights, but Smith saw action at the battle of White Plains in mid-October. Again he was so busily engaged that he failed to receive the order to retreat until almost too late. Although slightly wounded, he managed to extricate himself and his command after it had given a good account of itself.[3]

By this time Smallwood's regiment was badly battered. Nearly five hundred strong when it joined the army, it had lost 250 men at the battle of Long Island, and sickness, desertions, and casualties in the action around New York had taken 150 more. Replacements brought its strength up to about 250 men. There was no time for the regiment to pause and catch its breath, for the loss of Forts Lee and Washington, guarding the Hudson River, compelled the American commander to cross over into New Jersey and late in the fall he began to retreat southward. For the trusted but difficult rearguard post Washington again chose the Maryland troops. Smith and his men were in constant contact with the pursuing enemy. Day after day they retreated, stood and fought, and retreated again. The strain of constant skirmishing told heavily. Gist, promoted to colonel, was now acting as commander of the regiment, since Colonel Smallwood had been wounded at White Plains. Accompanied by Captain Smith and Captain Stone, he called on Washington and requested that the regiment be relieved of rearguard duty for a time. The commander in chief met the request with a refusal that was both tactful and kind: "I can assign no other regiment in which I can place the same confidence and I request that you will say so to your gallant men."[4]

The dreary retreat continued through the cold December rains over roads deep in mud. Lack of proper clothing, sickness, and desertions reduced the army from 11,000 to 3,000 men. At midnight on the ninth of December, 1776, Smallwood's skeleton "regiment" of 190 men reached Trenton to find only Washington and his staff on the New Jersey side of the Delaware River. Again Smith crossed in the wake of the retreat and, with the rest of the American army, went into winter quarters.

Sam Smith must have been discouraged at the pitiful aspect which Washington's little army presented. Ragged, beaten, and discouraged, the men who propped the falling cause that black winter of 1776–77 had to call up the full measure of their courage to fight down the despair they must have felt. For Smith, at least, there was some satisfaction in being promoted to major early in December, and shortly afterward he was assigned to Baltimore for recruiting duty. Thus he missed the Trenton campaign, the one bright spot in that otherwise disheartening winter. There was a promotion to lieutenant colonel awaiting him when he rejoined his regiment, which had been assigned to General Sullivan's division in February, 1777, at Morristown, New Jersey.[5] Here he remained with the American army through the spring and early summer while the American commander in chief awaited the movements of the British.

Howe renewed his activities in the middle of July when he embarked his troops in the transports of his fleet. Washington remained uncertain of his intentions until August 21, when Howe disembarked at the head of the Chesapeake and it became clear that Philadelphia was his objective. Washington moved south to intercept the enemy. Winter recruiting had brought his force to a respectable 11,000 men and he paraded part of it through the capital to boost the morale of its inhabitants. Sam Smith had cause to be proud of his men that day; for, as one historian has observed, "The best clothed men were the Virginians and the smartest looking troops were Smallwood's Marylanders."[6]

Washington placed his army across Howe's route at Chad's Ford on Brandywine Creek. Colonel Smith was with Sullivan's division, which made up the right wing of the American army. Howe repeated his Long Island tactics of engaging the center while moving a flanking force against Sullivan. Washington perceived the plan and prepared to cross the creek and smash the British center. But the incompetent Sullivan sent false information to Washington, informing him that no flanking movement was developing. Washington changed his plan and was therefore unprepared when the attack burst against Sullivan and threw him into disorderly retreat.[7]

Colonel Smith and his men were formed in a valley somewhat separated from the scene of Sullivan's disaster. In the disorder and confusion which followed, he received no word of the general retreat. He soon found that he and about thirty of his men had been by-passed by the British advance and were cut off from the main army. He retreated with his little force to the top of a nearby hill, checking several attempts by British detachments to surround him. As he withdrew, he collected the stragglers from the various disorganized units and by the time he reached the hill he had assembled a force of about a thousand men. Here he found that General Stirling had organized part of Sullivan's shattered command. They held the hill against enemy attack until General Greene came up in support. Darkness finally ended the battle, with the American army defeated but still intact. Washington retreated to Chester, and Howe was left free to advance on Philadelphia.[8]

On September 8, 1777, the British Army entered the capital. But Washington did not intend to let Howe occupy Philadelphia unmolested. As with all great generals, his reaction to the disaster on the Brandywine was to cast about for the means of delivering a counter-stroke. He realized that Howe's position was untenable unless he could get supplies overland from New York or up the Delaware river. Washington therefore moved his army north of the city blocking the way to New York and made plans for closing river to the British fleet. If he could hit the British hard before their supply line was cleared, Howe's tenancy of the capital might be very uncomfortable indeed.

The key to the river defense was Fort Mifflin, and for the command of this post Washington chose a Polish immigrant officer, Baron d'Arendt, recently commissioned a colonel in the American army.[9] Since the baron was ill and it was necessary to occupy Fort Mifflin at once, Washington gave the immediate command to the young colonel of his crack Maryland troops, Samuel Smith, who had earned a promotion from major to lieutenant colonel in less than two months. Smith received his orders from the commander in chief detaching him from his regiment on September 23. His instructions were detailed and explicit:

> You will proceed with the detachment under your command to Dunk's ferry on the Delaware, if you find in your progress the way clear and safe. When arrived there you will take the safest and most expeditious method of conducting the detachment to Fort Mifflin. . . . you will also take every necessary precaution to prevent the enemy from surprising you on the march, by keeping out small van, flank and rear guards and sentries when you halt.
>
> The keeping of the fort is of very great importance, and I rely strongly on your prudence, spirit and bravery for a vigorous and persevering defense. The Baron Arendt will be appointed to the chief command; when he arrives you will give him every aid. . . .[10]

Colonel Smith arrived at Fort Mifflin on September 27. He had under his command a force of 200 men under Major Robert Ballard of the First Virginia Regiment and Major Simeon Thayer of the 2nd Rhode Island. Captain Samuel Treat was his artillery officer and he later received assistance from Major Louis Fleury, a French marquis who was serving as an engineer, and whom Washington recommended very highly.[11]

The fort which Smith had to defend lay on the lower end of Mud Island. This island was little more than what its name implied—a bar of mud and silt thrown up by the converging currents of the Delaware and Schuylkill rivers which joined about three miles below

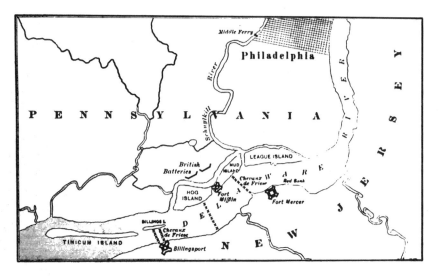

River Defenses of Philadelphia

Philadelphia. Fort Mifflin was thus located in the throat of a Y whose upper arms were the two rivers and whose tail was the Delaware proper. The Pennsylvania militia had already done much to help the blockade. They had placed two lines of *chevaux-de-frise* in the channel of the river, one at Fort Mifflin and the other about three miles farther down the river at Billingsport. These *chevaux-de-frise* were constructed of heavy wooden logs set in the river bed and projecting upward to the surface at a forty-five degree angle. Their upper ends were sharpened and iron-shod, and were capable of piercing the wooden side of any vessel which rammed them.

The lower row of *chevaux-de-frise* at Billingsport was protected by a fort on the New Jersey side garrisoned by militia. The upper row blocked the main channel of the river on the eastern side of Mud Island and was covered by Fort Mifflin on the Pennsylvania side and Fort Mercer on the Jersey mainland, the latter commanded by Colonel Green of Rhode Island. The river to the west of Fort Mifflin was too shallow for navigation.

Key to the defense of Fort Mifflin was Province Island, which lay west of the Fort on the Pennsylvania shore. It was called an island only because a shallow backwater slough passed around it from the river. Its flat, marshy expanse was virtually part of the Pennsylvania shore and on it were located two dry hummocks. If the enemy could establish a battery there, the works of Fort Mifflin would be enfiladed.[12]

As long as the forts protecting the *chevaux-de-frise* held out, their artillery fire would discourage any effort on the part of the British to remove the obstructions from the river or to move their ships up to Philadelphia.

Smith found Fort Mifflin occupied by forty militiamen whom he immediately detached as unfit for duty. He was also obliged to send thirty of his own men with them because sickness and exhaustion had made them useless.[13] The fort itself was badly constructed and totally inadequate for the task at hand. Deficiencies of food, clothing, blankets, and ammunition, and, most of all, lack of experienced artillerists to man the guns made the outlook discouraging.

The fort was walled with freestone masonry on the Jersey side and by pine stockades on the west. The main works of the fort faced downstream to guard against ships moving upriver. The upstream approach was protected by a ditch and three wooden blockhouses mounting French eighteen-pounders. An open platform mounting two eighteen-pounders and one thirty-two bore on Province Island to the west.[14]

The day following Smith's arrival he received a visit from Commodore John Hazelwood, who commanded the naval forces of the state of Pennsylvania in the river. This force consisted of several row galleys mounting heavy guns, two floating batteries, some fire ships, and two small frigates. Although under the nominal authority of the state, this force had promised Washington its full cooperation. Colonel Smith and the commodore went on a tour of inspection covering Mud and Province Islands. Smith recognized the importance of the two dry hummocks on Province Island some 500 yards from Fort Mifflin. He suggested to the commodore that steps be taken to neutralize the position but the commodore assured him, "A mosquito could not live there under the fire of my guns." With this assurance Smith set about making the fort suitable for defense. He wrote to Washington of his supply shortages and of his pressing need for trained artillerists. Washington immediately dispatched what supplies he could and two artillery sergeants. Smith selected sixty of his best men and set the sergeants and Captain Treat to training them to serve the guns.

His next step was to strengthen the works themselves. He had earthworks made of pine logs and dirt erected between each battery to prevent the guns from being enfiladed by possible fire from Province Island. He also had built a number of earth and log revetments in which the men could take shelter during heavy bombardments. Finally, he erected a blockhouse to the northwest of the main fort and established a small battery to strengthen the defense against Province Island.[15]

While Smith was thus strengthening his defenses, setbacks to supporting forces were making the situation worse. The American flotilla above the island made an attack on shore installations begun by the British below Philadelphia. One of the two American frigates, using the flood tide to move inshore for bombardment, went aground when her commander failed to get her back to deep water on the ebb. The vessel was forced to surrender, and so one of the two large American naval units on the river was lost. Hard on the heels of this disaster came another. The Pennsylvania militia garrisoned the fort guarding the lower line of *cheveaux-de-frise* at Billingsport. Lord Howe on October 4 sent a slightly superior force against it. When the militia saw the British approaching, they spiked their guns and abandoned the fort without a shot. No delaying action could now be counted on below Fort Mifflin itself.

On this same day Washington struck at the British in Philadelphia. Advancing into the city from the north, separate American columns surprised British outposts in Germantown and briefly drove the enemy. But the plan for a coordinated attack fell apart in the midst of foggy weather and confusion among Washington's lieutenants, and the attack failed. Yet the aggressive commander in chief urged Smith to maintain the river blockade in the hope that a new opportunity would present itself.[16]

Conditions on the island were deplorable. Ammunition and clothing were scarce. Every day men were coming down with malaria and twenty more had to be evacuated because of the disease. There was no more time for preparation. The British began their attack.

The enemy established a battery on Province Island in the first week in October. Despite his previous assurances, Commodore Hazelwood made no attempt to hinder the British. Timidity seems to be the only reason for the commodore's inaction for the ground around the enemy position was boggy and they would not have been able to establish supporting batteries. Smith realized that his whole position was threatened by the presence of the battery and he acted promptly.[17]

He managed to secure a few gunboats from the unwilling commodore. On October 10 he ordered an assault by the gunboats on the right or upstream side of the British position. He kept the center under the fire of the thirty-two pounder and its smaller supporting guns while Major Ballard with a force of one hundred men vigorously assaulted the left in small boats. The battery surrendered within half an hour after the attack had begun. An enemy reinforcement appeared to retake the guns but Smith halted them with a well-directed fire from the fort. The British then sent a small boat under a white flag requesting that the firing cease since they were coming to surrender. But instead of surrendering, the British reinforcements evacuated part of the guns and Smith had to be content with a handful of prisoners.[18]

The British soon renewed their attempt to establish their guns on Province Island. By October 14 they succeeded in throwing up an earthwork behind which they mounted a battery. Smith tried to dislodge them by fire from his few guns at the northwest blockhouse, but after it had been shot to pieces and two of its guns dismounted he abandoned any attempt to dislodge the British. He felt that he did not have the necessary strength for a second attack. All that the 156 defenders could do was to build more blinds and earthworks to protect the gun crews and hope that the British did not learn the Americans' real strength and overwhelm it with a landing force.[19] By the middle of October Smith was writing again for urgently needed supplies of clothing, food, and ammunition. The blankets and clothing requested earlier had not been received and "at least 60 of our small force are without breeches, many of whom have scarce so much as to cover their nakedness."[20]

The British fleet, having uprooted the obstructions in the river at Billingsport, moved upstream to a position just below Fort Mifflin and began to ferry supplies into Philadelphia under cover of darkness through the shallow western channel. On a calm night Smith detected the dip of oars and immediately realized what the British were doing. He went at once to Commodore Hazelwood and informed him that not only were supplies getting through, but there was danger of a night assault on Fort Mifflin which the garrison could not withstand. He suggested that the commodore send some of his galleys and gunboats to block the channel at night. The guns from the fort could cover it by day and darkness would shield the American boats from the fire of British warships. Hazelwood refused to comply with Smith's recommendations. He told Smith that a single shell would sink one of his galleys and he refused to risk it. Smith's indignation got the better of his tact. "Yes," he retorted, "and a shell falling on your head or mine will kill but for what else are we paid or employed?" He left the interview bitter in the knowledge that the whole purpose of the operation was being defeated by the willfulness of one man.[21]

Smith wrote to Washington of the situation and of the commodore's refusal to cooperate. Hazelwood excused himself to the commander in chief by saying that "the weather" had prevented him from cooperating fully with the army but that he would render every assistance possible. Washington's reply to Smith was an encouragement that supplies and reinforcements were on the way. He begged that both commanders not allow jealousies and quarrels to undermine the operation.[22] Since Hazelwood was a state officer, there was little else that Washington could do.

Washington also ordered the overdue Baron d'Arendt to proceed to his assignment. The baron, a tall imposing Pole, appeared at Fort Mifflin in the third week of the siege. Colonel Smith and Major Fleury took him on a tour of inspection. When they entered the shambles of the northwest blockhouse, the baron inquired what had happened. Colonel Smith replied that it had been shelled and that the British occasionally fired into it to discourage the Americans from rebuilding it. The baron leaped through the window and left the vicinity of the blockhouse with such alacrity that Major Fleury was led to remark, "Par dieu! C'est un poltron." "Yes," replied Colonel Smith, "and we must frighten him away from the Fort; or he will do more injury than good."[23]

D'Arendt's first move was to criss-cross the flat beach with pits and trenches making it impassable for an attacking force. He then turned his attention to the dyke, the only remaining means of approach to the fort. It was an earth wall erected around the fort to prevent it from being flooded by storms or unusual rises of the river. The Baron decided that this approach should be cut. Smith pointed out to him that any force approaching along the dyke would have to advance two abreast under direct fire from the fort's main battery. A breach in the dyke would put the entire island under water at the first heavy rain. But the Pole was adamant and the gap was made.[24]

Sam gave up in disgust. Apparently his own efforts were being wasted because of the stubbornness of his commanding officer and Hazelwood. He wrote to Washington that, since the commander in chief had seen fit to supersede him, he could see no further need for his presence at Fort Mifflin. His own detachment was reduced to eighty men, whom Thayer could adequately command. He therefore requested that he be allowed to rejoin his Maryland regiment. Washington's reply was a mild reproof. He reminded Smith that the original orders had specified that d'Arendt was to command the post and his arrival was in no sense a reprimand to Smith. On the contrary he was to be congratulated for a job well done. He left it to Smith "to determine upon that which, in your opinion, is most serviceable and consistent with the character of an officer."[35] Sam Smith decided to stay.

Admiral Richard Howe, commander of the British fleet and brother of the British army commander, determined upon a combined land and naval assault on Forts Mifflin and Mercer to attempt to force the passage. He sent the ship-of-the-line *Augusta,* the sloop *Merlin,* and four smaller vessels to a position where their fire would neutralize that of Fort Mifflin. The lighter draft sloop *Vigilant* then forced passage between Province and Mud Islands to gain a position upstream and attack Fort Mifflin from the rear. The current in the unblocked western channel had been made stronger by the obstruction of the *chevaux-de-frise* in the main channel, and the depth of the western channel had been increased enough to allow the *Vigilant* to pass. Simultaneously a British land force attacked Fort Mercer. But the river, which had played its tricks on American ships, now turned against the enemy. A change in the channel went undiscovered by the British until too late to save the *Augusta* and *Merlin* from going aground. Pressure from the attacking American naval units forced the British to abandon and burn them. The *Vigilant,* unable to force the passage unsupported, had to retire downstream.[26]

Colonel Green's Rhode Islanders, defending Fort Mercer, were aided by the timely arrival of a Virginia regiment of 150 men. They withstood the attack of the British land force although at one point they were dangerously short of ammunition. When Colonel Green sent to Fort Mifflin for a fresh supply, Baron d'Arendt refused the request until the pleas of Smith and the other officers finally forced his compliance.[27]

Not only was the victory a boost to the small defending force but it relieved Colonel Smith of the baron. As the *Vigilant* retired downstream after her unsuccessful attempt to force the passage, she loosed several broadsides into Fort Mifflin. The baron became greatly excited and began to give frantic orders in a mixture of German, French, and English. Sam saw his opportunity. "If I understand you, you mean that I should assume the command for the day." "Yes, sir," was the Prussian's reply and he sought shelter behind one of the revetments. Another broadside from the *Vigilant* sent a flying fragment of brick smashing into the baron's groin. He was evacuated to a nearby village on the Jersey shore. He did not return to Fort Mifflin and was later appointed an army inspector by Washington.[28]

The victory could not disguise from the defenders their continued precarious condition. Incessant pounding by British shore and ship batteries blasted defense installations almost as soon as they were repaired. Clothing became so scarce that early in November the Americans began to confiscate apparel from the inhabitants of nearby villages and farms. Some relief was afforded by the arrival of another group of 100 Virginians, but Smith knew that his total force was only one fourth of what was needed to hold out indefinitely. An early November gale added to the troubles of his little garrison. As Smith had predicted when d'Arendt had ordered the cutting of the dike, the ground in and around the fort was submerged under two feet of water.[29]

It occurred to Smith that if Mud Island were flooded, Province Island must be in the same situation. He immediately communicated with Commodore Hazelwood and suggested that a landing force using small boats might easily take and destroy the troublesome battery. The following night, the sound of firing told him that the Americans were attacking. Plunging into the water, Colonel Smith waded toward the sound until he was waist deep in the river. He hailed the American boats and told the officer in charge that the British had only a howitzer above water and that his gun could not be depressed sufficiently to bear on the boats. "We will go no nearer," was the answer. It was the last chance the Americans had at the battery. As soon as the water subsided, the British began adding more guns to the position, for they had decided to rely on the battery to reduce the fort.[30]

General James Varnum arrived in the second week of November with two regiments to reinforce Fort Mercer. Part of this force was diverted to Fort Mifflin, but it was too small to be any real help. The garrison had been eating ship's biscuit and salt herring for days. There was no place left above water to light a fire without endangering the wooden barracks and the magazines. Smith and his officers were in constant fear that the enemy would learn their true strength and make a landing which the weary, sick defenders would be powerless to oppose.

The British constructed floating batteries to supplement the batteries on Province Island. By day and by night the withering hail of fire smashed into the little fort. By the eleventh of November the three blockhouses had been destroyed and the rest of the defenses riddled.[31]

Colonel Smith was wounded on the eleventh. A brick chimney beside him was struck by a shell and collapsed on him, burying him beneath a pile of rubble. Although he was not critically injured, he had to be carried to a boat and sent to the Jersey shore. The command of the fort devolved upon Major Thayer.

Smith had one more round with Commodore Hazelwood. The day after he was wounded, he recovered sufficiently to enlist the aid of General Varnum in procuring some hot cooked food for the men on the Island. The general gladly consented but Hazelwood refused to furnish the boats to transport the food. Smith procured enough ex-seamen from the garrison at Fort Mercer to make up boat crews. He then persuaded Hazelwood to give him the boats without crews, and the food was finally sent.[32]

No historian could describe the last hours of the defense of Fort Mifflin better than Major Fleury, who left the following account in his journal:

> *November 10th, at noon.* I am interrupted by the bombs and balls, which fall thickly. The firing increases, but not the effect; our barracks alone suffer . . . a dozen of them are broken down; one of our cannon is damaged; I am afraid it will not fire straight. *Eleven o'clock at night;* The enemy keep up a firing every half hour. Our garrison diminishes; our soldiers are overwhelmed with fatigue. *11th . . . at night;* the enemy fire and interrupt our works. Three vessels have passed between us and Providence [*sic*] Island without any molestation from the galleys. Colonel Smith, Captain George, and myself wounded. . . . *12th.* Heavy firing; our two eighteen-pounders at the northern battery dismounted. . . . *13th.* The enemy have opened a battery on the old Ferry Wharf; . . . the block houses ruined; Our garrison is exhausted with fatigue and ill-health.—*14th.* . . . .Daylight discovers to us a floating battery placed a little above their grand battery. . . . *At noon;* we have silenced the floating battery. A boat which this day deserted from the fleet, will have given the enemy sufficient intimation of our weakness; they will probably attempt a lodgement on the Island, which we cannot prevent with our present strength.[33]

On the fifteenth General Varnum reported to Washington: "We were obliged to evacuate Fort Mifflin last evening. Major Thayer returned from thence a little after two this morning. . . ."[34]

For seven weeks Sam Smith, twenty-five-year-old colonel of the Continental Army, had defended Fort Mifflin against the might of the British army and navy with a force of ill-clothed, ill-fed, disease-ridden men that never numbered more than 350. During the last two weeks, he and his men were subjected to an enfilading fire from Province Island at a range of 500 yards and from British ships below the island at a range of 100 yards. The bombardment, possibly the heaviest cannonading that occurred during the war, sometimes reached the rate of fifty rounds a minute. Yet on the last day of the fight, Thayer silenced a British battery that ventured too close and withdrew his entire force with all their personal equipment.

The defense of Fort Mifflin was an episode of the kind that frequently occurs in war—a gallant effort to no apparent purpose.

Even after his failure at Germantown Washington had continued to seek an opportunity for a blow against Howe. Such a stroke would have been especially effective if the British supply line had still been threatened by the blockade at Fort Mifflin. Washington planned and probed, and urged Gates to bring his victorious army down from the north to augment the forces before Philadelphia. But Gates remained aloof and the chance never came.

Colonel Smith received a sword from Congress in recognition of his conduct in the Delaware campaign. "The glory of that defense," said the commendation, "is inseparable from you and your brave companions."[35]

3

Profits,
Property, and Privateering

WHEN COLONEL SMITH returned to General Washington's headquarters at Whitemarsh after the fall of Fort Mifflin, the commander in chief congratulated Smith on the excellence of his performance during the siege, and both he and Lafayette offered Smith places on their staffs. Smith, however, preferred to return to the Maryland regiment although still suffering from the aftereffects of his injury.[1] After marching with his regiment to winter quarters, Smith was detached to Baltimore for recruiting duty. Late in January of 1778, he returned with 400 recruits and finished out the bitter winter at Valley Forge training his men for the summer campaign.

Smith marched once more with Washington in an army that was somewhat recovered from the disastrous winter and stronger in discipline and training, if not in numbers, than it had been the previous year. When Sir Henry Clinton, who had replaced Howe as British commander in chief in Philadelphia, evacuated the city in June of 1778 and began his withdrawal overland to New York, Washington moved to overtake him. The army crossed the Delaware into New Jersey and took up the pursuit of the British.

Smith's regiment, the First Maryland, was assigned to General Charles Scott's division. When Washington came to the vicinity of Monmouth, he ordered forward several divisions, one of which was Scott's, to engage the enemy rearguard. On June 28, 1778, this force of somewhat more than 5,000 men, under the command of General Charles Lee, came upon a British force near Monmouth Court House. Conflicting reports estimated this detachment of the enemy at between 1,500 and 6,000 men. Lee disposed his forces for an attack, placing the First Maryland with Scott's division on the left, concealed in a patch of woods from where they could launch a flank attack. As the British advanced, General Scott ordered the flanking force out of its concealment prematurely. Simultaneously Lee decided that the force in front of him was far greater than his own, and he ordered a retreat.[3] Lee's order came just as Colonel Smith and his men had begun skirmishing with the enemy. The engagement was broken off and Lee fell back until he was joined by Washington. Smith's regiment was again thrown into line on the left and, after repulsing an attempt of the enemy to flank the American left, combined with another regiment of Scott's division to drive in the British flank. Darkness came before the Americans were able to press home a full scale attack and, under cover of night, the British withdrew.[4]

Clinton led his army to Sandy Hook, on the Jersey coast, and the British fleet transported it to New York. Washington marched his army northward through New Jersey and up to the Hudson River Highlands. He spent the remainder of the summer strengthening the defenses which would block the British navigation of the river and in establishing a strongly fortified defense line extending from Morristown to White Plains, New York. Both armies remained inactive the rest of the year; and, late in the fall, Colonel Smith was sent back to Maryland to superintend recruiting.[5]

Early in December he returned to Baltimore and to his sweetheart, Margaret Spear, who was famed for her beauty in a town that prided itself on its beautiful women. A young French aide-de-camp to Rochambeau, visiting the city a year later, said: "Permit me to remark that, for my taste, the ladies of Baltimore are more charming than the rest of the fair sex of America. Most of them have very white skin. . . . Also, they enchant by their freshness and the brilliant vivacity of their eyes. One may see many of them with svelte, perfectly proportioned figures, with beautiful little white, dimpled hands; with dainty, exquisite feet."[6] No doubt, Margaret Spear was among the number of Baltimore belles who charmed the aide-de-camp. She must have seemed even more beautiful and desirable to Sam after the bitter misery of one defeat after another and the drudgery of army campaigning. But he could not marry on the pay of a Continental officer. His own fortune and that of his father had been wiped out by the depreciation of Continental currency. John Smith had been one of the richest men in Baltimore, but a great deal of his money was tied up in debts owed by farmers from whom he bought his exports. These debts, when redeemed at all, were paid in worthless Continental paper. The choice which Sam faced was more campaigning on the pay of a Continental officer, or staying in Baltimore with Margaret and building for the future. Sam chose the latter course, and on Christmas Eve, 1778, they were married.[7]

He finished his recruiting duties for the winter and, on May 10, 1779, submitted his resignation to General Washington:

Impressed with a due sense of the duty I owe my country it gives me the greatest uneasiness that my circumstances will not permit me to serve it longer. When I first entered its service I thought my fortune sufficient to support me. . . . Our State I flattered myself would have done something towards enabling its officers to remain in the service. They have done the contrary. They have rescinded a law made for that purpose. . . .

Mrs. Samuel Smith, nee Margaret Spear
copy by W. E. West of the painting by Gilbert Stuart

I still hoped, on examination, that I might be enabled by our fortune to serve another campaign. I find I cannot. I hope this will meet Your Excellency's approbation and that I will continue to hold a place in your esteem. It would be adding too much to my present unhappiness should I meet with your disapprobation or disapproval. . . . I beg Your Excellency's permission to keep my commission, not that I ever expect any rank from it, but I wish to retain some mark of an honorable service. . . .

Washington replied:

I can only lament the necessity which has produced your letter of the 10th and obliges you to offer your resignation at the opening of a cam-

Robert Smith
engraving by St. Memin

paign—at a crisis in which good officers might render most essential services by their continuance and example in the army.

The proofs you have heretofore given of your abilities as a good and brave officer, I am happy in acknowledging; and could wish that circumstances . . . were such as to afford you the opportunity of closing the war with your military companions. . . .[8]

Smith continued his military service as an officer in the Maryland militia and was appointed commanding officer of the Baltimore brigade. Under his leadership and training, the unit became noted for its discipline and military appearance; and, at the end of the war, Smith was commissioned a brigadier-general.[9]

As Smith surveyed the opportunities for recouping his personal fortune, he perceived that a quick and lucrative profit lay in privateering. This practice was being carried out along the whole Atlantic coast. The Maryland privateers differed from those of the other states in that the capturing of prizes was more or less incidental to their trading activities. The restrictions of British trade before the war had already forced Baltimore merchants to seek more favorable trade to the south, particularly in the West Indies.[10] Now they redoubled their activities in this area.

The Baltimore schooners and brigs often sailed with a cargo which would yield a good value in regular trade, while the Yankee ships were going out with empty bottoms, merely hoping to capture prizes. The armament of a Baltimore ship was as much for defense as it was for offense, although the superior sailing qualities of the Baltimore-built ships made them dangerous in a fight. Such Maryland privateersmen as John Rodgers and Joshua Barney were the exception rather than the rule, and even they often carried cargo to the West Indies before starting out on a cruise for prizes. An estimated total of 248 privateers carrying a total of 2,450 guns sailed from Baltimore between 1778 and 1783.[11]

Samuel Smith's first venture after his resignation from the army was in a consignment of cargo on a French privateer which sailed from Baltimore in the summer of 1779. His profit was £5,000, sufficient, as he wrote to his friend, Otho H. Williams, "to help me set up house-keeping."[12] Such an enormous profit was unusual, but it gave Sam an idea of the possibilities. Smith secured letters of marque from both the state and national governments for the ships of John Smith and Sons. Late in 1779 he was issued a Maryland letter of marque for the sloop *General Wayne*, four guns, of which he was sole owner. The brig *Cato*, fourteen guns, of which Smith was one-fourth owner, received a letter of marque from the state council in

1780. In the same year the *Rambler*, ten guns, was authorized as a privateer. In this letter the state also issued arms and equipment to Smith to outfit gunboats for the purpose of raiding enemy shipping in the Chesapeake.[13] There is evidence that a total of ten vessels owned either wholly or in part by Smith engaged in privateering activities in the last four years of the war. This probably represents somewhat less than the number from which Smith derived a profit.[14]

The return from privateering and wartime trading was tremendous. Smith had one vessel, the *Otho*, the cargo of which trebled its investment in a single voyage. But the risks were great and a series of misfortunes could be ruinous. In 1781 within a period of a few months, the *Cato* with a cargo worth £3,000 was driven ashore in the Chesapeake, and the *Statia* and *Fiery Dragon* were captured.[15] Later two brigs, the *Otho* and the *Race Horse,* which had set out from Baltimore, were never heard from. Smith was often so discouraged that he wished he had remained in the army. In one such period of despondency he wrote to General Otho H. Williams, who was serving in the Southern Department, that he could have made as much money and more reputation by staying in the service. Nevertheless, the profits were so great that they absorbed the losses, and he could count a nice gain at the end of the war, certainly enough for him to be regarded as one of the wealthiest young men of the town.[16]

Another natural line of business for Smith was in supplying civilian and military needs, particularly the latter. In 1779 Smith became the agent for the state of Virginia in the purchase of Maryland flour. So strictly did the Council of Safety guard its precious grain supply that it was unlawful to ship grain out of the state without the Council's permission. When Smith attempted to remove the flour which he had purchased for Virginia, it was immediately confiscated by the state. Smith was able to show that it was part of an allotment made by the Council in reply to Governor Thomas Jefferson's request for food for Virginia, but many months were needed for Smith to unsnarl the red tape and recover the flour. After that Smith confined his dealings to the state of Maryland.[17]

John Smith and Sons possessed the ships and equipment to run its business, but wartime economic conditions had wiped out the necessary operating capital. Late in 1780 Smith, along with other Baltimore merchants, approached the Maryland authorities with a proposition whereby the state would furnish the money necessary for the purchase of cargoes, in return for which the merchants would bring in much needed foreign goods and also allow a profit to the state treasury. Markets were to be found in the West Indies and France, where the British blockade made food a profitable import. The state replied favorably; it purchased flour for cargo and allowed five percent to Smith as their agent. The profit from the cargo was split half and half, and the state was allowed to import one-third of the return cargo for its own profit, free of freight charges. The agreement included a provision that the state would receive one-third of all prizes taken.[18]

This trade was hindered not only by the British blockade of the Chesapeake but by British gunboats which lurked off the mouth of the Patapsco. Both merchant ships and the state's gunboats were frequently damaged in encounters with the British, and many of them put into Baltimore for repairs. Smith secured the appointment as state agent for ship repairs and also became its agent for handling of cargo not only for Smith and Company but for other companies.[19]

By virtue of his position as commanding officer of the Baltimore militia, Colonel Smith became active in the apprehension of Loyalists who were dealing with the enemy. British strategy was now concentrated against the Southern colonies and, in the spring of 1781, Lord Cornwallis, at the head of a British Army, had pushed north from the Carolinas into Virginia. This British thrust, although it never reached Maryland in any force, led the Council to warn Colonel Smith of those agents, in particular, who were selling flour to the enemy. Smith succeeded in apprehending several of them and turned them over to the Council. That body treated such persons with great severity, and a number of the prisoners were executed.[20]

As Cornwallis' advance continued into Virginia and seemed about to sweep northward unchecked, enemy naval forces appeared before the city in March, 1781. Smith mustered his detachment of 650 militiamen and prepared to repel a possible landing, but the enemy vessels contented themselves with a tight blockade at the river mouth. For almost a month, the town was completely cut off from outside communications except such as could move over the extremely poor roads.[21] Smith and his small force were greatly relieved when Cornwallis retreated to Yorktown and the blockading vessels moved down the bay, removing pressure from the upper Chesapeake.

Still later in the summer, the arrival of a French fleet at the mouth of the Chesapeake enabled Washington to abandon his position around New York and hurry south to join Lafayette for an attack on Yorktown. He looked to Pennsylvania and Maryland for supplies and equipment for his campaign. The State Council appointed Colonel Smith agent for the procurement of clothing, ammunition, and other supplies for the troops of the Maryland line.[22]

Smith was unable to get the merchants to accept the depreciated state currency in return for supplies. The merchants' point of view is understandable in the light of the following instruction which Smith received from the Council:

> It is necessary immediately to assist Mr. Green to purchase forty Reams of Paper fit for the Purpose of printing Money, we must therefore request you to assist Mr. Green in procuring a sufficient Quantity upon the best terms you can find and we will see that Payment is made immediately after the Money is printed.[23]

He solved the situation by recommending to the Council that they issue bills of credit on flour and tobacco which the state had in its warehouses. The price paid was slightly higher than current in order to expedite procurement. Under this arrangement Smith was able to get clothing, ammunition, and military equipment of all kinds for the troops marching south. In one month he supplied 5,000 items of equipment making up full marching gear for 700 men.

Smith found an investment for his profits in the purchase of confiscated Tory property which the state seized in order to help meet the expense of civil government and military operations. For small down payments and easy installments, Smith was able to purchase six lots in Baltimore for £712 and 470 acres in Baltimore County for £1300. Smith emerged from the war, therefore, in good financial condition considering the poor economic straits of the country. By taking advantage of the business opportunities in privateering, trade, and real estate investment, he made John Smith and Sons a going concern and laid the foundation for his peacetime career.[23]

When Baltimore, in 1783, celebrated the end of the war with a torchlight parade, the town was no longer a hamlet by Jones' Falls, but a bustling, thriving port. Said the Baltimore author and essayist, John P. Kennedy: "It was a treat to see this little Baltimore town just at the termination of the War of Independence, so conceited, bustling, and debonair, growing up like a saucy, chubby boy . . . fat and mischievous, and bursting incontinently out of his clothes in spite of all the allowances of tucks and salvages." And the Baltimore gallants are thus described:

> . . . most of them the iron gentlemen of the Revolution, with leather faces—old campaigners renowned for long stories; not long enough from camp to lose their military *brusquerie* and dare-devil swagger; proper roystering blades, who had not long ago got out of harness and begun to affect the elegancies of civil life. Who but they!—jolly fellows, fiery and loud, with a stern glance of the eye and a brisk turn of the head, and swashbuckler strut of defiance . . . all in three-cornered cocked hats and powdered hair and cues and light-colored coats with narrow capes and

marvellous long backs . . . with striped stockings, with great buckles on their shoes, and their long steel watch chains . . . and they walked with such a stir, striking their canes so hard upon the pavement as to make the little town ring. . . . There was such a relish of peace about it, and particularly when one of those weather-beaten gallants accosted a lady in the street with a bow that required a whole side pavement to make it in, with the scrape of his foot, and his cane thrust with a flourish under his left arm, till it projected behind, along with his cue, like the palisades of a *chevaux-de-frise*. . . .[24]

Sam Smith was probably not among the number of "roystering blades," for by 1783 the thirty-year-old merchant was the father of three children, Louis, St. John, and Elizabeth. He had already made a place for himself among the town's prominent citizens. In 1783 he was elected one of the port wardens of Baltimore. Two years later, Robert Hunter, a young London merchant visiting in Baltimore noted: "Baltimore is now a very considerable place, but, in the course of a few years, when these elegant houses are finished, it will be one of the first towns in America. . . . We dressed ourselves at two o'clock and at three went . . . to Colonel Samuel Smith's to dinner. I was introduced to his lady, a genteel, elegant woman. . . . We had a very elegant dinner, and a most agreeable company. . . . We sent for a violin in the evening and had a most agreeable dance. . . . At ten we walked downstairs to an elegant sideboard instead of formal supper."[25]

The gay social life was accompanied, nevertheless, by intense business activity. In 1784 the elder Smith retired from the business, and most of its direction fell to Sam. As head of the firm he faced the perennial problems which confront every merchant and, in addition, those difficulties attendant to putting the company back into operation on a peacetime basis.[26]

One of the most troublesome factors in this postwar business was market fluctuation. Faulty judgment on Smith's part or bad luck in foreseeing changes in price level might easily determine whether the company would show a loss at the end of the year. Price variations followed a general pattern. Imports sold best in the spring and fall when farmers brought their crops to market. Tobacco was much the same the year round, as it could be stored and sent to Europe when there was a good market. Flour could be purchased cheaper in the spring months when the famous Maryland winter wheat was harvested.[27]

Closely related to this problem was the laxity and inefficiency of ship captains, particularly those hired by charter. A captain who arrived late with manufactured goods from Europe often found that his cargo had missed the peak of the market and that the owner would lose a large profit because he had nothing to trade for an export cargo. Charter captains, naturally easygoing and independent, often caused great losses to owners, and Smith and Company therefore came more and more to own its ships and employ its own masters. By 1790 about twenty ships were sailing under the flag of Smith's firm. Even the company captains were liable to be dilatory and extravagant with expense money. Smith considered speed in loading and unloading the highest quality in a ship captain. "Any fool can navigate a ship," he said.[28]

In addition to these ever-present problems Smith, immediately after the war, faced a monetary condition which was worse than at any time in the nation's history. The depreciation of all kinds of American currency and the general instability of the small amount which, at the moment, possessed some value made any American money unacceptable to European merchants. Trade became a matter of barter and bills of exchange. The system is shown in the circular letter which Smith sent to the company's European correspondents in 1784 when he announced the reorganization of the company under the name of Samuel and John Smith.[29] The company would continue to handle cargo at its usual commission of five percent. Any cargo which they received would be allowed two-thirds value in return cargo even though it could not be disposed of immediately. For the remaining one-third, Smith issued a bill of exchange on one of his correspondents in London, Paris, Leghorn, or other centers of European international trade. These bills were issued for payment at sixty to ninety days sight. European agents in turn drew on Smith and Company for cargoes purchased in Europe.

The system worked in this fashion: When Smith and Company received a cargo from Europe, they would pay the agent for that cargo two-thirds value in export crop. Smith would then give the agent a bill of exchange for the remaining value which allowed the agent to draw on the Smith and Company account at one of the large European houses. When the cargo had been sold in the United States and Smith had sent a cargo to Europe, he established a credit value with the European firm on which the bill was issued, and this allowed debit and credit to cancel each other. Thus, large commercial firms both in Europe and the United States came to perform the function of international bankers. It was on this basis alone that many

American houses could carry on a large-scale trade; Smith was forced to turn down business with firms who wished to deal in cash.[30]

He also took care to establish sight notes as the basis of credit. The elapsed time between the receipt of goods and the date of the bill of lading was so great that, on nine-months' credit, the debtor would often have less than a month to meet his bill. No mail packet lines had been established, and business correspondence depended on slow and often irresponsible carriers for delivery. Such circumstances prompted the following letter sent in 1784 to John Noble and Company:

> We fear it will be out of our power to make payments punctually in less than a year. Your invoice is dated in February and we have but received the good now [June]; thus five months are elapsed, remittances are in 60 day bills so that were we to remit this day we would hardly be in time. . . .[31]

Another problem which was brought on and aggravated by postwar conditions was the prohibitive tariffs levied by other states. There was no national control over import duties, or over duties on interstate commerce. Cargoes which came from Europe and entered the country via other ports such as Philadelphia or Norfolk bore excessive interstate charges as well as high freighting costs before they reached Baltimore; hence, all profit on such goods was lost.[32]

The most important problem, and the one which taxed Smith's ingenuity and resourcefulness to the utmost, was finding trade outlets. Peace marked the beginning of a decline of the French trade. As long as the war lasted, Baltimore merchants enjoyed a preeminence in the grain trade which supplied food for France and the West Indies. Two circumstances changed the conditions which made this trade so successful. The first was, of course, the recognition by Great Britain of American independence, which resulted in the reestablishment of trade with Britain and a steady stream of British vessels into Baltimore loaded with English manufactured goods. British merchants wanted tobacco in return for these exports. The second circumstance was the continued prohibition by Great Britain of American imports into the West Indies and the additional imposition of similar restrictions by France. Now that the war was over, French merchants could satisfy the demand for flour from the planters in the islands, and they exerted pressure on the French government to exclude Americans from the trade. In addition, England's policy dictated that American supplies to the British West Indies cease, for England hoped that all such supplies, particularly flour and lumber, could be supplied by her Canadian colonies. Forced out of exporting to the West Indian market, Smith had to turn to the tobacco trade, in which England was the chief buyer.[33]

This trade carried with it many disadvantages. Continued British restrictions reminiscent of colonial times resulted in countermeasures by the Maryland legislature in the form of import duties not only on British goods but on British bottoms. Confusion and sharp practice on the part of customs officials resulted in excess charges. Articles were listed for duty by weight, stowage space, and "package." English agents were in the habit of adding insurance premiums to commission charges although this was supposed to be included in the commission. Excessive charges, made on the slightest excuse, finally forced Smith to discontinue shipments when one agent took one hogshead of tobacco out of every five and charged insurance premiums over and above this amount, "without," noted Smith bitterly, "departing one iota from 'custom'." Nor could an outlet for tobacco be found in France. During the war, the French Farmers-General had acquired large supplies of tobacco and established a monopoly in the market. They used their reserve supply to level off prices and did not purchase a leaf of tobacco from January to April, 1783. When they did come back into the market, Robert Morris of Philadelphia secured from them the right to be their sole purchasing agent in the United States. To all these difficulties in the tobacco trade was added the fact that tobacco planters were tending more and more to build their own private wharves along the river and bay front and ship direct to the foreign market. By 1786 Smith had difficulty in getting consignments anywhere.[34]

All these conditions were forcing the trade of Baltimore into channels that were neither natural nor very profitable. Smith decided that, one way or another, trade with the West Indies in export wheat and flour must be resumed. West Indian goods procured for food could be reexported to Europe. The prosperous trade which the company subsequently enjoyed in this direction was due to a combination of circumstances that allowed Maryland wheat to arrive in the West Indies with a higher quality than any other kind. This superiority was due not only to the quality of the wheat and flour but to its shorter time in transit. Baltimore, located some 200 miles nearer to the West Indies than its nearest northern competitor, had its crop source, the Monocacy valley, virtually at its back door. Southern ports such as Charleston and Norfolk, while nearer to the market than Baltimore, had to depend on time-consuming overland freight to reach their wheat areas in the Piedmont. Despite French and British trade restrictions, the island planters paid good prices for Maryland wheat when they could get it.

Sam Smith, like other Baltimore merchants, was a man of easy conscience where obedience to British and French law was concerned. His own government was too weak to protect him, so Sam made his own laws. Where privateering had served during the war, similar, if slightly less belligerent, methods were used in peace. A few examples of Smith's excursions into the West Indian trade will serve to show the ingenuity and skill with which he found a new market and extended the trade to the Continent.

In 1784 a company ship was sent to France, where it picked up a cargo of manufactured goods and proceeded to the West Indies. There it took aboard a cargo of sugar and molasses and cleared ostensibly for a return voyage to France but put into Baltimore "under stress of weather" where her cargo sold for one-third to one-half profit. Captain Dean of the *Unicorn* was directed to proceed to the West Indies and exchange his cargo of flour for molasses, continue to France, and pick up a cargo of wine for the return voyage to Baltimore. Captain Denny of the *Louis* was instructed to conceal an illegal load of dry goods under barrels of spoiled fish. One can imagine the reluctance of customs officers to inspect the holds of the *Louis* very carefully. Obviously, Smith and Company captains were using every trick of the trade: "stress of weather" to enter ports normally closed to American shipping; false papers and concealment of illegal cargo; and, as always, a considerable amount of luck. The triangular route enabled Smith to enjoy a very profitable trade, particularly in those years when crop shortages led the governors of the West Indian Islands to issue proclamations declaring an emergency, thereby justifying a suspension of all restrictions.[35]

The West Indian trade was profitable but risky. Sam found it necessary to supplement it with legitimate trade with southern Europe. He had found on his European tour that lumber was always welcome in Spain and Italy and that frequent crop failures offered a market in wheat and flour. Increasing demands by Americans for French and Spanish wines gave him a profitable import in exchange. By 1787 Smith was observing that "wet goods" were almost entirely replacing dry goods from the countries of southern Europe.[36]

In 1787 Smith extended his commercial activities still further by gaining access to the eastern Mediterranean. Up to this time, the activities of the Barbary pirates had forced him to purchase spices, fine textiles, and other products of the Near East from western Mediterranean ports. In 1787 he managed the purchase of licenses from representatives of the Barbary states in London which allowed him to trade without fear of seizure. He assigned one ship, the *Unicorn*, to this area exclusively. Smith's versatility and sagacity in his business enabled the firm to show a profit through the unsettled times and poor economic conditions of the Confederation period. His worst year was 1787, when currency inflation reached its height in Maryland. Toward the end of the year, the decline of real prices forced Smith to sell goods at a loss and the company experienced difficulty in paying its debts.[37]

Smith, along with the other merchants of Baltimore, was vastly encouraged when the Constitutional Convention met at Philadelphia in the summer of 1787 to revise the Articles of Confederation. The situation in the commercial relations of the states had reached such a point that Maryland, for instance, where navigation laws were concerned, considered citizens of other states as aliens. The interest of Baltimore merchants like Smith was less in political theories than in a centralized government which would aid shipping and manufacturing interests. When the work of the Philadelphia Convention was submitted to the states for ratification, friends of the proposed federal government set to work. Although some elements in Maryland, as represented by Luther Martin and Samuel Chase, feared that a strongly centralized government would subordinate the small states to the large, there was never much doubt that Maryland would ratify.

Although there is no record of Smith's campaigning for the Constitution, as the time for the ratification convention approached he probably joined with the merchants and manufacturers in Baltimore who urged that citizens vote for those candidates who favored the Constitution and who would pledge their support in public. The two delegates who were elected were so pledged. It is difficult to tell definitely, but it seems probable that the movement for unconditional ratification started in Baltimore. This movement succeeded; for, when the convention met at Annapolis on April 21, 1788, the Federalist members held a caucus and determined to block any move to discuss the document item by item. In several states the battle was so close that a quick and decisive vote from Maryland might turn the scale elsewhere. Anti-Federalist leaders in the convention, therefore, met with only a clam-like silence when they propounded their objections. After sitting for three days, the convention gave a 66 to 11 vote for ratification.[38]

News of ratification was received in Baltimore with wild enthusiasm, and the town celebrated with a parade of mammoth proportions. Sam Smith and the other Baltimore merchants saw in it not only

an instrument through which the evils of tariff barriers imposed by
the states during the Confederation could be alleviated but also an
agency through which to bargain in the diplomatic market. Smith
predicted to one of his business correspondents that trade would
soon be on a sounder basis "than the heterogeneous one it now
enjoys."[39]

Yet business had already begun to improve. There were currency
troubles, there were good times and bad times. But the United States
has always experienced its economic ups and downs. Although its
difficulties were different in nature from those of subsequent years,
the fortunes of Smith and Company during the decade of the eighties
and after belied the thesis held then and later that the Union was
an economic wreck and that the replacement of the Confederation
government by that inaugurated under the Constitution of 1787 was
responsible for the salvation of the United States, at least from the
economic point of view.

This promise of better days helped commercial interests so that
Smith and Buchanan enjoyed an extensive and profitable trade. But
at first the new government fell far short of living up to expectations.
Many people were extremely pessimistic as to the ability of the national
government to survive the sectional dissensions which arose. This
pessimism was transmitted to foreign consuls and other official emis-
saries of one sort or another; and, as a consequence, America enjoyed
scant respect abroad. It appeared to some as if Americans seemed
to be relapsing into their former colonial condition from sheer inability
to keep out of it.[40] For a time the Nootka Sound controversy, which
involved Spanish efforts to keep Britain out of the Oregon country,
caused the latter to make overtures and raised American hopes that
England might grant commercial concessions. Spain appealed to
France for help and received a reply which frightened her into withdrawing from her position. Great Britain's overtures ceased.

In France, 1789 marked the overthrow of the Bourbon dynasty
and the establishment of the new revolutionary government. This
seemed at first to augur well for American trade, since the new
revolutionary government indicated its friendliness to the United
States. But before any diplomatic commitments could be made, Great
Britain challenged the French revolutionists. In 1793 war burst upon
Europe, and the United States found itself in the position of being
the largest neutral carrier of goods, and almost the only one capable
of supplying the West Indies. Reprisals by both the French and the
British in attempting to restrict each other's trade marked the appearance of privateers as well as warships to threaten neutral American

vessels. Britain was particularly fearful that the United States would honor the commitments which she had made to France in the Treaty of 1778, under which French possessions in the Western Hemisphere were guaranteed American protection in case of war. France, despite her hopes and expectations of American aid, continued to prey on the latter's ships which traded with the British West Indies.

Smith and Buchanan adopted a policy of observing restrictions as far as was practically possible and of continuing a profitable trade. Company ships were nevertheless subjected to a great deal of British highhandedness. In the first two years of the European war, Smith and Buchanan suffered more losses than the total since 1783. In 1793 the brig *Peggy* was stopped in the West Indies and the company agent was interned at Jamaica. Although he was soon freed, the British conficated the ship and condemned her cargo. In the following year the brig *Sidney* was delayed at St. Kitts while the British admiralty court held her master for trial for violation of an embargo on the French West Indies. The brig *John* suffered a similar fate.[41]

French behavior was almost as bad as the British. The Smith and Buchanan ship *Jane* arrived in France and found that port orders prevented her from landing her cargo. Before she could depart, French authorities seized the ship and confiscated her cargo. The revolutionary government of France seemed to have as little respect for the Americans as the British since it usually ignored protests of such episodes as the *Jane*. Smith openly expressed his disgust at the failure of the United States to protect its own commerce.[42]

The returns of neutral trade, however, were more than sufficient to make up for the losses sustained. Smith and Buchanan flourished, and from the profits of the firm Smith was building a fortune which was to make him one of the wealthiest men in Baltimore.

4

Mr. Smith
Goes to Congress *

IN 1792 at the age of forty Samuel Smith began his national political career, a career which was not to terminate for forty-five years. His only previous experience had been two one-year terms in the Maryland legislature to which he had been elected in 1790. Here he did a notable amount of committee work and generally aligned himself with the conservative, hard-money men. He lent his efforts to the establishment of the Bank of Maryland and opposed the efforts of soft-money men, led by Samuel Chase, to secure relief for insolvent debtors.[1] But this conservative leaning did not prevent him from serving on a committee to set up a plan for free public education nor from doing important committee work for the improvement of the state's public roads.[2]

When Smith announced his candidacy for Congress from the Baltimore district in 1792, Dr. James McHenry, a leading Baltimore Federalist who later served as Secretary of War in Washington's and Adams's cabinet, wrote to his friend Alexander Hamilton: "Col. Smith has entered for this district. Mr. [Charles] Ridgely, you know, also stands. Ridgely, I am told, is a friend to further assumption. Samuel Smith is not. He is, however, a good federalist. As a merchant he will not like any increase of duties on dry goods. . . . He is a man of great wealth, unskilled in public affairs." Smith was elected, polling 1615 votes to Ridgely's 1027. The election was a dull one and only about half of the city voters and one fourth of those from the county participated.[3]

The duties and assumption to which McHenry referred were part of the program which Hamilton, the first Secretary of the Treasury, had drawn up to put the new nation on a sound financial basis. General Washington, who had been the overwhelming choice of the

---

* Parts of this chapter appeared previously in "Aaron Burr: Would-be Usurper," *William and Mary Quarterly*, 3rd series, vol. 8, 1951, 205–209.

nation for its first chief executive, had recognized that the desperate economic condition of the country required immediate and skillful attention. The brilliant New Yorker, whom he had placed at the head of the Treasury Department, responded with a program that embodied the assumption of state debts by the national government, a tariff on imports to produce revenue, a national bank, and the funding of the national debt. But alleviating the financial distress of the nation was not the only purpose behind Hamilton's plan. He saw in it a means of effecting his whole political philosophy. He had little faith in the mass of the people, believing that only a strong, vigorous government capable of controlling the states and asserting its authority over the people could save the nation. He directed his efforts, therefore, toward gaining the support of all the strongest elements in society, what John Adams called "The rich, the well born, and the able...."[4] These Hamilton sought to bind to the national government by economic ties so strong that it would be to their interest to support it.

Hamilton had gone a long way toward achieving his goals when Smith arrived in Philadelphia in the fall of 1793 to take his seat in the Third Congress. He was certainly interested in the kind of energetic national policy which Hamilton advocated, for it was obvious that the commercial and business interests must benefit from the kind of promotional legislation which the Hamiltonians proposed. Yet his judgment was tempered by several factors, not the least of which was his admiration for Thomas Jefferson, the Secretary of State. The two men had first become acquainted almost ten years before when Jefferson had been a guest in Smith's house in Baltimore. He was aware that there was a growing rift between the two distinguished members of Washington's cabinet, and that Jefferson and Hamilton were each attracting a political following that eventually formed the basis of the nation's first two political parties.[5]

Jefferson was alarmed at Hamilton's governmental engine, which he thought would lead to a concentration of power that, in the end, would destroy republicanism and democracy. He feared that the elitist leadership which the Secretary of the Treasury was promoting would lead to a domination by the rich and wellborn. To Jefferson the role of government was one which contented itself with protecting men's rights, but which otherwise left them free to pursue their own destiny. It was essentially the question that always confronts men who govern themselves: to what degree may men be allowed to do as they please and to what degree must they be restricted in the interest of an orderly society? In attempting to achieve a balance between liberty and order, Jefferson believed that the people were the only safeguards against tyranny. The democracy might be at times unruly and wrong-headed but it would always reject any form of absolutism.

Hamilton insisted that men could be free only in a society of order and security. Only the rich, the wise, and the good were capable of formulating those broad and far-reaching policies which Hamilton called the "common good" or "the public interest." These policies included those immediate and short-term interests which the people perceived and demanded but also included permanent and far-sighted goals which the people could not perceive. To Jefferson this embodied a kind of statism which was deadly to individual freedom. Thus Jefferson was convinced that Hamilton aimed at monarchism. Hamilton was just as sure that Jefferson's democracy led down the road to mob rule and anarchy.[6]

When Smith entered upon the national political scene there were no real political parties, but the outlines of party structure were beginning to take shape. James Madison had already organized a formidable opposition to Hamilton's program in Congress. While a number of members followed Madison's leadership and others took their cue from Hamilton, a majority followed no consistent pattern of voting and the new member from Baltimore also found himself voting sometimes one way and sometimes another. In many respects Smith had the makings of a good Hamiltonian. He was a wealthy merchant and therefore was interested in a strong national government which would protect and develop commercial interests.

But the great international struggle which was beginning in Europe in 1793 between France and her allies on the one hand, and England and her coalitions on the other, began to have a profound impact on American politics. Jefferson himself observed that "the form our own government was to take depended much more on the events in France than anybody had before imagined." Jefferson and many other Americans not only remembered the aid which France had rendered during the War of Independence but saw its revolution, like that of the United States, as a war against absolutism. The Hamiltonians, on the contrary, sympathized with Great Britain. To them England represented the forces of order and stability which alone would save Europe and Western civilization from the chaos of democracy.

Although France did not call upon the United States for aid such as had been rendered by France in 1778, Washington thought it wise to declare the government's intention to stay aloof and impartial in the quarrel between England and France. To this end he issued the Neutrality Proclamation of 1793 which seemed to Francophiles a repudiation of American obligations under the Treaty of 1778. Whatever Smith may have thought of the President's action, his pro-French feelings were offended by the actions of the French envoy, Edmund Charles Genêt. Arriving in May, 1793, Genêt appealed to the popularity of the French Revolution and showed scant respect for the administration. He attempted to force the United States into acting as a base for depredations on British commerce and advocated American aggression against Spanish and British colonies. Smith strongly disapproved of Genêt's conduct.[7] Eventually even Jefferson was forced to reprimand Genêt and the President demanded his recall. Subsequent actions of the Jeffersonians, however, did little to strengthen Smith's sympathies for their views. He, like other merchants, viewed the commercial situation with alarm. With the outbreak of the war in Europe both French and British vessels, principally the latter, began to detain American vessels and confiscate their cargoes with such dispatch and ruthlessness that trade was almost paralyzed. Secretary of State Jefferson submitted a report to Congress outlining the history of American commercial relations with the two belligerent powers and recommended that Congress establish a system of retaliatory measures which could be used to wring concessions from both England and France, although the report left no doubt that the principal enemy was England. Jefferson realized that commerce was not only a source of wealth but of coercion and he believed that the trade of the United States was sufficiently valuable to other nations so that reciprocal favors or restrictions could be used to reinforce American neutral rights. James Madison, Jefferson's chief lieutenant in the House, submitted a bill, clearly aimed at Britain, which imposed duties on goods and tonnage of the vessels of all nations which did not have commercial treaties with the United States. The President was authorized to impose additional reciprocal restrictions upon the ships of any nation which discriminated against American commerce.[8]

This proposal signalled Smith's first major appearance on the floor of the House on January 15, 1794, and the occasion was his unqualified opposition to the Madison bill as a proper solution to the commercial problem. It was a businessman's speech showing little consideration for either pro-British or pro-French feeling. He stated bluntly that it was necessary to recognize the proposal for what it was, an attack on Great Britain. He would be the first to acknowledge that she had treated the United States badly. But the inescapable fact remained that since the passage of the first tariff law our trade had increased as much again in four years as it had in the forty years prior to 1789. "Why," he asked, "should we jeopardize this phenomenal progress by entering into a commercial war with half of Europe or even with England alone? . . . Mr. Madison was killing the goose that laid the golden egg."[9]

The resolutions were tabled for more than a month. Sentiment against England increased but when Madison renewed his fight for the bill in March Smith was still firmly opposed. With hardheaded practicality he observed that the measures were sufficient neither for a policy of war nor for one of peace. However much the advocates of the proposal might prate of national dignity and honor, Smith thought that if the United States were to take issue with England it would either have to fight or conduct a stringent commercial war. The former was not the will of the people and the latter would not be served by the resolutions of Mr. Madison. The resolutions were tabled again and before they could be reconsidered developments of overshadowing importance made them inconsequential.[10]

Late in the spring of 1794 news reached Congress that not only had further depredations been committed on American shipping in the Caribbean but that Lord Dorchester, Governor-General of Canada, had made an inflammatory speech intended to arouse the Indians in the American Northwest. Americans had long suspected that the British army, which still held forts on the American side of the Canadian border in violation of the Treaty of 1783, had been inciting the Indians against American settlers on the frontier. This latest news from Canada seemed to confirm the suspicion. Smith voted with the Jeffersonians who, backed by a wave of indignant public opinion, pushed through a temporary embargo, non-intercourse act with Great Britain, and appropriations for an increased army and navy.[11]

At this juncture a brief interlude of domestic strife temporarily removed Smith from his seat in Congress. Part of Hamilton's financial program had included an excise tax on distilled spirits. This had aroused the farmers of western Pennsylvania and Maryland to the extent that a number of riots and clashes between the Pennsylvania distillers and government officers had broken out. President Washington called on the militia of Virginia, Maryland, and Pennsylvania to march against the insurrectionists. Samuel Smith was commissioned a major-general by Maryland Governor Thomas Stone and hastened to Baltimore to place himself at the head of five hundred troops. On September 15, 1794, he prepared to march against a body of the insurgents who were reported to be advancing on the federal arsenal at Frederick, Maryland. A correspondent of the *Maryland Gazette* described the parading of the troops in Baltimore:

> A more warlike appearance, perhaps, our town has not exhibited since the year '76, than it did yesterday, in consequence of an express from the Governor to General Smith. The militia of this town were requested to meet on the parade, near the old Theatre, at 4 P.M. They met accordingly . . . and General Smith, in a short but energetic address, informed them of the object of their meeting. . . . "It is not," said he, "against an enemy that we have to march, but a set of men more daring than the rest, a lawless banditti, who set themselves up to govern."

The Maryland troops met those of the other states at Cumberland, Maryland, and the whole, under the command of Alexander Hamilton, advanced westward. The army, however, had a difficult time finding any rebels. Two of the "ringleaders" were arrested and convicted of treason but were pardoned by the President.[12]

When Smith returned to the opening of the second session of the Third Congress he found that the Federalists, backed by public reaction to the Whiskey Rebels, proposed a further increase of excises by levying a tax on the manufacture of sugar, snuff, and several other articles. Smith recognized the fact that manufacturers were enjoying protection under the duties of 1789. In the excise he saw the elimination of all the benefits of tariff protection. Joining with the Jeffersonian opposition, in a speech against the tax in January, 1795, he pointed out that manufacturers, assured of a profit because of the tariff, had set up their businesses and invested their capital. "Well, you have got the manufacturer engaged," he said. "Their capital is fixed; and then you come down on them with an excise that destroys the whole. . . . The system was absurd, because the object of revenue would be destroyed. It was in the highest degree unjust and tyrannical." Smith's motion for reduction was lost and the excise bill was passed.[13]

Whatever hesitations Smith may have had about aligning himself wholeheartedly with the Jeffersonians were swept away with the next developments in commercial intercourse between the United States and Great Britain. President Washington had dispatched Chief Justice John Jay, an Anglophile Federalist, to the Court of St. James as special envoy to mediate the differences between the two nations and write a treaty. The two main points of contention were the British occupation of American territory in the Northwest and the restrictions and depredations which had been directed at American merchant ships by Great Britain. Jay's Treaty reached the United States early in 1795. The

Chief Justice had succeeded in getting the British to abandon the forts in the Northwest but the commercial provisions caused a burst of indignation from all over the nation. Jay had agreed that enemy property on neutral ships might be seized by Great Britain and that food might be confiscated if paid for. This opened the way for further seizures and secured justice for American merchants only after long and tedious court actions. As to the West Indian trade in which Smith was so vitally interested, Jay secured permission for direct trade for Americans to British West Indian ports, but only in vessels of less than seventy tons. In return for this Jay pledged that the cotton and sugar and other competing tropical staples would not be exported in American vessels from the United States.[14] The sum of these provisions was virtually to wreck the American reexport trade with the West Indies, a trade especially vital to Baltimore.

When the text of the treaty became known Samuel Smith may well have felt like the indignant citizen who said: "Damn John Jay! damn everyone that won't damn John Jay!! damn everyone that won't put lights in his windows and sit up all night damning John Jay!!!" But the Senate consented to the treaty and Washington signed it on the ground that it was better than no treaty at all.[15]

Smith did not have a chance to voice his protest until the next year. In order to carry the treaty into effect it was necessary to appropriate money for the various commissions which were appointed under the treaty to iron out specific grievances. The Republicans in the House saw their chance. Led by Madison they refused the appropriation until Washington should furnish the House with all documents and instructions relative to the negotiations. In this way they hoped to show that the Federalists had been responsible for the failure to secure better terms. Washington refused the demand and the issue was joined. Smith supported the Republicans in two speeches in March, 1796, which showed his intense disgust for the conduct of the administration. In one of them he said:

> When the Envoy was sent to Great Britain, he was principally to demand restitution for the depredations on our commerce. We find that object attended to so vaguely that our best informed men seem doubtful whether much will ever be recovered under the Treaty. . . . We find, that by a fair construction, we have acknowledged ourselves to have been the infractors of the Treaty of Peace. . . .[16]

The United States, he continued, instead of securing advantages and restitutions, had been restricted in the West Indian trade which was vital to the prosperity of Baltimore and other southern ports. He was willing to concede that it might be the best possible treaty that could be obtained under the circumstances. But what were the circumstances? The executive did not see fit to say. He recollected that the clamor of public opinion on the Neutrality Proclamation had been stilled by the submission to the people of pertinent information which justified the executive decision. Why did not the President see fit to do likewise in the present case unless there was something discreditable in the transaction? Secret and confidential, seemed to be the administration's only answer. Said Smith:

> . . . gentlemen had taken a ground that appeared alarming: That the President of the United States and two-thirds of the Senate may, by the aid of a Treaty, do anything and everything not morally impossible (provided they do not infringe on the Constitution,) and that the immediate Representatives, forming this House, have only to be informed thereof, and to obey. . . . Could this be the fair construction of our so much boasted Constitution?[17]

With this heavy attack of the Republicans blocking the appropriation, the Federalists maneuvered the issue away from the treaty and toward the President. The question became one, not of accepting or rejecting the treaty, but of accepting or rejecting President Washington. The Republicans were forced to admit defeat after Hamilton had rallied the country behind the Federalist cry of "The Glory of the President and the safety of the Constitution."[18]

So successful was this Federalist strategy that Smith encountered dissatisfaction with his position among his own Baltimore constituents. Citizens of the town instructed him by petition to vote for the treaty. On April 22, 1796, he denounced the treaty in the strongest terms but ended by saying that he could not repudiate his former commander in chief, and so would vote for the appropriation.[19]

This lame reversal weakened his position in Baltimore so much that a strong opposition candidate could have defeated him. James Winchester and Colonel John Eager Howard were both spoken of as candidates to oppose him but Federalist leaders were concentrating their efforts on the election of their presidential candidate, John Adams, to succeed Washington. Winchester refused to neglect his business for politics and Howard was elected to the Senate, so Smith was reelected to the House unopposed although the Federalists secured the state for Adams, who defeated Jefferson for the Presidency, by an electoral majority in Maryland of seven to four.[20]

Meanwhile, events in France were shaping themselves to the detriment of the Republicans and to the delight of the Federalists. Reacting to Jay's Treaty, and its stipulation that provision ships sailing for

France might be confiscated if cargoes were paid for, the Directory of France declared that it would treat American ships in the same manner when they were bound for British ports. James Monroe, the American Minister, whose sympathetic assurances of American friendship seemed to be denied by Jay's Treaty and by the election of the Federalist candidate to the presidency, was recalled. Wholesale French depredations on American shipping and the refusal of the Directory to receive Monroe's Federalist successor, Charles C. Pinckney, gave the Federalists ample excuse to whip up anti-French sentiment. They immediately introduced into the last session of the Fourth Congress a series of resolutions for additional appropriations for the army, navy and fortifications.[21]

Smith did not follow the Republicans in their opposition to this increase in the defense program. His vote and voice are recorded in favor of all such measures. It was the beginning of a long series of disagreements between Smith and the Republican party on the country's defense establishment, and the disagreements continued for the next thirty years. He could not conceive of a policy which looked to preeminence in commerce without a sufficient naval force to protect it. "They had been asked by the gentleman from Pennsylvania (Mr. Gallatin), in what nation, besides Great Britain, their Navy went hand in hand with their commerce," he said in the debate over the naval appropriation in the spring of 1797. "He would ask that gentleman in what nation commerce had flourished, to any extent, without a Navy. He knew of none. . . . It was ridiculous to think of supporting any considerable commerce without a naval force." His vote appeared also against a reduction of the army and it was largely through his efforts that the reduction, after it had been approved once, was reintroduced and rejected.[22]

He was equally vehement, however, against the Federalists when they proposed offensive measures which would force the country into war with France. The newly elected president, John Adams, refused to follow his party's line and determined to avert a war. He sent two special envoys, John Marshall of Virginia and Elbridge Gerry of Massachusetts, to join Pinckney, who had remained in Paris despite the French government's refusal to receive him. They were to attempt to renew efforts to negotiate with France. He also called Congress into special session in the summer of 1797 and issued a proclamation forbidding the arming of merchant ships. He considered that clashes between American and French ships were basic factors in the bad feeling between the two nations, which, if continued, would surely mean war. The Federalists in Congress immediately countered by introducing a bill which authorized the arming of merchant ships. But they gained no support from Smith. He drew the line between preparedness and belligerence, and joined the Republicans in supporting the President's action. On June 5 when he faced the Federalist opposition he proved that he had become an accomplished debater, and the scorn with which he upbraided the Federalists in support of Adams' bill warmed many a Republican heart.

In answer to opinion voiced by pro-British Federalists that the hardships of war were as nothing beside the injuries to national honor which the United States suffered at the hands of France, Smith taunted them with the reminder that during the debate over the Jay treaty when war with England threatened, "there was not a British tear that was not called forth on this same ground." Honest merchants, he continued, did not want to arm their ships. It not only increased insurance rates but endangered the lives of the ships' crews by inviting attack from hostile men-of-war. His own constituents, forming the population of one of the largest commercial centers in America, had specifically instructed him to do everything in his power to keep peace. If Congress wished to legislate in favor of privateers and filibusters and thereby ignore the wishes of honest citizens, then the President's proclamation should be defeated. The Congressional bill was rejected but the Federalists did not abate their efforts.[23]

However, events were against the Republicans. In France Talleyrand, the French foreign minister, overreached himself when he demanded from the American mission a *douceur* in addition to a loan as the price for opening negotiations. Such high-handed conduct, when it was reported in America, raised the cry "Millions for defense but not one cent for tribute."[24] When Adams laid the reports of the ministers before Congress in the spring of 1798, designating the French go-betweens in the negotiations as X, Y, and Z, the Federalist majority had 12,000 copies printed and distributed. Riding the wave of indignant public opinion, they authorized the calling out of a provisional army, levying of additional taxes, non-intercourse with France, and a bill which authorized American vessels to retaliate against French armed ships.[25] Smith and the other Republicans tried in vain to stem the tide. Only on the bill to authorize American naval vessels to convoy merchant ships did he vote with the Federalists.[26] When the Federalists tried to pass a bill authorizing the President to issue letters of marque to privateersmen in a vain effort to precipitate hostilities, Smith lashed out:

> What are our means of war? We have means sufficient for defence, but we have none for offence. Have you a sufficiency of arms? I know you

have not. Have you cannon? No; you have been obliged to dismantle your
fortifications to supply your ships of war. Have you a fort that is able
to repel the attack of an enemy? In short you are devoid of every means
of aggression. You may protect yourselves, but you cannot hurt your
enemy.[27]

Finally, the Federalists, like Talleyrand, overreached themselves.
In June and July they passed four laws calculated to reduce what
the Federalists conceived to be a grave danger from foreigners in
the United States. The Naturalization Act required a minimum of
fourteen years' residence for citizenship, and two Alien Acts gave
the government power to deal with aliens, and the President the
power to remove undesirable foreigners from the country. In addition
to these the Sedition Law was passed which, after providing against
subversive activity of foreigners against the government, contained
a clause which stated that any speech or writing against the President
or Congress with intent to defame or bring them into disrepute was
a misdemeanor punishable by fine and/or prison. It was in this latter
provision that the Republicans saw an attempt by the Federalists to
gag the opposition and perpetuate themselves in power. Smith voted
with the rest of the Republicans in their attempt to block the law,
but the Federalist majority triumphed.[28] There was a wave of Republican reaction headed by the resolutions from the Virginia and Kentucky
legislatures declaring the acts unconstitutional and void.

1798 was a Congressional election year and the Republicans seized
upon the issue to arouse public opinion. Samuel Smith, now that
he was wholeheartedly in the Republican ranks, realized that he would
have a hard fight to retain his seat in Federalist Maryland. His opponent, James Winchester, a Republican turned Federalist, attacked him
with such virulence that Smith was led to publish a defense "to the
voters of the city and county of Baltimore":

The various shifts that my opponent has from time to time reverted to,
are neither honorable to himself nor complimentary to your understanding.... In the beginning of his opposition he declared in the public
papers that my reelection would depend upon my votes and observations
in debate and not on anything that had ever escaped me in the levity of
unguarded conversation. Upon this high ground he commenced his
attack. But from this he very soon found it necessary to descend and has
suffered himself to be the organ of the most pitiful slander against
me....[29]

When Smith attacked the Sedition Law in his campaign speeches,
the *Federal Gazette* promptly denounced him:

General Smith voted against what is commonly called the SEDITION law. I desire no stronger evidence of his hostile disposition to the *administration* of the federal government, and of his *political* principles, than his vote, *and* his speeches to his constituents in justification of it. It has been the *catchword* of the antigovernmental party, to brand this law by the appellation of the gag law, that is, that it is made to *gag* or *stop the mouths* of the people; to take away the liberty of speech, and to prevent inquiry into the misconduct of the government and its officers. Gen. Smith has had the effrontery to make use of such *language* before several meetings of his constituents. There is no language too severe, no epithets too coarse, for such base attempts to deceive and mislead the people. . . . General Smith ought to blush for attempting to imput [sic] upon his constituents, a belief that the law was intended, or can possibly have any effect to restrain in any degree the freedom of SPEECH.[30]

But neither the General nor his fellow Republicans were deterred. William Hindman, Baltimore Federalist, reported to McHenry that they were "Riding Day and Night" to blacken Federalist reputations,[31] Smith's influence with the lower class laborers, mechanics and sailors, "a dreadful Mob that made every thinking Person apprehend Mischief," as George Salmon wrote fearfully to McHenry, enabled Smith to defeat his Federalist opponent. He was a popular man with the people of the city, despite his wealth and position—or perhaps because of it. It cost money to produce all the age-old tricks of campaigning such as free whiskey, barbecues, rallies, and the like. His opponents accused Sam of spending $6,000 on the election. The Federalist Hindman noted, on the other hand, that the election in 1798 of the four Maryland Republicans, half of her representation in the House, was due to "the Want of Exertion on the Part of the Federalists, whose Purses ought to be open for the Occasion."[32]

Smith's victory marked an important watershed in his career. He had earlier been attracted to the Hamiltonian policies of sound money and fiscal responsibility, something to be expected of a man of his commercial background. But by 1796 he had broken with the Federalists, primarily on questions of foreign policy. His pugnacious temperament was affronted by the attitude of appeasement which Hamilton had adopted toward Great Britain. More important was the fact that Baltimore's trade with the West Indies, including the British West Indies, was severely damaged by British policy. American merchantmen in the Caribbean, if bound for the French islands, were seized for trading with the enemy; if bound for the British West Indies, for violating Jay's Treaty. In contrast to the merchants of the Northeast, Smith's profits were not so dependent on a large carrying trade with England.

Nor could Smith forget the sentimental attachment to America's wartime ally, France, a sentiment which was strong among the people. Episodes like the XYZ affair might bring on temporary attacks of the "black cockade fever," but Britain could always be counted upon to commit acts which even Alexander Hamilton characterized as "atrocious" and "tokens of deep-rooted hatred."[33]

Happily for Smith, sentiment accorded with political advantage. He thus found his support among the laborers, mechanics, and sailors of Baltimore and there is no reason to believe that he found the association distasteful. Like many Americans the general was proud of his military career and thought of himself as an "old soldier." He was commander of the Maryland militia and he was not above using his position for political purposes. His opponents were admitting a fact of political life when they complained that "after drinking the general's whiskey or rum" the militiamen were not likely to vote against him.[34] His election secured Baltimore for Jefferson's party in a year which was generally marked by Federalist victories. Thus the election of 1798 marked him as a Republican leader of considerable consequence.

Smith took little or no part in the Congressional debates in the sessions of the Sixth Congress. His appointment to duty as a major general in the Maryland militia in accordance with Congress's recent bill authorizing the activation of the provisional army kept him busy. But a more probable reason for his inactivity was that he, like some of the other Republicans in Congress, gave up trying to oppose the Federalist majority and began to concentrate his efforts on the approaching Presidential election of 1800.[35] The war with France failed to materialize because John Adams refused to yield to the pressure from the Hamiltonian pro-war Federalists and had sent another special mission to negotiate a settlement with Napoleon. The Federalists suddenly found themselves responsible for an increased army and navy—and taxes to pay for them—but diminishing prospects for war. As the election approached, the Republican forces gradually gained strength. A Republican caucus in the capital placed Thomas Jefferson and Aaron Burr, the master politician of New York, in nomination to oppose the Federalist ticket of John Adams and C. C. Pinckney.

Party divisions in Maryland in the campaign of 1800 followed geographic lines to some extent. The relatively small independent farmers of the western counties combined with anti-British Republicans of Baltimore. Conservative planters of lower Maryland and Annapolis tobacco interests looked to Great Britain for their economic support. Federalist leadership was vested in such men as Charles

Carroll of Carrollton, a planter and the richest man in America; Samuel Chase, anti-constitutionalist, but now a member of the federal judiciary and anxious to retain his influence; Luther Martin, another anti-constitutionalist, but hating and fearing Jefferson and Virginia to the extent that he became the "bulldog of Federalism"; James McHenry, the ex-army surgeon who was Adams' Secretary of War.[36]

Smith knew a close fight when he saw one and in the campaign he stumped the state for weeks at a time. He and his fellow-Republicans, Charles Carroll, Jr., Gabriel Duvall, Joseph Hopper Nicholson and others, had good grounds for their attacks on the Federalists: the Alien and Sedition laws, the unjustified war measures, and the whole Federalist program of centralization of the national government. The Alien laws were particularly objectionable in Baltimore where many agents for foreign commercial firms were forced to leave, thus disturbing international trade.[37] Another Federalist mistake which the Republicans capitalized on was the plan instituted by the elder Carroll and McHenry to pass a law through the legislature to have electors selected by that body. The Federalists felt that there would be a better chance of getting a majority by this method than in a statewide election. But the bill failed to pass the legislature and the knowledge of such tactics turned many votes to the Republicans, who took full advantage of the situation to show that the Federalists were depriving the people of their liberties.[38]

The Maryland electors cast five votes each for Adams, Pinckney, Jefferson and Burr.[39] By the total count of the electoral college Burr and Jefferson each received seventy-three votes and the election was thrown into the Federalist-dominated House of Representatives, which had been elected in 1798. When the Federalists decided to throw their support to Burr, the stage was set for one of the most dramatic presidential elections in American history. Jefferson was the choice of his party by intent and already acknowledged by many as a hero of the Revolution. Aaron Burr, not yet the slayer of Hamilton nor tainted by the charge of treason, was suspect as a cynical, new-school politician. Jefferson thus becomes the hero and Burr the quasi-villain. Yet, in the tangle of partisan historiography, obscure half-truth, and personal rivalry, the hero has emerged a little tarnished and the villain with more than the suggestion of a halo.

Apoligists for Burr have claimed that he never sought the election and that he did not connive with the Federalists who, seeing in him a pliant if not a corrupt politician, gave him their support in the House as a last ditch effort to retain a portion of power. Detractors of Thomas Jefferson hold that he secured the election by a corrupt bargain with members of the House who extracted certain promises from him as conditions for their support.

One of the key figures in the situation was General Samuel Smith, influential in securing five of the ten electoral votes of the state for Jefferson. It was to him that Burr addressed his first disavowals of ambition for the presidency, and through him Jefferson is alleged to have made the corrupt bargain. Burr wrote to General Smith on December 16, 1800, shortly before the final electoral count had been determined:

> It is highly improbable that I shall have an equal number of votes with Mr. Jefferson; but if such should be the result, every man who knows me ought to know that I should utterly disclaim all competition. . . . As to my friends, they would dishonor my views and insult my feelings by harboring a suspicion that I would submit to be instrumental in counteracting the wishes and expectations of the U.S. and I now constitute you my proxy to declare these sentiments if the occasion shall require.[40]

But two weeks later the repudiation was not quite so positive. The results of the election were then known, and in a letter which Smith received from Burr on December 29 there was a definite flavor of contradiction. Since the letter itself is vague in its protestations of wounded dignity it is here quoted in full:

> I advised you from New York of my intended journey hither [Trenton] and offered if you should please to meet you in Philla.—I shall remain here until the 3 Jan. expecting your answer.
>
> At the moment of leaving town I received a great number of letters on the subject of the election, and I perceive a degree of jealousy and distrust, irritation by no means pleasing or flattering—The letters are however generally answered by those which I have written you; but one gentleman (of our party) has asked me whether, if I were chosen President, I would engage to resign—The suggestion was unreasonable, unnecessary and impertinent, and I therefore made no reply. If I had made any I would have told that as at present advised, I would not. What do you think of such a question? I was made a candidate against my advice and against my will; God knows never contemplating or wishing the result which has appeared—and now I am insulted by those who use my name for suffering it to be used. That is what we call going on principle and not on men—I presume however that before this time you are satisfied that no such event is or ever was to be apprehended by those who laugh at your absurd claims —Write me therefore of something else—Who is to fill Wolcott's place? What will become of the french treaty—of the judicial bill—etc., etc.[47]

In other words, the Republican party had technically, if not by actual intent, nominated Burr for president, and he was insulted that they should now imply that he was not qualified. Note indeed the phrase "as at present advised I would not [resign]," in contrast to "I should utterly disclaim all competition" of December 16 when the electoral ballots had not been counted and an equal vote was "highly improbable." The least anyone can suppose at this point was that Burr regretted his previous disclaimer.

The next development was the arrival of "a Mr. Ogden" in Washington, who, Smith informed Burr on January 11, 1801, "has undertaken to say that he came to Trenton with you, that you conversed pretty freely on the subject of the tie, from which he meant I presume, to insinuate that he had your confidence." The gentleman in question was David A. Ogden, prominent New York attorney and a staunch Federalist. Ogden sought out the New York Republicans and represented to them the advantages to their state which would follow Burr's election. When the New Yorkers announced their intention of standing firm for Jefferson, Ogden then approached a New Jersey Republican but met with a similar response.[42] Such activity immediately raised in General Smith's mind the possibility that Burr was secretly coalescing with the Federalists to win their support. And there was ample ground for this fear, as seen in James A. Bayard's letter to Alexander Hamilton, January 7, 1801, which read in part: "By persons friendly to Mr. Burr it is distinctly understood that he is willing to consider the Federalists as his friends." There was a further report that Burr had "expressed his displeasure at the publication of his letter [of December 16] by General Smith."[43] As early as the 24th of December Robert Goodloe Harper, Maryland Federalist, had written to Burr: "I advise you to take no step by which the choice of the House can be impeded or embarrassed. Keep the game perfectly in your hands, but do not answer this letter, or any other that may be written to you by a Federalist man, nor write to any of that party."[44] Nathan Schachner, in his biography of Burr, takes note of this letter and says: "There is no record of an answer. It asked for none nor did it require any."[45] Certainly it did not require an answer if indeed Burr were deep in the Federalist game and if he wished not to have his ambitions "impeded."

General Smith, even though he did not know of this correspondence, became concerned with the appearance and activities of Ogden and he wrote as much to Burr.[46] Burr's answer of January 16 was as immediate as it was brief: "I have said nothing of a Mr. 'O'—nor have I said anything to contravene my letter of the 16 ult. but to enter into details would take reams of paper and years of time."[47] But James A. Bayard later said of Ogden: "I remember Mr. Ogden's being in Washington.... It was reported that he was an agent for Mr. Burr, or it was understood that he was in possession of declarations of Mr. Burr that he would serve as president if elected."[48]

The appearance of Ogden created enough confusion to send General Smith to Philadelphia to keep the appointment with Burr suggested in the latter's letter of December 24. The details of this meeting are set forth by George Christie, Republican representative from Maryland, in a letter written at the General's request for use in a libel suit:

> You informed us . . . after telling us that you relyed on our not divulging the conversation you had with Mr. Burr that you went to Phila. on the day appointed . . . you had a long conversation with him on the subject of the Election of the President of the U.S. but you could not imagine what Col. Burr meant for some time as he had not made any observations but what might as well have been made by letter. At length you inquired of Col. Burr what was to be done if the Federal members did not give up, in that case Col. Burr (greatly as you said to your surprise) told you that at all events the House could and ought to make a choice, meaning that if they could not get Mr. Jefferson they could take him. . . . You told us that you came away much mortifyed as when you went up to Philadelphia you expected that Col. Burr would give you full authority to say that he would not serve if Elected President. . . . But instead gave you to believe that it would be best not to rise without making a choice even if that choice should be him. . . .[49]

The balloting in the House of Representatives began on February 11, 1801. Although the Federalists had a majority of members in the House, the Republicans carried eight of the sixteen states for Jefferson in the first ballot. Two states, Vermont and Maryland, were divided and the Federalists voted six states for Burr.[50] Since a majority of nine was necessary for election Jefferson needed one more state. But the Federalists grimly persisted in maintaining the deadlock, and ballot followed ballot with no change in the result. It is inconceivable that had General Smith been authorized by Burr to rise in the House and announce that the latter would not serve if elected, the Federalists would have continued to vote for him.

Burr's action can be explained only on the assumption that he desired the election. Not daring to campaign openly against his own party, he could only secure the Presidency by getting Republican votes in both of the divided states and also gain an additional state which had previously voted for Jefferson. Only by maintaining a public silence and by hinting in private that he was available could he hope to succeed. This was his precise course of action.[51]

That Burr was working hand in glove with the Federalists is more difficult to substantiate. Against the statement of Bayard quoted above, the implications of Ogden's activities, and the strategy mapped out by Harper's letter, may be set forth the following comments. Jefferson expressed the opinion to his daugher, Martha Jefferson Randolph, on January 4, 1801, that "The Federalists were confident at first that they could debauch Col. B. . . . His conduct has been honorable and decisive, and greatly embarrasses them."[52] Caesar Rodney, in a letter to Joseph Hopper Nicholson, said on January 3, "I think that Col. Burr deserves immortal honor for the noble part he acted on this occasion."[53] And General Samuel Smith wrote to his son John July 19, 1804, "I have said that none of his correspondence or conversation with me would warrant the charge made against him of having intrigued with the Federal party for his Election."[54]

Two observations should be made, however, in connection with the statements of Jefferson, Rodney and General Smith. First, it must be constantly borne in mind that Burr was a Republican nominee and that if he became President he would have to institute a Republican administration. He must have been highly regarded by party leaders to have received the nomination. The Republicans were in the unenviable position of backing Jefferson without being able to oppose Burr. Had they not defended the conduct of Burr in the absence of any real evidence of his bargaining with the Federalists, their party's position would have been absurd. Such a defense, moreover, was the best means of counteracting an intrigue if one, in fact, did exist. Even if Burr had actually come to an understanding with the opposition the best way to retaliate was to defend him as a staunch Republican.

On the thirty-sixth ballot, February 17, 1801, the Federalist members of the two deadlocked states, Maryland and Vermont, cast blank ballots, thus allowing the election to go for Jefferson. The question at once arose as to what made the Federalists give in. Perhaps it was simply that they realized their cause was hopeless. But some contemporaries, including Burr, insisted that Jefferson made a corrupt bargain.

Politics in 1801 were conducted, ostensibly at least, on a much higher level than in our own day. Just as Aaron Burr would have been condemned had it been proved that he made political promises to the Federalists, so Jefferson would have been equally tainted had he attempted to influence members of the House by appealing to them directly.

While rumor and veiled hints flew thick and fast in Washington all during Jefferson's first term, it was not until 1805 that the corrupt bargain charge was publicly made. Hostility between Jefferson and Burr had begun shortly after they took office and had grown to such an extent that Burr was dropped as vice-presidential candidate in 1804. Already in the midst of his preparations for going "down the river," Burr, in 1805, instituted a suit against James Cheatham, editor of the *American Citizen,* to publicize and confirm the charge of bargain against Jefferson. Burr contended that James A. Bayard, Federalist and sole representative in Congress of the state of Delaware, had approached Smith two days before the final ballot was cast and had asked him for assurance as to Jefferson's views on certain questions. Bayard told Smith that if Jefferson would pursue a policy in line with his own ideas on the funding system, the navy, and the retention of Federalists in public offices he would withdraw his support from Burr. Smith was able to satisfy Bayard in a general way, but the Federalist insisted on more definite assurance. According to Bayard, "The next day, upon our meeting, General Smith informed me that he had seen Mr. Jefferson and had stated to him the points mentioned and was authorized by him to say that they corresponded with his views."[55] The result of Bayard's having been thus informed is related by George Baer, Maryland Federalist:

> On February 16 a consultation was held by the gentlemen I have mentioned, [Baer, Craik, Dennis and Thomas, Maryland Federalists; Bayard and General Morris, Federalist of Vermont] when, being satisfied that Mr. Burr could not be elected. . . . it was resolved to abandon the contest. . . . A general meeting, however of the federal members was called, and the subject explained, when it was admitted that Mr. Burr could not be elected. . . . *Having also received assurance from a source on which we placed reliance that our wishes with regard to certain points of federal policy in which we felt a deep interest would be observed in case Mr. Jefferson was elected,* the opposition of Vermont, Delaware and Maryland was withdrawn.[56]

Bayard, by 1805 a political enemy of Jefferson, set forth his account of the "bargain" in a deposition which Burr intended to use in the Cheatham case. General Smith, being the other principal in the transaction, was called upon for his account of the incident. He agreed that Bayard had met him on the fifteenth and had indicated that he might withdraw his support from Burr if he could ascertain

Jefferson's views on the aforementioned subjects, But Smith sharply disagreed with Bayard's account of subsequent events. Smith explained that he went to Jefferson "without his having the least idea of my object" and ascertained his views by engaging him in a general discussion on the various topics. Smith continued: "I communicated with him [Bayard] the next day—from the conversation I had had with Mr. Jefferson I was satisfied in my own mind that his conduct... would be so and so. But I certainly never did tell [Bayard] that I had any authority from Mr. Jefferson to communicate anything to him."[57]

The question seems to turn upon whether Jefferson knew that Smith came from a Federalist member and whether or not Jefferson authorized Smith's reply to Bayard. "Which," says one of Burr's biographers, "on the face of it seems a rather academic distinction. Certainly Jefferson was too smart a politician not to have realized why Smith sought him out in special conference to discuss certain matters which could only have emanated from Federalist sources."[58] There was, however, no need for Smith to seek him out since Smith and Jefferson lived in the same boarding house. Nor was there any need for, or record of, a special conference. Jefferson himself said that "the general subject and all its parts were constant themes of conversation in the private tete-a-tetes with our friends. But certain I am, that... he nor any person was ever authorized by me to say what I would or would not do."[59]

Adding a final bit of weight to General Smith's version was an incident which occurred at the time of the Cheatham trial. When Smith was asked to furnish his deposition, he prepared a rough draft in his own hand. Colonel Burr obligingly called and offered to take the General's deposition to a clerk to be put in final form. When Smith received the prepared copy he found that his deposition had been altered to agree more nearly with that of Bayard. Burr presented the two depositions only to have Smith withdraw the altered copy and replace it with a draft of the original.[60] With this conspirator's touch, the charge against Jefferson was momentarily buried, yet to be revived on later occasions by general historians, biographers, and even members of Congress.

Jefferson's inauguration as the third President of the United States marked the triumph of the Republican revolution. It also marked the mature development of Samuel Smith as a politician of consummate skill. He had established himself as an expert on commercial affairs in Congress and, with his colleagues, had begun the Federalist overthrow in Maryland. He had created a Republican stronghold in Baltimore which never wavered during subsequent resurgences of Federalism in Maryland; and if he had not carried the state for Jefferson, he could claim a large share of credit for keeping it from voting for Adams. For these services to his party Samuel Smith stood in the front rank of the Republican leaders who now shed their opposition roles and, as Jefferson's lieutenants, set about the work of positive accomplishment.

Samuel Smith was not given to expositions on political philosophy, although he was capable of the kind of florid oratory which politicians of that day considered to be standard equipment. (Perhaps the twentieth century historian, rendered altogether insensitive by political demagoguery and television commercialism, takes too cynical a view of such eloquence.) Smith represented a mixed constituency. His business associates and friends, such as William Patterson, James A. Buchanan and Jonathan Hollins, who supported him throughout his long career, obviously thought he was "sound" on issues which affected them as merchants and businessmen. Yet his Republican antagonism for Great Britain was as much the old soldier's memory of an enemy as the merchant's shipping losses. He shared the popular and essentially emotional sympathy for France and he obviously had strong support from the "dreadful mob" of Baltimore, as any perennially successful politician in that turbulent city had to have. He was a wealthy merchant but he was only a generation removed from John Smith's trading post on the Pennsylvania frontier. Sam Smith probably never heard the phrase "grass roots" but he understood its meaning very well. So his politics was partly intuitive and partly the politics of business, and he never bothered to build a philosophical framework for it.

5

Jefferson's Lieutenant

"THE RAPID INCREASE OF BALTIMORE has even surprised its friends," says a contemporary chronicler, "and it now ranks as the third commercial port in the Union." Jefferson's chief lieutenant in Baltimore was Samuel Smith, ex-soldier, merchant, and man of affairs. Besides his partnership in Smith and Buchanan, he held an interest in Buchanan, Spear and Co., another commercial house organized by his cousins.[1] He had investments in road and canal companies, was a bank director, and had far-flung real estate interests.[2]

Among his Maryland holdings were several town houses in the city of Baltimore and one of these, on Exchange Place, he had bought in 1796 for himself and his family. He continued to live there, while the town around him grew into a city.[3] But the residence to which he gave the most meticulous care and lavish expense was his summer home, "Montebello," completed in 1800. Differing from the colonial tradition of most of the large houses near Baltimore, the house was divided into two parts. The front half, of one story, had a columned, marble-paved porch running in a semicircle across the width of the house. The rear half, which rose two stories high, was rounded into bays at either end and had a central bay extending outward in the rear. This allowed a ground floor interior composed of a central oval dining room with flanking half oval drawing rooms. "With its unusual mass, its white walls, its long stretches of fine balustrade, and its oddly curved porch . . . Montebello must certainly have produced a much gayer and more villa-like effect than its refined and stately neighbors," says a twentieth century architect.[4] "Montebello" was located a few miles northeast of Baltimore and for many a summer it was to provide a haven from the heat of the city for General Smith and his family.

The Smith family had become quite large by 1801. Margaret had eleven children, the youngest born in 1797. Of these apparently only six survived childhood accidents and diseases, and Louis, the eldest and Sam's favorite, died in 1805 of consumption at the age of twenty-one. Anne, the youngest, lived only five years.[5]

Of Sam's ten brothers and sisters only five were alive in 1801. Mary, who had married George Nicholas of Virginia, later a prominent lawyer and Jeffersonian stalwart in Kentucky, died in 1800. Margaret married George Nicholas' brother, Wilson Cary Nicholas, an aristocratic Virginia planter, also a staunch Jeffersonian, and close friend and political associate of Smith in Congress. John, Sam's former partner, deserted his merchant career in 1789 and was now a Baltimore attorney.[6] Most conspicuous of Sam's brothers was Robert. Five years younger than Sam, he had been in school during the Revolution but had taken time out to participate in the battle of Brandywine as a private. After the war he came to Baltimore and, by 1801, had developed the city's most extensive admiralty law practice. He was chosen an elector in 1788 in the nation's first presidential election and had an outstanding career in the Maryland legislature for over ten years. A man of great personal charm, liked by almost all who met him, Robert Smith was, at forty-four years of age, a successful man. New honors awaited him and he was, during the next decade, to be intimately associated with Sam's political career and with Jefferson's Republican party.[7]

The President called upon Samuel Smith just one month after his inauguration as the third president of the United States. Robert Livingston of New York had refused to accept the position of Secretary of the Navy so Jefferson offered it to General Smith. "It is the department which I understand the least," Jefferson wrote to Smith, "and therefore need a person whose complete competence will justify the most entire confidence and resignation." Smith refused the offer, saying that the state of his private affairs was such as to preclude his doing full justice to that office.[8] This may have been the reason or it may have been Margaret Smith's distaste for the crude little capital, for Albert Gallatin wrote his wife, "Mrs. Smith is here and hates the place."[9] But in all probability, Smith turned down the post because he realized that Jefferson was waiting only until the Federalist-dominated Congress adjourned before nominating the brilliant Swiss-American, Albert Gallatin, to the position of Secretary of the Treasury. The new administration was pledged to strict economy and Gallatin and Jefferson both favored reductions in the army and navy as the first and most productive fields of budgetary retrenchment. Smith himself believed in a defense establishment capable of protecting the nation's commerce and had not hesitated to go against the party to vote for its increase. Had he accepted Jefferson's offer he would have been hampered by restricted appropriations which would make it impossible to conduct the department as he wished.[10]

Jefferson did appoint Gallatin to the Treasury. To lead the Department of State he chose his life-long friend and fellow-Virginian, James Madison. Two New Englanders, Levi Lincoln, Attorney General, and Henry Dearborn, Secretary of War, filled out the cabinet except for the Naval Department vacancy. After offering the latter post to John Langdon of New Hampshire and William Jones of Philadelphia, Jefferson turned once more to Smith. The latter still refused but agreed to run the department for a short time until a suitable permanent appointee could be found.[11] The only major problem with which Smith had to deal during his few weeks in office was the Tripolitan War. A series of outrages by the doughty Mediterranean corsairs of the North African coast had been committed upon American merchantmen who had grown tired of paying the commercial blackmail demanded by the Barbary States. Finally, on March 14, 1801, the Pasha of Tripoli declared war on the United States.

Before the news of the actual declaration had reached America, Smith had acted. On May 15 he dispatched Commodore Thomas Dale with three frigates to the Mediterranean with orders to meet force with force. Dale destroyed a Tripolitan corsair on the way and when he reached his station he set up a blockade on the port of Tripoli. Subsequent events leading to a complete victory for the United States occurred after Smith retired from office in July, 1801.[12]

Sam's successor was his younger brother, Robert. Jefferson wrote to the elder Smith early in July: "Mr. Langdon having ultimately refused ... by this mail I propose the office to your brother, Robert Smith.... Let me beseech you, dear sir, to give us the benefit of your influence to prevail on his acceptance...."[13] Robert Smith succeeded his brother on July 15, 1801.

Relieved of his undesirable post in the Navy Department, Smith resumed his seat in Congress in the fall of 1801, where the Republican members were girding themselves for the overthrow of Federalism. General Smith and William Branch Giles were the oldest and most experienced of the Republican leaders in the House. Here began a close alliance between the Maryland merchant and the Virginia planter which was to last until the latter's retirement from public life. In many ways they were alike and in many ways opposites. Both were wealthy, both marked by an open, jovial nature that was robust and genial. Giles's dress was carelessly plain, after the manner of many Virginians. His eyes were dark and retreating, his form robust and inclined to bulkiness, his hair sandy in contrast to his dark complexion.[14] In debate Smith was tenacious, but inclined to facts and figures to prove his point, Giles was more flamboyant and dramatic, yet possessing "a well-digested and powerful condensation of language, he points out his objections with calculated force and sustains his position with penetrating and wary argument."[15]

Not the least impressive of the Republican House leaders was the slight, elegant figure of John Randolph. The slender, boyish body and the equally boyish face belied the lightning brain and the slashing tongue of Randolph of Roanoke. Seldom has the national legislature seen his equal in administering verbal assault on an opponent. Joseph Hopper Nicholson of Maryland, Samuel Mitchill of New York, and Michael Leib of Pennsylvania made up for their lack of parliamentary brilliance by their skill and hard work in committee.

Speaker of the House Nathaniel Macon of North Carolina appointed John Randolph as Chairman of the Ways and Means Committee. Second in importance was the Committee on Trade and Commerce, and the Speaker acknowledged General Smith's preeminence in this field by placing him at the head of that committee.[17] Under this leadership the Republicans, with a majority of 69 to 36, set about the fulfillment of Jefferson's pledges. The first object of their attack was the repeal of internal taxes.

Knowing that such an attack was coming, the Federalists introduced a series of resolutions for the repeal of import duties aimed especially at such widely used articles as sugar, coffee and brown sugar. They hoped, by carrying such reductions, to place the Republicans in the position either of not repealing internal taxes or facing a deficit in revenue for the next year. The Republican majority, after a day of debate, simply refused to answer the assertions of the Federalists and quietly voted down each proposal for tariff reduction.[18]

But they faced a problem when the debate for internal tax repeal came up in March, 1802. The chief point made by the Federalists was that these taxes represented an income of $650,000 a year. How was this revenue to be replaced? Even the astute Secretary of the Treasury, Gallatin, refused to commit himself for he had estimated the income from import duties at a very conservative figure, and in doing so, had been unable to satisfy himself that the deficit could be met. It remained for Randolph to provide the solution by securing a pledge from Robert Smith and General Henry Dearborn, Secretary of War, that they would effect such economies in their departments as would balance the estimates of Gallatin.[19]

One by one the Federalists, led by James A. Bayard of Delaware and Roger Griswold of Connecticut, defended the items to be repealed, and one by one they were voted down by the Republican majority. Sam Smith summed up the Republican argument on March 22. His statistics showed, he said, that seven states, New Hampshire, Connecticut, Vermont, Delaware, New Jersey, Georgia and Tennessee together paid only $52,000 in internal taxes as compared with Maryland's $72,000. "Are we then, to be surprised if those States which pay scarcely anything . . . should be found voting against the repeal?" And to the opposition's contention that the articles taxed were luxuries, he added slyly, "I have yet to learn what luxury there is in drinking whiskey."[20]

He then went into the matter of the deficit which the repeal would create. Here he turned the Federalist tactics back on them, for were not these the gentlemen who had advocated the lowering of tariff duties only a month ago, a reduction which, if it had been carried would have created a deficit of $2,000,000? He was surprised that the gentlemen worried about a paltry $650,000. "The President has recommended the lessening of other expenses," he concluded, "which Congress have adopted, and will adopt, such as will, I expect, amount to one million dollars. Let us therefore give his honest endeavors to save the public money, and to relieve the burdens of the people, our warm support and assistance."[21] The repeal was carried by better than a two to one majority.

The Judiciary Act, next on the Republican repeal agenda, was a partisan Federalist measure passed in the closing days of Adams' administration. It was designed to create a number of new federal judgeships with the attendant clerks and court officials. Many of the new judgeships may have been needed. Certainly it was necessary to relieve the Supreme Court justices from the arduous travel necessitated by holding court throughout their circuits. But what infuriated the Republicans was that these positions had been distributed to Federalists by Adams on the eve of his retirement, so as to provide a stronghold for Federalism in the courts which the Republicans would be unable to touch because of the fact that judges held office for life. The Republicans sought to nullify its effect by repealing it. The Federalists were virulent and violent at the thought of this attack upon an independent branch of the government. "Once touch it with unhallowed hands; sacrifice but one of its provisions, and we are gone," said that tower of Federalist strength in the Senate, Gouverneur Morris.[22]

The Senate bill for repeal was reported to the House in February, 1802. For the Republicans, William Branch Giles led the fight. For the Federalists, the brilliant young man from Delaware, James A. Bayard, guided the opposition. Giles exhorted his fellows to repeal an act "passed in the highest paroxysm of party rage" which produced "a gradual demolition of the State Courts." Bayard replied with the exposition of the theory that aggrandizement of state power would destroy the Union.[23] Randolph sneered that President Adams had used his power of patronage to create "the veto of the Roman Triumvirate over your laws," and had given "to the publicans and sinners the privilege of priesthood."[24] Bayard replied with a devastating catalogue of positions now held by Republicans who were the key figures in swinging Jefferson's election in the House.[25] The debate went on, with personalities exchanged and speakers often called to order. The Senate met and adjourned hastily in order to attend the House sessions.

Samuel Smith took little part in this debate. He was "unequal to the constitutional question" by training and preferred to leave the burden of the argument to his colleagues. His only speech was in reply to his Federalist Maryland colleague, John Dennis, who charged the new administration with excessive use of patronage, and the President with officious interference in submitting to the House relevant documents showing that the new judgeships were unnecessary. Said Smith:

> Is it not fair, then, to conclude . . . that the law which the gentlemen
> from the Federal Party would not themselves permit in 1800 when they
> retained the power, they did pass in 1801 when they knew that all power
> had been taken from them? Is it not fair to conclude that the law was
> passed for the sole purpose of embarrassing the new executive, by a
> corps of men, clothed with omnipotent power, and hostile toward it?

Although the executive never had submitted a judicial document to the House, Smith "could not but express . . . regret that the last President had not, when he pressed the law upon Congress, supplied such documents; if he had, every gentleman would have seen how unnecessary the law was." After a bitter debate lasting nearly a month the triumphant Republican majority won their fight for repeal.[26]

At the close of the first session Jefferson's lieutenants could take pride in the institution of a new financial program, which promised economy and early extinction of the public debt. To this was added the repeal of internal taxes and of the Judiciary Act.

General Smith returned to Baltimore to bolster Republican sentiment in Maryland. Two accomplishments marked the efforts of Smith and his fellow Republicans. The first of these was the appointment of Smith himself to the United States Senate by the legislature in March, 1802 to replace Federalist John Eager Howard.[27] The other was the elimination of property qualifications for voters. This measure had, strangely enough, been introduced by the Federalists in 1797 under the leadership of Michael P. Taney, father of the future Chief Justice of the Supreme Court, Roger B. Taney. The conservative senate of Maryland had voted the measure down after it had passed the House of Delegates. The Republicans, having gained a majority in the lower House in the elections of 1799, adopted the measure for their own but when it was introduced in 1800 the senate still blocked it. This attitude on the part of the state senate, whose members were elected for five years, made it so unpopular that a wave of indignation swept the Federalists out of office in 1802 and the elimination of property qualifications was passed.[28]

When Congress convened late in 1802 the Jeffersonians lacked the able leadership of William Branch Giles, who had become ill during the summer. This put a greater burden on Smith and Randolph, but the solid Republican phalanx insured a continuation of Jefferson's program.

New diplomatic developments in the summer of 1802 preluded delicate maneuvering in this second session of the Seventh Congress. The Spanish governor at New Orleans, acting on his own initiative, had denied to Americans the right of deposit of their goods, thereby closing the mouth of the Mississippi to the West. This action, if permitted to remain in force, would effectively throttle Western trade. To complicate the situation Spain had, by the Treaty of San Ildefonso, secretly ceded the Louisiana Territory to France. When rumors of this action reached America the spectre of a French colonial empire to the west of the United States rose to haunt the administration.[29]

The Federalists were delighted. Seizing upon the issue, they proclaimed themselves the friends of the West and proposed that the United States assert its rights immediately and, if necessary, by force. Their purpose was twofold. First, they hoped to attract westerners to the Federalist party and weaken Republican strength in that area. Second, they hoped that a war scare would force large defense appropriations which would upset Gallatin's carefully laid financial plans.

When Smith arrived at Washington in December of 1802 he soon discovered that Jefferson had pursued a wise but very delicate course. In his message to Congress the President referred to the situation in Louisiana merely as "a change in the aspect of our foreign relations."[30] Meanwhile, he had been assured by the Spanish minister in Washington that the order of the governor at New Orleans would be withdrawn and a peaceful settlement would result. But the cession of Louisiana to France, the order for which was signed by Charles IV of Spain on October 15, 1802, led Jefferson to the decision that New Orleans must be purchased. Before any action could be taken, however, the Federalists in the House, led by Roger Griswold of Connecticut, opened their attack. Griswold demanded all executive papers connected with the cession of Louisiana to France. He was forestalled momentarily by Randolph and Smith, the latter harking back to the debate over the Jay Treaty when the Federalists had denied submission of executive documents:

> According to his recollection, one side of the House had called for papers on the principle that, after negotiations were terminated, the House had a right to information before they made a grant of money under a treaty. He . . . thought it improper, and had then so declared, to call for papers during a pending negotiation.[31]

Griswold's motion was set aside momentarily on a point of precedence and Randolph immediately moved to clear the galleries for a secret session to consider a confidential message from the President. This was done, and the Committee of the Whole adopted a resolution that the United States did not believe that there "was any want of good faith on the part of his Catholic Majesty, and, relying with perfect confidence on the wisdom and vigilance of the Executive, they will wait the issue. . . ."[32] This resolution was passed by sections. The Federalists voted for that part expressing belief in the "good faith on the part of his Catholic Majesty" but opposed the expression of confidence in the executive.

The tactics behind this sparring were dictated by the fact that the Republicans knew that Jefferson was determined to act with great vigor, even with force, against Spain if the order revoking the right of deposit were not withdrawn. But he did not wish to exhibit this hostile attitude through the revelation of executive documents in a public session which might upset negotiations which he hoped would be successful. The Federalists wanted publicity of all the circumstances of the situation so that they might inflame the country and force a war. But they were forced to concur in all parts of the resolution passed in the secret session except that expressing confidence in the executive. When Griswold again put forward his resolution for documents, Smith cut the ground from under him by reminding him of the paradox of his position:

> Does not the gentleman who drew this resolution believe, from the express words in it, that the conduct of Spain has been unfair, and that she may have adopted measures derogatory to her character and honor? . . . Is the gentleman really in earnest in his inquiries at this time? and if the effect of his resolution should be to show that the stipulations are injurious to our rights, would he know how to act? he would be for acting spiritedly, no doubt; and yet, at this very moment, when he professed such a declaration, he declares to the world that he has no confidence in the Executive, who is now pursuing the proper measures! . . . I cannot consider [his] conduct as intended to promote the real interest of the country; but as calculated to bring the country into a situation from which it cannot withdraw without . . . expense and blood.[33]

On the same day, January 11, 1803, General Smith moved the House into another secret session during which $2,000,000 was appropriated for negotiations "between the United States and foreign nations." The way was thus paved for the most brilliant achievement of the first Republican administration. Shortly afterward Jefferson nominated James Monroe, of Virginia, to aid the American minister in Paris, Robert Livingston, who had already begun to negotiate for the purchase of New Orleans and the Floridas. Monroe, trusted friend of Jefferson and popular in the West, was confirmed after a brief but bitter debate in the Senate. He departed shortly after a public dinner had been given in his honor at which General Smith summed up the administration policy in a toast: "Peace, if peace be honorable; war, if war is necessary."[34]

Having failed to discredit the administration in the Louisiana situation, the Federalists, in the closing hours of the session, tried a new attack. Bayard of Delaware demanded an investigation of a sale of United States Bank stock made by the commissioners of the sinking fund for the retirement of a loan in Holland. By leaving no time for an investigation, the implication of improper conduct would remain until Congress could reconvene. Smith here demonstrated his special value to the Republican party. Speaking without preparation and drawing solely on his extensive financial knowledge, he showed that Bayard's conclusions had ignored such varying factors as the rate of foreign exchange and the difficulties attendant to the transfer of so large a sum in international bills. The commissioners had acted wisely, and had actually saved the government money.

Then he labelled the resolution for what it was: "But, sir, I will ask, what does the gentleman mean. To find fault, is it? His resolution, in truth, means nothing. We are told, ten hours before adjournment that an inquiry is to be made...." By whom, if not by the present Congress? "Does the gentleman mean to send the question to the Supreme Court of the United States? Or does he mean that the House shall immediately judge of the legality? If he does... I am ready to declare the sale to have been legal...."[35] A majority of the House thought so too, and the next day Congress adjourned.

During the following summer Jefferson's hopes for Louisiana were fulfilled. As he had foreseen, the war between England and France was resumed, and Napoleon was forced to abandon his hopes for an American empire. As an initial step toward establishing France in America, Napoleon in 1802 had sent one of his best generals, Marshal Leclerc, to recover French possession of St.-Domingue (Haiti) which had successfully revolted against French rule in 1793. Leclerc managed to subdue the forces of Toussaint L'Ouverture after a hard fought campaign but the weakened French army was further decimated by an outbreak of yellow fever which also took the life of Leclerc. With the outbreak of the European war, Napoleon was obliged to abandon St.-Domingue and with it, Louisiana. Livingston and Monroe were able to buy not only New Orleans but the whole of Louisiana for $15,000,000.[36]

Another circumstance attendant to the French withdrawal from St.-Domingue was the release from duty in Leclerc's army of Jerome Bonaparte, youngest brother of the First Consul. In the summer of 1803 young Bonaparte came to New York, where he was cordially received. He soon appeared in Baltimore and was entertained by Commodore Joshua Barney, who had known him when that famous American sea fighter had been in the French Navy during the 1790's.

The social whirl produced by the young Frenchman's arrival was one of the most notable in the annals of Baltimore. Early in the fall, at a party at the home of Judge Samuel Chase, Jerome met Betsy Patterson, daughter of William Patterson, a prominent Baltimore merchant who had married General Smith's sister-in-law. Although her father foresaw the displeasure of Napoleon, he could not dissuade Betsy from accepting the attentions of the handsome Frenchman. After a whirlwind courtship which was the talk of Baltimore, Jerome married Betsy on Christmas Eve, 1803.[37]

The reactions were immediate and numerous. When the young couple reached Washington, President Jefferson and society in general received the bride and groom with the utmost cordiality. Pichon, the French minister, was aware that Napoleon would probably be furious but he also showed the proper attentions.[38] He wrote to Talleyrand:

> It appears, Citizen Minister, that General Smith, who in spite of the contrary assurances he has given me, has always had this alliance much at heart, has thrown his eyes on the mission to Paris as a means of appeasing the First Consul. He has long since aimed at the diplomatic career, for which he is little qualified; this motive and the near return of Mr. Livingston have decided his taste. For some time there has been much question of this nomination among the friends of General Smith.[39]

In the meantime, the Federalists had found a target for their scorn. John Quincy Adams sourly confided to his diary: "Curious conversation between S. Smith, Breckenridge, Armstrong and Baldwin about 'Smith's nephew, the First Consul's brother.' Smith swells on it to extraordinary dimensions. . . . it was really the young man who was seduced. . . . The Smiths are so elated with their supposed elevation . . . that one more step would fit them for the discipline of Dr. Willis."[40]

Smith did have diplomatic aspirations to the position in England. In the summer of 1803 he wrote to his brother-in-law, Wilson Cary Nicholas, who he knew had influence with the President, concerning the possibility of his appointment as minister to the Court of St. James. Nicholas advised Smith not to apply since he would have to give up his commercial connections or put himself in an ethically questionable position of conflict of interest if he received the appointment. He enclosed a letter to Jefferson, in which he warmly recommended Smith, leaving it up to the latter's judgment as to whether it should be sent.[41] Smith took Nicholas' advice and did not apply; but the incident foreshadowed the events of the next five years, which were to be marked by an increasing disposition on the part of Smith to question the wisdom of the Sage of Monticello in his conduct of foreign affairs.

6

Leader of the "Invisibles"

"IF WE CAN KEEP the vessel of state as steadily afloat in her course for another four years," wrote Thomas Jefferson to Elbridge Gerry on March 3, 1804, "my earthly purposes will be accomplished...."[1] There was in the year of 1804 certainly nothing to dismay the most pessimistic of the Republicans. Campaigning on a record that boasted the purchase of Louisiana, internal taxes repealed, twelve millions on the national debt paid, the Mediterranean pirates chastened, and Federalism overthrown, the Republican party swept Jefferson into office for a second term. In Maryland Sam Smith and his fellows secured nine of that state's eleven electoral votes for the Virginian.

In the Congress which met just after the election of 1804, a Congress in which the Federalists would muster only nine out of thirty-two Senators and twenty-five out of one hundred and forty-one Representatives, the Republicans made a final attack on the Federalist-dominated judiciary. Samuel Chase of Maryland, Supreme Court Justice during the Adams administration, who had several times invoked the Sedition law against Republican editors, had continued even after Jefferson's election to use his charges to juries as political harangues to courtroom audiences on the wickedness of Republicanism. At the President's suggestion, the House appointed a committee, headed by John Randolph, that brought impeachment charges against Chase which were sustained by the House. The trial before the Senate consumed most of the session of 1804–1805, with Randolph heading the prosecution and Bayard, Harper, Luther Martin, Philip Barton Key of Maryland, and Charles Lee of Virginia representing

Chase. The prosecution bungled the proceedings badly and the Federalists answered brilliantly. Randolph's arrogance, invective, and insults alienated many otherwise staunch Republicans. Senators Smith and Giles tried desperately to muster the necessary two-thirds votes for conviction, but they managed a bare majority on only four of the eight counts.

The significance of the vote was not so much that Justice Chase was acquitted but that Randolph temporarily lost his control of the Republican party in Congress. Even President Jefferson remained aloof and Secretary of State Madison was openly amused. The failure indicated the first serious rift in the Republican ranks and foreshadowed Randolph's break with the administration in the next session.[2]

In this session, which began in December of 1805, General Smith was elected president pro-tempore of the Senate in the absence of Vice President Clinton,[3] and from this vantage point he noted the signs and portents that foretold a conflict within the Republican party. John Randolph was becoming more and more alarmed at the increasing tendency of the administration toward what he conceived to be Federalist policies. Gallatin, personally friendly to Madison, was nevertheless a supporter of Randolph because of the latter's efforts to keep down expenses and economize in appropriations. The other potential alignment included Samuel and Robert Smith who, together with Northern Republicans, foresaw the necessity of a commercial and, possibly, a fighting war with England which would require an increase in the defense establishment of the country. To complicate matters Jefferson, encouraged by his success in the purchase of Louisiana, determined somehow to acquire East and West Florida from Spain.[4]

As the first step in his effort to purchase Florida, Jefferson sent two messages to Congress. The first, his regular message at the opening of the session, referred to Spanish aggressions along the southern frontier and was definitely belligerent in its tone. The second, a secret message, hinted at the need for money for diplomatic intercourse with which he hoped, with the aid of French pressure, to secure the Floridas.[5] Jefferson had been assured of French cooperation from a secret communication from Talleyrand, who requested the same privileges for French merchants in Florida as they then enjoyed in Louisiana, in return for which France would cooperate in securing Spain's assent to the sale. As an additional gesture in securing the good offices of Napoleon, Jefferson recommended to Congress, through George Logan of Pennsylvania, that trade between the United States and St.-Domingue be suspended as an aid to France in recovering that island.[6]

However much Smith may have known of the circumstances surrounding the Spanish negotiation, he opposed Logan on this latest administration measure. On December 20, 1805, he vigorously denounced the President's proposal. The people of St.-Domingue, he said, had won their independence. A suspension of our trade would be justly considered by them as an act of war. Half a million people depended on direct trade with the United States for their food. But in addition to this moral reason the United States would be doing France a favor at the expense of its own lucrative trade. And Sam Smith, though he did not say so, knew from experience just how lucrative this trade was. Not only would this eliminate one corner of the triangular trade, he continued, but we would give to England, our worst enemy, an opportunity to take over this trade which precluded our ever getting it back.[7] The bill passed, however, when Jefferson sent to the Senate notes from the French ministry saying that the trade "must" be suspended.[8]

With the way thus paved, the House went into secret session; but the administration ran into further opposition in the person of John Randolph. Suspicious of the whole affair, Randolph had gone to Madison, who had told him that France had to have money from the United States if she were to aid us in the Spanish negotiation. Randolph thought that if the President wanted money he should ask for it openly and expressed his disgust by simply departing from Washington, leaving the House Ways and Means Committee immobilized because of its chairman's absence.[9] When he finally returned and prepared an adverse report from the Committee, enough Jeffersonians in the House adhered to the administration to thrust Randolph aside and appropriate two million dollars for the Spanish negotiation.[10] In the Senate the measure passed with three Republicans absenting themselves from the voting and four voting with the Federalists. Smith was among the Republicans who supported the administration.[11]

Yet when the President appointed John Armstrong, the American minister at Paris, to aid James Bowdoin at Madrid, Smith again went into opposition. Armstrong had succeeded Livingston in France and had received a great deal of blame from American merchants for his handling of the French spoliation payments provided for under the Louisiana Treaty. Although most of the blame really lay with Livingston, who had begun the adjustments in a very slipshod manner, Armstrong was intensely unpopular in commercial centers.[12] "Armstrong is again honored at a time when all America believes he should be recalled," Smith observed to Nicholas, adding that his appointment had seriously undermined Jefferson's popularity in Baltimore.[13] The nomination was saved in the Senate when, despite Smith's efforts to defeat it, Vice President Clinton, who had resumed his duties as presiding officer, broke a 17 to 17 deadlock by voting for approval.[14]

While the decision was being reached on the Florida Purchase issue, General Smith became involved in the knotty problem of commercial relations with England. After resuming her war with France in 1803 Great Britain, for almost two years, took no steps to interfere with the neutral carrying trade of the United States. Even more advantageous to American shipping interests was the action of France in opening her trade to the West Indies, normally closed to all save French merchants. Unable herself to supply her colonials, she was forced to admit American ships to keep them from starving. Britain countered by invoking her Rule of 1756, which stated that trade not open in time of peace could not be permitted in time of war. Although this put a halt to the reexport trade, Americans soon resorted to the expedient of landing cargoes in ports of the United States and then reloading them, often in the same ships, and sending them to France as American goods. Great Britain now took more stringent action. In 1805 a British admiralty court decision in the case of the merchant ship *Essex* held that unless produce carried by American ships in broken voyage between two enemy ports paid bona fide American customs duties, the ships were engaged in direct trade and therefore violated the Rule of 1756.[15]

Coupled with this decision was an increased activity of the British navy against the American merchantmen. Ships were stopped on the slightest suspicion of violation and sent to the nearest British port to await the decision of Admiralty Court. If they escaped condemnation, they still experienced inconvenience and delay. To add insult to injury Great Britain increased her impressments of seamen from American ships to fill her short-handed navy. This was done under the pretext of recovering British deserters, but about six thousand American citizens fell victims to the press gangs during the entire period prior to the war of 1812.[16]

In January of 1806 Jefferson sent a message to Congress asking that it take the grievances against Britain under consideration but offering no lead as to what should be done. In the Senate the message was referred to a committee headed by General Smith. Since the President seemed unwilling to take the lead, Smith reported out a bill the first section of which recommended non-importation of British woolens, silks, glassware, and a long list of less important articles. These were later revised on the floor of the Senate to provide for much milder restrictions. But the heart of Smith's retaliatory action was aimed at James Monroe, American Minister in England, and at Secretary Madison, whom Smith held partly responsible for permitting British high-handedness. He recommended that the United States "demand" indemnity for England's abuses and seizures and that some arrangement be made which would put Anglo-American relations on a satisfactory basis. These arrangements were to be made by a special mission which was to supersede Monroe. He concluded his report by pointing out the ignominy of the present position of the United States in her relations with Great Britain by saying, "We are in truth more useful to her than if we were again her colonies, for she enjoys all the benefits of our commerce and incurs no expense in our protection.[17]

After the resolutions had passed, Smith, accompanied by Senator Samuel L. Mitchill of New York, called on the President to present his case and to add his own advice to the official word of the Senate. Two years later Jefferson wrote Monroe of the interview:

> After delivering the Resolutions the committee entered into free conversation, and observed that although the Senate could not in form recommend any extraordinary mission, yet that as individuals there was but one sentiment among them on the measure and they pressed it. I was so much averse to it, and gave them so hard an answer that they felt it and spoke it, but it did not end there. The members of the House took up the subject and set upon me individually. . . . I found it necessary at length to yield my own opinion to the general voice of the national council. . . .[18]

Having carried the point which he and his friends had advocated, Smith's next move was to seek appointment on the special mission for himself. He was not qualified as a diplomat, but he thought that, since the object of the mission was to conclude a commercial agreement, someone should be appointed who understood commercial affairs. But President Jefferson gave Smith a sharp rebuff by retaining Monroe in his position as minister and appointing William Pinkney, Maryland Federalist from Baltimore, to aid him. Smith wrote indignantly to Nicholas:

> When I actually heard that the President had written privately himself (to the astonishment of all his cabinet, when he told them) to William Pinkney of Maryland, a warm Federalist, who had answered consenting to succeed [sic] Monroe and when I was informed that the only difficulty was to find a capable merchant to join the mission for the purpose of making a commercial treaty—and that no member of the cabinet could think of a proper character. . . . I confess I was mortified and I could not but ask myself "what have I not done to serve these men? What have I done to be thus insultingly slighted?"[19]

Although Pinkney was one of the most distinguished members of the Maryland bar and had served on the commercial commissions set up under Jay's Treaty, Smith was thoroughly disgruntled and disgusted. He confided to Nicholas his conviction that the mission of Monroe and Pinkney could not succeed. "Neither of them can know anything of the practical commerce of the country, and must make mistakes."[20] Nor did he fail to point out the political implications of the appointment of a Federalist. "If . . . the President selects from the Federalists his most confidential servants, may not Baltimore be pardoned if the people should select their servants from the same party?" And he showed his growing contempt for Madison by concluding, "I can never coalesce with the Feds. but not so M[adison]. I believe he is almost ripe for it."[21]

Smith's insurgency, however, was mild when compared to that of John Randolph, who charged that Madison and Jefferson had done little more than spell Federalism backwards during the first term and now were spelling it forward. When Andrew Gregg of Pennsylvania early in March brought before the House a resolution for non-importation similar to that passed by the Senate under Smith's leadership, Randolph attacked not only the bill but the administration and its entire policy. Madison, Monroe, even Jefferson himself, were arraigned by him with virulence and sarcasm such as the House had seldom heard directed at an administration. The chief burden of his argument was against the administration's conduct of the Florida negotiation, and he took the opportunity to mention all the details of the secret session and even the private conversations which he had held with the Secretary of State on the subject.[22] In his vindictiveness he overreached himself, for Smith and other Republicans might have been willing to follow him had his revolt and the manner of its execution stayed within reasonable bounds. But, as Smith wrote to Nicholas of Randolph's denunciation of the Florida negotiation, "The question was simply, Buy or Fight! Both Houses, by great majorities, said, Buy! . . . Mr. Randolph expects that . . . a public explosion of our views and plans will render abortive this negotiation and render the executive and poor little Madison unpopular. . . . However, he spares nobody and by his conduct has compelled *all* to rally around the Executive *for their own preservation*."[23]

Gregg's resolution was set aside and Smith's non-importation bill, as amended by Nicholson, was passed by the House.[24] The net result of the stormy session was a futile appropriation for the purchase of the Floridas and a watered-down non-importation act against Great Britain while, in London, Pinkney and Monroe attempted negotiations with the British Ministry.[25]

The President's annual message to Congress, when it convened in December, 1806, did nothing to strengthen Smith's faith in the wisdom of the administration's foreign policy. In fact, foreign relations were almost ignored in favor of recommendations for abolition of the slave trade, expenditure of the surplus in the Treasury on internal improvements, and the establishment of a national university.[26]

The first action of Congress was to suspend, at the administration's request, the non-importation act of the previous session.[27] Smith felt powerless to oppose it in view of his recent rebuff by the President. Revolt at this time would be fatal. "We have established theories," he wrote to Nicholas, "that would stare down any possible measures of offense or defense. Should a man take a patriotic stand against these destructive and fine spun follies, he will be written down very soon. . . . Never was there a time when Executive influence so completely governed the nation."[28] Smith did, however, succeed in introducing a bill which was subsequently passed increasing the army by one regiment of infantry and one battalion of cavalry.[29]

General Smith's judgment of the abilities of Monroe and Pinkney was justified when news of the negotiation, which they had concluded on the last day of 1806, arrived in the United States early in the spring of 1807. Madison sent the Monroe-Pinkney Treaty to General Smith for his comment, perhaps as a belated recognition of the latter's influence in the Senate and to soften the rebuff by the administration.

Smith denounced the treaty in the strongest terms. In two letters to Madison, April 3 and 18, he pointed out that the treaty said nothing about the two chief points upon which Monroe had been instructed to secure satisfaction, impressment and indemnity for British confiscation of American goods. Article III, which provided that American ships in the East Indian trade proceed directly from British possessions to the United States, eliminated inter-island trade in the Far East and reduced this trade to the point where it would be of no value. There was no reference in the treaty to the discriminatory export duties which Britain charged against the United States, a point which the Senate had considered of the utmost importance. Finally, there was the humiliation of Article XI in which Great Britain required that all French or Spanish colonial products be required to pay a minimum American duty, with no drawback, when reexported through American ports. This ruling was intended to last for the duration of hostilities between France and England. This virtually closed the West Indian trade, since the treaty did nothing to alter the British West Indian trade provisions of Jay's Treaty.

Most important of all, Smith recognized, as Madison apparently did not, that the treaty was an expression of England's basic policy:

to destroy or seriously cripple American commerce—not so much as a means of defeating Napoleon, but as an end in itself. No one reading the debates and correspondence of Spencer Perceval, Lord Hawkesbury, George Rose, and George Canning during the formulation of the British Order in Council of the following November can doubt that Smith was right. Monroe's treaty, Smith wrote, would "completely prostrate our trade at the feet of G. B.... at no time have the British enforced a system so completely injurious to the U. S.... We ought to risque every consequence that can possibly result to us, even war, rather than commit the honor & interest of the nation by binding ourselves to such an instrument."[30]

Jefferson was almost as disgruntled by the terms of the treaty as Smith. He not only rejected it, but refused to submit it to the Senate, not wishing to subject Monroe to the criticism of that body which he knew would result. William Branch Giles, a friend of Monroe, wrote to him frankly that the treaty had "excited universal disappointment and astonishment."[31] But Smith foresaw the implications of this action, perhaps far more clearly than did Jefferson himself. On March 4 he wrote a remarkably prophetic letter in which he said:

> The Senate ... did *unanimously* advise the President to negotiate a treaty with Britain. The Senate agreed to his nomination of the negotiators. A treaty was effected. It arrives. It is well known that he was *coerced* by the Senate to the measure; he refuses to submit it to their approbation. What a responsibility he takes! By sending it back he disgraces his own ministers and *Monroe is one.* Monroe and Pinkney come home and in justification publish the treaty. It may appear good in the eyes of unprejudiced men.—I suspect it will. By refusal to accede to it the British continue their whole system of "You will not trade in time of war where you [were] refused in time of peace;" the impressment is carried on to an extent un-unbounded in their power; ... a general outcry will ensue; all will say, "If Monroe's treaty had succeeded, those losses would not have happened; why was it refused?" Jealousy of Monroe, and unreasonable antipathy by Jefferson and Madison to Great Britain!—This will be said, this will be believed. And Monroe will be brought forward; new parties will arise, and those adverse politically will be brought together by interest ... Monroe will be called a martyr and the martyr will be the President. And why? Because he has done right, and his opponent has advised wrong....[32]

In other words, Jefferson was demanding blind obedience and in so doing was leaving the way open for a party split which would surely come, once Monroe returned to the United States. Jefferson was shielding Monroe at his own expense. The President may not have feared any Federalist resurgence but Smith knew that the Maryland Federalists were still strong. "The Republican party is a rope of sand," wrote Smith, "only to be held together by federal opposition. The moment that ceases, it will go to pieces and something new will start up in its place."[33] The Federalists had gained ground when Justice Chase was acquitted, and they waited only for a Republican breakup to recover their ascendancy.[34] Had Jefferson allowed the treaty to be submitted to the Senate and had its faults brought forth in debate, or had he studied it more carefully before his summary rejection, the belief that it was merely his hatred for England that lay behind his action would not have gained so much ground.

It is possible at this point to discern that group of Congressmen who came to be known as the "Invisibles." The term was coined by Nathaniel Macon in 1809 to designate a rather nebulous group of Washington politicians who frequently opposed the policies of the Jefferson and Madison administrations.[35] The "Invisibles" were just that—difficult to identify because they often disagreed among themselves and because it was hard to recognize or classify them. In the forefront of this group was Samuel Smith. It was natural to assume that his brother, Robert, Secretary of the Navy under Jefferson and Secretary of State under Madison, was also in the clique. Wilson Cary Nicholas, close friend of Thomas Jefferson and brother-in-law of General Smith, was another "Invisible." William Branch Giles, Senator from Virginia, was to be found lending his incisive mind and biting tongue, while Michael Leib's voice and vote marked him as an adherent. Dr. Samuel Mitchill, Vice President George Clinton, and even John Randolph of Roanoke sometimes supported the group, although Randolph cared little for "the doughty General" who was "vulnerable at all points and his plausible brother not much better defended."[36] Indeed, the more effort one makes to track down this shadowy coterie, the more one is impelled to the conclusion that Macon's appellation was justified. It may be assuming too much to call Sam Smith "leader" of a group as independent and strong-willed as the people singled out above.

The rift between the "Invisibles" and the President seemed on the point of becoming an open break when, on June 22, 1807, the country was shocked into a violent wave of anti-British feeling by the British man-of-war *Leopard's* firing on the American *Chesapeake*. The outrage was all the more humiliating because it occurred inside the Chesapeake Capes. Jefferson registered the American protest in London and resisted the war-like imprecations of Congress. Said Wilson Cary Nicholas: "If I directed affairs of this Country I would instantly employ force to avenge the injury which has been done us. I would not ask, I would take satisfaction."[37] William Branch Giles presided over a meeting of Virginia citizens in Amelia County which resolved that "this meeting consider the attack on the Frigate Chesapeake, as the commencement of a war on the United States by the British Government."[38]

Jefferson and his cabinet hesitated. The President must have been painfully conscious of the lack of preparations for a war which he himself had so steadily resisted. He may also have considered the fact that the Napoleonic Decrees were in many ways as objectionable as the Orders in Council, although Napoleon had committed no such overt act as that perpetrated by the *Leopard*. All summer the American government waited to see what the response of England to the American protest would be. In December it found out just how penitent His Britannic Majesty was. Britain's reply was in the form of a new Order in Council which in the severity of its restrictions outdid anything she had yet contrived. The Order provided for a "paper" blockade of all ports closed to British vessels by Napoleonic decree.[39] This meant that any neutral vessel could be seized anywhere on the high seas if there was evidence that it was bound to or from a port declared under blockade. In effect, American goods could be legally exported to the continent only through English ports, a situation which, as Sam Smith later noted, bore a striking resemblance to "regulations made for us when we were colonies." This practice, eventually exercised also by Napoleon against vessels bound to or from ports "paper" blockaded by France, conflicted with United States interpretation of international law. According to Madison, a blockade, to be legal, must be real; that is, the offending vessel must be apprehended in the act of entering the zone declared to be under blockade. Caught between the possibility of seizure of their vessels by either belligerent, American merchants were "damned if they did and damned if they didn't." To meet this dilemma Jefferson promptly recommended, and Congress passed, an embargo on all United States trade abroad.[40]

The Republicans enthusiastically supported the embargo. Smith, Giles, Nicholas, and Vice President Clinton all closed their ranks around the President against the outcries of the New England Federalists. Baltimore, third largest port in the nation, sent the Maryland senator expressions of its approval in the form of a petition signed by 5,000 citizens of the city. The measure did much to heal the incipient schism created by the fiasco of Monroe's mission. The "Invisibles" also used the situation to press their demands for stronger measures of defense. The results were not particularly gratifying: $850,000 for gunboats; $1,000,000 for land fortifications; $200,000 for arming the militia; $2,000,000 for eight new infantry regiments. In particular, the naval appropriation, which John Randolph said reduced the Navy Department to the Gunboat Department, must have been disappointing to Secretary of Navy Robert Smith. Little had been done to rectify the situation described by Samuel Smith in 1806: "The law of nations is with us, the law of power is against us."[41]

If the new-found solidarity in the Republican ranks was brought about by Jefferson's firm stand against England, it was soon dispelled by the prospect of Jefferson's retirement and his obvious choice of James Madison as his successor. There were strong undercurrents of dissatisfaction, but the election of 1808 proved only that, while Madison was highly unpopular in sections of his own party, his opponents in the party were of many minds as to a suitable substitute.

The "Invisibles" also split. To the dismay of Samuel and Robert Smith, Giles and Nicholas swung their support to Madison, and under their direction the Virginia General Assembly held a caucus calling for the nomination of the Secretary of State. Giles and Nicholas also inspired the calling of a Republican congressional caucus which was attended by eighty-nine senators and representatives, of whom eighty-three cast their votes for Madison.[42]

Against these tactics the opponents of Madison issued a protest, probably written by John Randolph, and signed by seventeen prominent Republicans, of whom Senator Smith was one:

> We ask for energy and we are told of his [Madison's] moderation. We ask for talents and the reply is his unassuming merit. We ask for his services in the cause of public liberty and we are directed to the pages of the Federalist, written in conjunction with Alexander Hamilton and John Jay, in which the most extravagant of their doctrines are maintained and propagated. We ask for consistency as a Republican, standing forth to stem the torrent of oppression which once threatened to overwhelm the liberties of the country. We ask for that high and honorable sense of duty which would at all times turn with loathing and abhorrence from any compromise with fraud and speculation. We ask in vain.[43]

But the opposition was to no purpose. Randolph supported Monroe, whom the Smiths despised almost as much as they did Madison. Their choice was George Clinton of New York. Wilson Cary Nicholas may have reflected Southern Republican opinion of the Vice President when he said, "I have never seen one respectable man from New York who did not speak disrespectfully of him and with horror at the means by which he established himself there. If, however, I had confidence in him as a man, I could not vote for him because I have no evidence we should better our situation.... Nor can I consent to any act of mine to throw the government into the hands of the Federalists...."[44] In the end the rebels were forced to close their ranks to prevent the Federalists from driving a wedge between the factions. Although the administration and Madison could claim a victory, there were ominous signs to be read from the election of 1808.

Federalist gains were registered in many areas outside New England. Using the rising tide of discontent with the embargo as their principal issue, Maryland Federalists picked up six seats in the lower house of the state legislature and two of Maryland's presidential electors defected to the Federalist candidate, C. C. Pinckney. The lower house of the legislature fell to the Federalists in the next election.

All this did not prevent Sam Smith from exercising successfully his old mastery at electioneering. Baltimore still remained a Republican stronghold and returned Republican representatives to the state legislature and to Congress. The victory was celebrated by bonfires, parades and a gin party on Gallows Hill, the spirits furnished by the senior Senator from Maryland.[45]

Meanwhile, the controversy over the embargo continued. Its opponents issued statistics to prove that while it was ruining the commerce of the United States, it was having no appreciable effect on Great Britain. Defenders of the measure contended with equal statistical authority that its effects abroad were serious and would soon be decisive. Even in those areas where the embargo had been enthusiastically supported, rotting hulls and idle seamen were creating waverers and skeptics, and merchants looked askance at their stuffed warehouses.

The summer of 1808 found Baltimore beginning to feel the pinch. The importance of Baltimore as a port has been obscured in many accounts of the commercial history of this period and particularly of the embargo itself. This is understandable in view of the fact that the most violent and extreme opposition came from New England. Nor was the latter section modest in proclaiming its commercial importance and the burdens which the embargo imposed upon it. Yet in 1806 1,043 seamen were registered in Baltimore as compared with 1,001 in Boston.[46] Baltimore's exports for the year 1805 amounted to $7,601,300 out of a total for the United States of $95,566,021.[47] The combined exports of the ports of Massachusetts amounted to $19,000,000 while Pennsylvania's exports totaled $13,700,000 and New York's $23,000,000. In the years 1806 and 1807 the figure for

Baltimore went over the ten million mark, an increase of over 30 percent. Boston's increase in the same period was appreciably less, about 20 percent.[48]

The commercial life of Baltimore, then, was considerable; and the economic blow struck by the embargo, crippling. In 1808 Baltimore's exports dropped to a pitiful $1,904,700, a loss of better than 80 percent. Total exports of the United States in the same period amounted to $22,430,960.[49] Farmers from nearby districts, particularly from the wheat country of the Monocacy Valley, complained of the lack of a market and of the high cost of manufactured goods.[50] "The Farmer is nearly ruined by Mr. Jefferson's experiments," cried the Baltimore *Federal Republican,* "who cannot sell his crop for half price, and whose grain is rotting upon his hands...."[51] On the Baltimore market prices of imported goods were climbing. The end of the year would find lemons up 168 percent, high grade brandy up 33⅓ percent, low grade 50 percent, and shoes up by 15 percent to 33 percent.[52]

"The only way for the people to save themselves from ruin is to turn such unworthy servants out of office and elect men who they know will vote against the embargo and all such measures as are intended to destroy commerce and injure agriculture which is her hand-maid," concluded the *Federal Republican.*[53] Robert Goodloe Harper, staunch Federalist and prominent Baltimore attorney, by way of protest, refused to drill his militia company of artillery during the Fourth of July celebration.[54] But then, as the *Evening Post* pointed out, "...toasts given by MERCHANTS of this city ...generally countenance and support the EMBARGO, while toasts drunk by LAWYERS ...generally reprehended the measure."[55]

Not the least vociferous of the "Lawyers" was Luther Martin, the old "Bulldog of Federalism" himself, who attacked the administration under the *nom de plume* of "Honest Politician." The *Evening Post* denounced him as "Luther, Lord of Slander Hall" and suggested a coat-of-arms: "Crest—decanter, *rampant.* Supporters—Dexter fide, *Bibo,* his brows entwined with wine glasses—on the sinister, *Belial,* richly ornamented with the insignia of 'OUR noble and ancient order' of Billingsgate. Motto—for my desserts."[56]

Despite the Federalist attacks and the staggering loss of trade, the merchants generally stood firm. "It is the height of folly," said the *Evening Post,* "to assert that the restrictions of the embargo are not hard to be borne—it is the summit of ignorance to believe that the people do not and will not suffer much." But people were still in favor of the measure as the best means to coerce the belligerent powers into concession. This was the view "among some of the greatest shipowners of this port." So Baltimore tightened its belt and determined "bravely to meet the throes and convulsions of the day."[57] It may be well to note that the *Post's* somewhat sanctimonious air was marred by the fact that Baltimore was included in the list of ports which the Secretary of the Treasury, Albert Gallatin, had reported as having been guilty of violations of the embargo.[58] And John Randolph announced on the floor of the House of Representatives that one hundred thousand barrels of flour were smuggled out of Baltimore during 1808.[59]

As Congress convened late in 1808, supporters of the embargo, including Giles and Samuel Smith, braced themselves for the assault. Smith firmly believed that the distress felt by the lower classes of English workers would soon be felt by those in power. But private expressions of opinion showed that Gallatin, Madison, and even Robert Smith were wavering. "Most fervently," wrote the Secretary of the Navy to Gallatin, "ought we to pray to be relieved from the various embarrassments of this . . . embargo. . . . Would that we could be placed on proper ground for calling in this mischief-making busybody."[60] Gallatin, gazing at the diminishing income to the Treasury, probably concurred.

But the challenge issued by the Federalists, through Senator James Hillhouse of Connecticut, was met with vigor. Senator Smith replied to the Federalist senator's resolution for repeal. Britain with her Orders in Council and France with her Berlin Decree, he said, made American trade "hazardous at all points." The only way in which the United States could trade with Europe was by paying high re-export charges in England and in the very act of touching an English port American vessels were made fair prize for French seizure.[61]

The gentlemen from New England, he continued a few days later, protested that the embargo worked discriminately against them. Perhaps these gentlemen had never heard of Baltimore or New York where the embargo was favored. For their information he would inform them that New York exported more than all the New England States combined and that Maryland alone exported three-fifths of New England's total.

He denounced the waverers in bitter terms for their lack of courage in the face of British restrictions and impressments, and for their craven fear that the embargo might lead to war:

> Where is the difference in principle between the regulations made for us when we were colonies and those made for us at this time? Does not Great Britain still assume the same rights? . . . They forget that we are

independent—I trust, Mr. President, that we shall not also forget it. . . .
  I have in my hand a public letter . . . by a Senator from Massachusetts
(Mr. Pickering) . . . 'I will close this long letter by stating all the existing
pretenses, for there are no causes for war with Great Britain.
  Great God! Mr. President, can that man feel for American seamen who
can say and write that the impressment of five thousand of our seamen by
Great Britain is no real cause but pretext only?

And finally, he chose the words of England's own Foreign Secretary, George Canning, applying them to what he thought should be the basis of American policy:

No doubt shall remain to distant times, of our determination and our
ability to have continued resistance; and that no step which could be
mistakenly construed into concession, should be taken on our part, while
it can be a question, whether the plan devised for our destruction has,
or has not, either completely failed or been unequivocally abandoned.[62]

Giles echoed these sentiments. The embargo, he said, "has preserved our peace—it has saved our honor—it has saved our national independence." As for the possibility of war, the people would endure it "rather than surrender their own liberties, and the nation's . . . sovereignty; let us then for a time, sir, bear our present privations—let war be the last experiment."[63] The Senate voted down Hillhouse's resolution twenty-five to six. Further proof of the strength of congressional pro-embargo sentiment came with the passage of the Enforcement Act in January of 1809, authorizing federal officials to make searches for illegally imported goods under the general warrants. The Federalists roared out their fury. The Baltimore *Federal Republican* hurled back at the Republicans the principles of the Virginia and Kentucky Resolutions, expressing the belief that the embargo was "a law which is to be enforced at the point of a bayonet [and] will bring on a struggle which may terminate in the overthrow of the government. Our rulers are answerable for the issue."[64] William Patterson, Baltimore merchant and Smith's brother-in-law wrote, "If continued [the embargo] will bring a revolution in government & perhaps civil war, at any rate it must throw the government into the hands of the Federalists . . . be assured that this state of things cannot be continued." Perhaps Patterson was remembering bitterly his sentiments in the previous spring when he had noted, "Every thinking man in the community be him Republican or Federalist sees and knows the propriety and necessity of the embargo . . . [and] it is very desirable that it should be continued until the powers at war shall feel the necessity of changing their conduct toward us. . . . But I have my doubts and fears that the people of this country have ... sufficient virtue and perseverance to wait this event."[65]

Then, in mid-February of 1809, support of the embargo suddenly collapsed. New England Republicans, frightened at the growing secessionist sentiments in their section, were convinced, and convinced others, that New England must be appeased. Equally important was the growing dissension, less openly expressed, among Republicans in the Middle and Southern states. Even Baltimore, which had held out under the leadership of Senator Smith, showed its impatience. More to salvage the party from division than to satisfy New England, the bill for repeal was introduced by Wilson Cary Nicholas, and Senator Smith admitted defeat.

What brought about this sudden collapse? One is forced to wonder at this rather sudden reversal, since Jefferson had only recently demonstrated the firmness of his control over the party. Jefferson told John Quincy Adams, sixteen years after the event, that he was profoundly disturbed by Adams' expressed conviction that unless the embargo was lifted New England would secede.[66] But at that time Jefferson was eighty-two years old and in the same letter he admitted that his mind was almost blank concerning events of former years.

There is more reliable evidence. Said the President on the 7th of February, 1809:

> I thought that Congress had taken their ground firmly for continuing their embargo till June, and then war. But a sudden and unaccountable revolution of opinion took place last week ... and in a kind of panic they voted the 4th of March for removing the embargo, and by such a majority as gave all reason to believe that they would not agree either to war or non-intercourse. This, too, after we had become satisfied that the Essex Junto had found their expectation desperate, of inducing the people there either to separation or forcible opposition.[67]

The "unaccountable revolution" was explained afterward.

> I ascribe all this to one pseudo-Republican, Story. He came on ... and staid only a few days; long enough, however, to get complete hold of Bacon, who, giving in to his representations, became panic-struck and communicated his panic to his colleagues, and they to a majority of Congress. They believed in the alternative of repeal or civil war, and produced the fatal measure of repeal.[68]

Both surprise and anger are mirrored in the above words. Surprise that the Republican majority had jumped over the traces, anger that the majority had been intimidated by the threat of secession—a threat which Jefferson believed no longer existed. The party machinery, or at least Jefferson's control over it, had momentarily collapsed.

It was the pressure of the economic conditions of the embargo upon the structure of the party, not so much in New England, but in the Middle States, in such Republican strongholds as Sam Smith's Baltimore, which led the members to accept the "out" supplied by Story and Bacon. Some may really have been convinced that secession was a near-reality. But the Essex Junto had been preaching secession since 1804. The Republican Party had defeated Federalism in New England before. But with the Federalists gaining ground in areas which had hitherto been solidly Republican, with rifts and rents appearing in the party structure itself, the rank and file may well have decided to remove the millstone from their necks as gracefully as possible. Party leaders felt the pressure of adherence to the embargo very keenly. In October, Smith's old friend Wilson Cary Nicholas had conveyed a warning to the President:

> If the embargo could be executed and the people submit to it, I have no doubt it is our wisest course; but if the complete execution of it and the support of the people cannot be counted upon, it will neither answer our purpose nor will it be practicable to retain it. Upon both these points I have the strongest doubts. . . .[69]

James Monroe warned Maryland Republican stalwart Joseph Hopper Nicholson on the eve of the 1808 elections:

> We are invited with great earnestness to give the incumbents all the support we can,—by which is meant to give them our votes at the approaching election; but it is not certain that we could give the effectual support to the person in whose favor it is requested. . . . After what has passed, [the Republican party] has no right to suppose that we will, by voluntary sacrifice, consent to bury ourselves in the same tomb with it.[70]

In other words, if Republican strength in the Middle States went the way of New England, the party was in serious danger of extinction.

Jefferson and the embargo both went out on March 4, 1809. The Baltimore *Federal Republican* exulted:

> The people will see that their interests have been betrayed and their rights have been infringed and the sacred provisions of the constitution violated, for the purpose of carrying into effect a visionary scheme, continued by the great enemy of the civilized world to prostrate the only barrier which opposes his ambition.—The indignation of an injured people will follow their betrayer to his retreat.[71]

The pressure of the embargo on commercial interests in Baltimore and other Middle Atlantic ports had a political importance which was far greater than that expressed by the vituperative rage of New

England with the result that the political effect and influence of other commercial areas has been underestimated.[72] It was the ominous note of discontent from the Middle States and the South, less vocal but far more serious to finely tuned political ears, like those of General Smith, that led to the Republican revolt and the repeal of the embargo on March 14.

The "Invisibles" did not intend, however, to abandon the strong position which the embargo represented. The Nicholas bill provided for measures of defense which would prepare the nation for war, continued non-intercourse with both England and France, and authorized the President to issue letters of marque and reprisal against the nation which failed to lift her restrictions against the United States. Giles thundered in the Senate, "the time is not past, but is fast approaching, when the whole energy of the nation must be called forth to save what we have left of our honor, independence, and dearest interests."[73]

But despite these efforts only non-intercourse was saved from the wreckage. Trade with both belligerents only was suspended and the President was authorized to resume trade with either, if it lifted its restrictions against the United States. Wilson Cary Nicholas, who retired from the Senate at the end of the session, later in the year stated his and the "Invisibles' " position: "I am decidedly of the opinion that every expedient short of war is submission disguise it as they will and that such expedients will tend only to our embarrassment and disgrace.... When I took the first step in the contest with these powers I foresaw the possible way, the ultimate resort to arms. It was our duty to avoid it if possible. But was equally incumbent upon us not only to be aware that this was the probable result, but to be prepared to meet it, and we ought not to have taken the first step unless we were determined to go to all lengths; that was then my determination and has remained so ever since."[74]

As Jefferson's second term came to a close, Samuel Smith and his colleagues determined not to surrender completely to Madison and Gallatin. The decision of the President-elect to appoint Gallatin to the State Department seemed to Smith and Giles catastrophic in its implications. Madison's willy-nilly foreign policy and, more particularly, his defense policy would be carried on as before, with Gallatin's eye ever on the budget and the national debt. It was determined, therefore, to make an effort to secure the appointment of Robert Smith to the Treasury as a sort of counterbalance to Gallatin. This was done, although over the protest of Nicholas,[75] and Madison was led to understand that Smith's appointment was a necessary condition of the Senate's approval of Gallatin. When the brilliant Swiss-American balked at the idea of Robert Smith, whom he considered incompetent and inefficient, meddling in his beloved Treasury, the insurgents insisted that Robert Smith be appointed Secretary of State and Madison grudgingly acquiesced.

The new Secretary of State had already been informally involved in the negotiations with the British minister, David Erskine, who seems to have discussed Anglo-American relations with various members of the cabinet. In the latter part of 1808 he had informed his superior in London, Foreign Secretary George Canning, that "hints... were thrown out by Mr. Smith, [then] Secretary of the Navy, in a conversation I had with him—that... he would wish that their ministers be recalled from England and France, and that preparedness be immediately made for a state of hostility." He also reported the belligerent spirit of the "Invisibles" and other like-minded Republicans.[76] Canning had been under fire from the opposition in Parliament who charged that his policy would provoke an American declaration of war. To what extent this pressure and Erskine's reports affected him is difficult to say. But on January 23, 1809, he issued a series of instructions to his minister in which the previously belligerent British tone was considerably altered. The dispatches, which did not reach Washington until early April, provided the basis for negotiations between Erskine and the new Secretary of State, Robert Smith. It should be noted that these instructions were drawn up before the collapse of the embargo and the failure of the aggressive measures proposed by Nicholas.

Erskine was directed to offer the repeal of the Orders in Council of November, 1807, in return for which the United States would lift its restrictions on British trade, while continuing them against France. In short, Canning was offering precisely the kind of settlement for which the Non-Intercourse Act was framed. In addition, in April, 1809, Britain modified her Orders in Council to the extent of restricting the blockade to France and Holland and allowing neutral vessels to proceed directly to ports not under blockade. The West Indian trade was, in effect, reopened and the Rule of 1756 implicitly abandoned, at least for the time being. Erskine's instructions, however, contained two conditions. One stipulated that the United States must acknowledge the validity of the Rule of 1756. The other would allow the British to seize American vessels engaged in illegal trade with France—in short, Britain would be allowed to enforce American law.[77]

Erskine opened a series of informal conferences with Robert Smith which led to the conclusion of what was known as the Erskine agreement. Knowing that the United States would take offense at Canning's stipulations, he did not even mention them. In an exchange of notes—which constituted the first executive agreement in the history of American diplomacy—Britain acknowledged her fault in the *Chesapeake* affair. The United States agreed to reopen trade with Britain and close trade with France, as provided under the Non-Intercourse Act. In the matter of impressments, there was a gentlemen's agreement that each nation would take scrupulous care to observe the laws and practices of the other; that is, the United States would try to exclude all but bona fide American citizens from enlisting aboard her vessels, and Britain would refrain from violating the rights of American nationals. Erskine agreed that the Orders in Council of January and November, 1807, would be immediately repealed. The agreement was to be followed by subsequent negotiations which would presumably lead to a formal treaty. Erskine may have reasoned that this would take care of Canning's unfortunate stipulations.[78]

For a brief time it appeared that the United States had won a resounding diplomatic victory. Madison issued the appropriate presidential proclamation and American ships joyfully put to sea for England. Then, at the end of July, came the stunning news. Canning had repudiated the agreement. Erskine was recalled and Francis James Jackson was sent to replace him. Canning justified the disavowal on the ground that Erskine had violated his instructions in not securing American compliance with the two conditions. But the Cabinet's decision was reached only after an extended discussion during which several of Canning's colleagues urged acceptance. And there is reason to believe that Canning did not consider the stipulations as *sine qua non* to an agreement.[79]

It is not difficult to conjecture a more obvious reason. When Canning wrote his instructions of January 23, no relief from the embargo was in sight and the possibility existed that the United States would go to war. When Erskine was repudiated, not only had the embargo been repealed but the belligerent sentiments of Smith and his supporters had been rejected. The General underscored the point during the next session of Congress: "The people were impatient under the embargo and you repealed it. Yes, sir, it was repealed at the very moment when Great Britain, smarting under its effects, was modifying her Order in Council; and she would have done us complete justice but for the wavering indecisive conduct that she saw we were pursuing."[80] One is forced to wonder what Canning's position would have been if the embargo had remained in effect until June 1, as Jefferson and the "Invisibles" wished, or if Nicholas' repeal had been passed without amendment. Jefferson's weapon of economic coercion came very close to success.

7

The Downfall of the "House of Smith" and the Rise of the "House of Austria"

AFTER THE DEFEAT of the embargo and the advent of the new administration, General Smith and the "Invisibles" went into open revolt against Madison and Gallatin. The political in-fighting which resulted in Robert Smith's appointment to the State Department has already been recounted. The Treasury, under Gallatin, had accumulated a surplus and had extinguished all but ten million dollars of the national debt. But this fiscal policy had also left the country virtually defenseless, with only a small standing army and a navy which consisted of a number of coastal and inland waterway gunboats plus six frigates which had been authorized by the Adams Federalists. Smith felt that strong measures were necessary to protect American maritime rights. While he did not, at this time, openly advocate war, he did feel that the country ought to be prepared in case war was forced upon it. This did not square with what he conceived to the the pinch-penny policies of the Secretary of the Treasury. When Madison yielded to the pressure of Smith and Giles by appointing Robert Smith as Secretary of State, he hoped that intra-party reconciliation could be reached. Albert Gallatin was in a different mood.

The Secretary of the Treasury lost no time in launching a counter-attack. The occasion was afforded by the fact that Samuel Smith had not been reelected to the Senate in 1808—but neither had he been superseded. This odd circumstance had come about because the Federalists had gained control of the lower house of the state legislature while the Republicans retained a majority in the senate. The Federalists refused to reelect General Smith and the Republicans refused to elect anyone else. The Republican governor gave Smith an interim appointment until the session of 1809 could decide the issue.[1] Joseph Hopper Nicholson, a Maryland Representative from Baltimore, decided to contest the General's reelection, which thus depended on whether he could command a majority in the new House of Delegates which would be elected in the late summer of 1809.

Gallatin had told Nicholas in the spring that he thought Robert Smith had been guilty of a conflict of interest while he had been in charge of the Navy Department. During the war with Tripoli Smith had found it necessary to establish a temporary naval base in Leghorn, Italy, in order to facilitate the maintainance of the American squadron in the Mediterranean. To expedite naval expenditures he had bought bills of exchange on Leghorn from several large mercantile houses, among them, Smith and Buchanan. Gallatin's charge was that these bills had been in the nature of an accommodation, that is, that government money had been left in General Smith's firm until it suited their convenience to remit it to Leghorn.

Upon learning of Gallatin's suspicions General Smith wrote angrily to him, "I believe it impossible that any man who has the least pretensions to character would commit an act so base as that charged on me."[2] Gallatin's reply was far from conciliatory. "The transaction . . . is, under all its aspects, the most extraordinary that has fallen within my knowledge since I have been in this department."[3] His specific charge was that Smith and Buchanan had drawn bills of exchange on Leghorn without previously transmitting funds to meet these obligations. The effect, said Gallatin, was at worst collusion between the naval agent in Leghorn and Smith and Buchanan, and at best an accommodation to give the firm the use of government funds.[4] It betrayed either Gallatin's rancor or his ignorance; for, if the naval agent had had to wait until the arrival of funds before reissuing the bills of exchange, the whole purpose of the transaction would have been lost. The system was used to avoid the frequent transmission of large sums of specie and to expedite the logistical support of the Mediterranean squadron.

During the special session of Congress called in the summer of 1809, Nicholson managed to obtain the appointment of a special committee to investigate. Its recommendation was in the form of a request for a report from the Secretary of the Treasury, a rather unusual proceeding in view of the fact that the charge originated with him. Yet Gallatin's report failed to indicate a specific instance in which the transaction had been questionable. Robert Smith reported that "instead of crimination, which was expected, [it] is evidently nothing but a labored apology for his former misunderstanding and misrepresentation of the subject." Gabriel Duvall, comptroller of the Treasury later wrote, "I never had any idea that there was anything in the whole transaction that in any way impeached the integrity of your character or that of your house [Smith and Buchanan]. The more the subject is examined, the more satisfactorily it appears that there is no ground for such an imputation."[5]

This episode furnished the basis for charges of corruption which were widely circulated throughout Maryland during the summer of 1809. The General replied by a vigorous campaign, which he had to conduct throughout the state if he hoped to win reelection to the Senate. The late summer and early fall found him engaged in "a little mission to ride about the Country, in order to solicit votes,"[6] and his energy was rewarded by a Republican victory. By the time the legislature convened Nicholson had given up the fight, and Smith's reelection was assured. His opposition to the administration was also assured. Covert sniping in the form of opposition to Madison in 1808 and the imposition of Robert Smith on the new President's administration had been at least partially atoned for by his loyal campaigning for Madison and the Republicans in 1808 and 1809. But Gallatin's broadside signaled open warfare. The General now felt no obligation of loyalty to the administration.[7]

The President's message to Congress when it convened in the fall of 1809 offered no clue as to what policy Madison wished to pursue. Congress floundered helplessly until finally Nathaniel Macon introduced a proposal which subsequently became known as Macon's Bill Number One. It provided for the exclusion of all British and French shipping from American ports and the exclusion of all goods from both countries and their colonies unless imported in American ships. The measure was suggested by Gallatin, who probably hoped to repair the growing deficit in the Treasury and who rightly suspected that the Non-Intercourse Act was being evaded on a massive scale.

When the bill passed the House and came before the Senate in the early months of 1810, Smith organized his forces and, with the aid of Federalist votes, attacked and defeated it. His opposition was based on more than simply his antagonism to Gallatin and the administration. He believed that it would be as ruinous to American commerce as previously unsuccessful measures, without being strong enough to coerce England and France into making concessions. He could not doubt, he said, that England and France would retaliate by excluding American shipping from their ports, for they had already confiscated American property amounting to $3,000,000. The net result would be a virtual embargo. Why not, then, impose an embargo

and be done with it? This was the policy that he had advocated all
along.

> Mr. President, I read this grand effort with attention. In vain did I look
> for something therein that would tend to obtain satisfaction for the
> Chesapeake; in vain for anything that would tend to prevent future
> impressment of American seamen; in vain for anything that would in-
> duce or coerce the belligerents to repeal their unjust orders and decrees
> against our lawful commerce.[8]

Smith's voice and vote decided the result. But the pro-British
Federalists, while sustaining him in the defeat of Macon's Bill, refused
to support his countermeasures for arming merchant ships and providing them with convoys. The measure barely passed the Senate
and died in the House.[9]

Conferences between representatives of the two houses, in which
the General participated, finally produced a measure which bore the
title of Macon's Bill Number Two, although Nathaniel Macon had
nothing to do with it. This was essentially the Non-Intercourse Act
turned inside out. Trade was resumed with both belligerents with
the proviso that if either relaxed its restrictions on the commerce
of the United States, the President was authorized to declare non-
intercourse with the other. Sam Smith opposed the proposal in committee and attacked it when it came to the floor of the Senate. He
attempted without success to amend it to authorize the President
to use naval forces to protect American ships. But Giles was silent
and Robert Smith was heard to say, "I intimated to Genl. Smith,
that as he could not support the Executive of his own choice he
ought to retire, and especially as the President had the support of
the Republican party with the exception of a few malcontents. He
treats the subject with disdain. . . . Unpopular as Genl. Smith obviously
rendered himself in the last session, his strange infatuation would
not allow him to admit it."[10] But there was no sign that Macon's
Bill Number Two represented Madison's policy and the President
himself characterized it as feeble and unlikely to improve the American
position. And if Sam Smith was unpopular he had no corner on
the market. "Submission is out of the question," he observed, "and
submission men are very unpopular. . . . In Penna. great exertions
are making against the friends of Mr. Gallatin who they charge, with
being the author of Macon's Bill. . . . He has become very unpopular."[11]

But there was one quarter in which Macon's Bill Number Two
was viewed with pleasure and approbation. In France Napoleon
thought he saw in its operation an opportunity to incorporate the

United States into the Continental System. With the shrewdness and unscrupulousness of which he was capable, the emperor issued an order dated May 1, 1810, seemingly revoking the Berlin and Milan Decrees as they applied to American commerce, the order to take effect November 1. The order was transmitted through Napoleon's foreign minister, the Duke of Cadore, to Jonathan Russell, the American minister. For a brief time it appeared that American policy was vindicated, and William Pinkney, the American minister in London, pressed England for reciprocal concessions. But it soon became evident that Napoleon was playing a devious game. Russell reported that despite the apparent assurances of Cadore, American ships trading with Britain were still being seized and that American property which he had been led to believe would be released was still sequestered. All this a full month after the revocation was to have gone into effect.

But James Madison decided to take a gamble. He was by no means convinced that Napoleon was sincere, but he was anxious for an excuse to bring commercial pressure to bear on Great Britain. It was a bad gamble, for Napoleon's record of diplomatic constancy was notoriously bad. Nevertheless, in November, 1810, the President issued a proclamation that the French decrees had been revoked. Under the terms of Macon's Bill, trade with England would automatically cease. It was a measure of the President's doubts that John W. Eppes, an administration spokesman in Congress from Virginia, introduced a non-intercourse bill when Congress convened for its next session. A law passed by Congress would eliminate the embarrassment which might arise if someone questioned whether Napoleon had, in fact, repealed his decrees and therefore satisfied the terms of Macon's Bill.

Sam Smith's dissatisfaction with what he regarded as Madison's willy-nilly policy was building toward a climax. Yet there was an inconsistency between the aims of the Senator and those of the Secretary which belied the general impression that the brothers were plotting the downfall of Madison and Gallatin. Robert Smith, failing to appreciate the delicate game the President was playing, was determined to present a note to the French minister in Washington, Louis Sérurier, in order to force a showdown. A commitment would confirm Napoleon's sincerity; evasion would demonstrate the reverse and the United States' position would be clarified. But the President demurred. "I was to my astonishment," said Robert Smith, "told by him that it would not be expedient to send Sérurier any such note. His deportment during this interview evinced a high degree of disquietude."[12] Madison was committed to his illusion and he did not want it shattered.

Robert Smith may have been technically and even morally right but as an effective instrument of his brother Sam he was altogether wrong. The Senator and his colleague, William Branch Giles, were forced into the unenviable position of seeing the man whose fortunes they had promoted, at some cost to themselves, blundering in the wrong direction. They saw Madison moving slowly into a position which differed from their own only in degree and force. And Sam Smith was already deeply committed to another fight with Gallatin.

The Secretary of the Treasury presented to the Eleventh Congress a request for the recharter of the Bank of the United States. First chartered under Hamiltonian auspices in 1791 as a Federalist measure, the Bank had won many converts, including Gallatin. In fact, the question of recharter had come up in the previous session of Congress. Sam Smith's Senate Committee on Banking and Commerce had taken up the question and the result had been a proposal to recharter the Bank with some alterations to repair what the General felt to be some serious faults. As a businessman he recognized the fact that the Bank had a stabilizing effect on the nation's financial system. It was Gallatin's monetary conservatism, reflected in the Bank's policy, that disturbed Smith. The large number of foreign stockholders, the limited note circulation, and the tight credit policies did little to furnish the kind of financial energy to the business community which had been one of the most persuasive of Hamilton's arguments when he proposed the original charter. Smith also believed that the Bank's directors were not above a little partisan politics designed to promote Federalist interests. Most important, he felt that the Bank had not expanded its capital or its services in order to meet the expanding needs of the nation's economy. Smith had therefore recommended in 1810 a recharter which he felt would overcome some of these deficiencies. The Senate could not reach an agreement and it was decided to extend the charter until 1812.[13]

During the summer of 1810 General Smith thought he detected more of the kind of pressure which he had criticized. He accused the branch bank in Baltimore of withdrawing funds from state banks and tightening credit among merchants. He warned the President that any appearance of political meddling by the Bank would lead members of Congress to "believe that the Sec. of the Treasury was thoroughly favoring the institution."[14] Madison made no reply. Thus, when the recharter was presented in 1811, the General could in good conscience oppose the Bank on its merits and at the same time deliver a blow at Gallatin.

For three days the General held the floor of the Senate. He

first attacked the monopolistic tendencies of the Bank, pointing out that in the United States, a nation of free enterprise, such an institution was dangerous. (This is a worn and hoary argument to modern Americans but it had especial appeal in the age of Jefferson.) He further cited the fact that until 1798 the branch at Baltimore had had only one Republican director and he had been dismissed when his Republicanism was discovered. The Bank was a Federalist institution and a partisan one at that.

As to the services that the bank was supposed to perform, there was not one which the state banks could not and were not performing equally well and in some cases better, said Smith. Nowhere, for instance, was the collection of duties handled better than in those ports where the Bank had no branch. The Comptroller of the Treasury himself was his authority for this statement. State banks accepted out-of-state currency for deposit to the credit of the Treasury. The Bank of the United States refused to do so. If the bank's currency pervaded the nation, it would be a satisfactory arrangement; but such was not the case. If the Bank refused to handle state currency without providing sufficient currency of its own, then it had better be abolished.

Page by page and paragraph by paragraph he refuted the recommendations of the Secretary of the Treasury, the whole tending to prove conclusively that there was no need for the Bank of the United States. He concluded by saying that the constitutional aspects of the argument were not in his province. He rather left those to the abilities of his colleagues who were versed on the subject. But their strong arguments on this aspect should lead any thinking man to vote against such an institution.

The vote in the Senate on the renewal of the charter was seventeen to seventeen. Vice-President Clinton broke the tie with his vote against, and the First Bank of the United States passed out of existence.[15]

The defeat of the Bank brought the political feud between Smith and the administration to a head. Robert Smith and Gallatin opposed each other in the cabinet. The President ostensibly remained aloof from the quarrel but was condemned, and all his measures for conciliation opposed, by the "Invisibles" in the Senate. And they openly expressed disgust with "the czar, meddler in foreign affairs, and obstacle in the way of energetic action," Albert Gallatin.[16]

Stung by the repudiation of the bank, Gallatin forced the President's hand. When the Eleventh Congress expired he offered his resignation to Madison, who now did not hesitate to keep Gallatin and get rid of Sam Smith's brother Robert.

He refused Gallatin's resignation and asked him to sound out Monroe on the possibility of his accepting the State Department.

Monroe indicated that he was willing and Madison then requested his resignation. When Smith protested the truth of this charge, the he pointed out to him that he had been acting in opposition to the administration for some time, no doubt referring to Smith's disagreement on French policy. In the interests of harmony he was requesting his resignation. When Smith protested the truth of this charge the President did not reply directly but became more pointed. He stated "that whatever talents he [Smith] might possess, he did not, as he must have found by experience, possess those adapted to his station . . . that the business of the Department had not been conducted in a systematic and punctual manner . . . and that I had daily become more dissatisfied with it." He offered Smith the post as minister to Russia.

A few days later Robert Smith resigned, refusing the sop which Madison offered him. He then published a bombastic defense of his career as Secretary of State which was answered by a vituperative article in the administration's *National Intelligencer* characterizing him as having "a turpitude of heart, or a blunted, muffled, wooden-headed power of penetration and feeling too disgraceful in itself to be able to disgrace the government it betrayed."[17]

Robert Smith had the last word. In the Baltimore *American* of July 6 he said:

> Were there any truth in this remark [charging want of integrity], it could not fail to convince every person of the utter unfitness of Mr. Madison for *his* office. It in plain English says that from the officious persuasion of a few intriguers he had appointed to the most important and highest station in the government a person without talents and integrity . . . one who had been his colleague in office during the long term of eight years, and of whose fitness he of course had better means of judging than any other person or persons whatever.[18]

Sam Smith perceived what he had long suspected. Admittedly a highly partisan witness, but for that very reason a good source in our account of the opposition to Madison, he related the circumstances as he saw them:

> A small conclave of men . . . saw a mode by which the Presidency might be retained in the House of Austria (for by that name Virginia was designated). The plan that they devised was, that the Secretary of State should be from Virginia, that his post should give him character, and, presuming him to have talents, consequence in the Union. Mr. Monroe was intended to succeed Madison as Secretary of State, but either Monroe was not then admitted to the secret, or, if the plan had been submitted to him, he thought he had a claim to the first term as President. . . . He therefore acted the very silly part of offering himself as the candidate for the Presidency and permitted his friends to assert that the administration had

acted under French influence. Mr. Monroe did not get a single vote and this restored him to his senses . . . and prepared him for a reconciliation with Mr. Madison which actually took place. . . . On the reconciliation having taken place I have no doubt that the system of the *House of Austria* was laid before Mr. Monroe and it was concluded to recommend its operation as originally contemplated, to wit—to make Monroe heir-apparent to the Presidency by appointing him Secretary of State. . . . It became, however, absolutely necessary to white wash Mr. Monroe before the appointment could take place. . . . It was necessary that Virginia should (by some act), show that Mr. Monroe was restored to the respect of his fellow citizens —an opportunity offered—the District Judge died, a successor was required. . . . The President appointed [Governor John] Tyler . . . this created a vacancy for which Mr. Monroe was chosen for there was nobody to oppose him. . . . Thus was M[onroe] completely *purified* and rendered a *proper candidate* in the President's opinion for any office. Some new difference of opinion operated to the disadvantage of Mr. [Robert] Smith and some tales were told to the President which altho wholly untrue were by him believed—all of which tended perhaps to hasten and countenance the measures long since contemplated.[19]

There is this to be said for Robert Smith. Historians have tended to base their opinions of his abilities largely on the testimony of Madison and Gallatin, of whom enough has already been said to demonstrate that they were hardly impartial witnesses. It should also be pointed out that before his entrance into government service in 1801 he had been one of the most successful admiralty lawyers in Baltimore. As Secretary of the Navy he had, in spite of the financial retrenchments of Gallatin, conducted a successful war against the Barbary corsairs which, while perhaps not an outstanding feat of arms, was an acknowledged accomplishment in logistics. He was popular with the administrative assistants in his department and with the professional seamen of the Navy.[20]

Madison charged that he himself had done most of Smith's work after the latter had become Secretary of State, and accused Smith of incompetence and inability even to draft state papers.[21] Diplomatic affairs were of first importance from 1809 to 1815 and Madison would have been a dilatory President indeed if he had not devoted a great deal of time to State Department affairs; nor was it unnatural that a Secretary of State become President should continue to supervise his former department. Thus Jefferson had taken personal charge of the Louisiana negotiations in 1802 and 1803, and Madison seems to have continued to write dispatches over Monroe's signature as he had done with Smith.[22] Robert Smith scored the only diplomatic success which the United States achieved in this period in the Erskine agreement. It was Madison's revision of the agreement, pointing out the duty of the king to visit further punishment upon Admiral George Berkeley, instigator of the *Chesapeake* affair, which Canning cited as justifying the rejection of the agreement.[23] Finally, Smith had attempted, in vain, to point out the fraud inherent in Napoleon's "revocation" of the Berlin and Milan Decrees. Madison, having committed himself to a false assumption, could not allow any action which would force France to admit her bad faith. He had taken a gamble, but, in the event, he had neither the staying power to run his bluff nor the willingness to accept the retreat which would have been justified by Robert Smith's confrontation with Sérurier. In accusing Robert Smith of opposing "administration policies," Madison was adopting as his own measures which he himself had called feeble and disgusting and which represented policies imposed on him by Congress in the absence of executive leadership.

The appointment of Monroe occasioned a good deal of surprise in some quarters. After his last diplomatic failure in 1806, Monroe had twice been offered the post of governor of Louisiana by President Jefferson, but had petulantly refused. As noted above, he had made an abortive attempt to challenge Madison's candidacy in 1808. However, when he became a candidate for governor of Virginia, he had expressed general approval of the administration and Madison votes had elected him. But privately he had opposed Madison's foreign policy, this as late as February, 1811. He favored an accommodation with England and a stiffer attitude toward France.[24] These expressions of disapproval were not so private that they were not known to Madison, and a hasty exchange of notes between the two was necessary for the President to exact a pledge from Monroe to support administration policy.[25] To Sam Smith and to others it clearly appeared that the "House of Austria" had welcomed back its errant archduke. Philip Norbonne Nicholas wrote to the General from Richmond that Monroe's appointment "confounds all party distinctions & proceeds on the principle that whether men support or oppose correct principles they are equally entitled to ministerial power."[26]

For the moment the Smiths were licked and Sam knew it. Robert Smith's rebuttal was sound on many points but intemperate and abusive beyond the limits of good taste. As one observer remarked, " ... It is one of the rare instances of a man's giving the finishing stroke to his own character, in his eagerness to ruin his enemy. I hear but one opinion of Smith: he has signed his death warrant...."[27] Sam Smith agreed. When Robert published his defense and the newspaper war broke out, the General wrote to his son, John Spear Smith, "I consider it a seal on the influence of the Smiths . . . it will leave you an uphill work if you wish public life." John's reply was perhaps the best commentary on the whole affair: "Wronged as he has been and justly as he may be incensed, yet surely when the country is surrounded with difficulties, when she is on the brink of a war, it is not for one who has had so great a part in her councils to be the cause of disunion and discontent."[28]

The General's eldest son was writing from London. He had already begun his career auspiciously in 1809 by securing a post in the diplomatic service as private secretary to the American minister in Russia and had served for a time with John Quincy Adams. By 1811 he had been transferred to London and was serving on the legation staff under William Pinkney. The latter's relationship with young Smith was apparently not affected by the General's political hostility; for, when Pinkney returned to the United States in June, 1811, he recommended John Smith's appointment as *chargé d'affaires*.[29] John later married the daughter of Wilson Cary Nicholas, but in 1811 Sam was writing with facetious anxiety to his daughter, Mary Mansfield, "All the fine fortunes will be picked up before John comes home. . . . Tell John that Judge Tilghman has a beautiful daughter of 16 or 17 years of age, highly accomplished with $200,000."[30]

Mary Buchanan Smith, Sam's eldest daughter, had made what Baltimore considered a "brilliant marriage" to James Mansfield, grandson of the famous Chief Justice. She was now living in England and had borne Sam's first grandchild.[31] Another daughter, Laura, had been quite a problem. After a violent love affair with young Christopher Hughes, Baltimore wit and bon vivant who later became a minor diplomat, she quarreled with him and the courtship was broken off, to the intense satisfaction of her father. However, the quarrel was later patched up and they were married late in 1811. Hughes was to be appointed three years later as secretary to the American peace commission at Ghent. Sidney, the youngest daughter, was still unmarried, but, as Laura wrote to her sister in England, she made great preparations for the season in Washington. In the manner of a *grande dame*, "at every new dress she scolds and groans over the trouble of going into company." And her father observed that she "begins to look at the glass en passant like Madame B." Betsy Bonaparte, "Madame B.," was also frequently in the Smith household. She charmed all around her and, as her uncle wrote, "laughs and talks, defends the Emperor and hopes he will destroy all his enemies." But there was no denying the fact that the social season in Washington that fall of 1811 found "the Smiths rather under a cloud."[32]

Although the cloud extended to the Smiths' political as well as the social life, the continued timidity of the administration, "this shilly shally, he-would-and-he-would-not kind of conduct,"[33] gave the "Invisibles" another chance and they took it. With the assembly of the Twelfth Congress in the latter part of 1811 there appeared a new faction in the House. The young gentleman from Kentucky, Henry Clay, had entered the national scene and, with John C. Calhoun of South Carolina and other young insurgents, was whipping his "Warhawks" into line for a showdown fight with the President. Angry at an administration that stood ineffective and undecided against the insults of Britain and France alike, spurred on by the agricultural distress which followed the decline of commerce, furious at the British-incited raids of the Indians on the frontier, they, too, denounced Madison and Gallatin. To these insurgents the "Invisibles" attached themselves; and Giles' Army Bill, reported December 9, 1811, and subsequently passed, was the first of a series of measures preparing the country for war.[34]

Although France, after Napoleon's "repeal" of the Berlin and Milan Decrees in response to Macon's Bill Number Two, had continued ship seizures and indicated her lack of good faith at every turn, only the Federalist minority questioned that the war was to be with Great Britain. It was Britain who had failed to repeal her Orders in Council and continued to seize American ships and impress American seamen. It was the British sloop-of-war *Little Belt* who, early in the summer of 1811, had fired on Captain John Rodgers' USS *President* and had been almost blown out of the water for her temerity. It was Britain and British rifles in the hands of American Indians that were murdering Western frontiersmen.

Supported by an ardent Republican press and urged on by continued British outrages, this alliance of veteran insurgents and frontier "buckskin statesmen," the one controlling the Senate and the other the House, began their program to force the President's hand.[35] Smith remained in the background and Giles became the spokesman for the "Invisibles." The alliance was not to be denied. Madison succeeded only in postponing the inevitable when he secured approval for a ninety-day embargo. In voting against it Smith remarked that it seemed to him to give Madison "a fair occasion to sneak out of war."[36] On June 1, 1812, Madison sent his war message to Congress, which four days later responded with a declaration of war.

But none realized better than Smith himself that his day as an influential politician was temporarily over. The "Invisibles" and the "War Hawks" had been successful, but at the cost of almost complete loss of influence for Smith. At the time when Robert Smith was trying to justify his conduct as Secretary of State, Sam had written, "Whether you succeed or not in your attack will depend largely on our foreign relations. If France completes her engagements, the President's measures will be eulogized—If a Regency should take place [in England] & the Orders in Council be repealed with the blockade, his Conduct and wisdom will be immortalized—If none of these should happen your attack may have some weight, but no considerable effect. The party must in their own defense have a point on which to rally, and that point will be Mr. M[adison]."[37]

As for Gallatin, he "will remove every person that has an opinion of his own—or whom he suspects of any attachment to us," observed General Smith to Mary Mansfield. "I do not think there ever was a court where so much pitiful little intrigue was going on as ours. A friend of Mr. M[adison] for twenty-five years—I mean Mr. Giles— has been put into the background because he remonstrated.... He also broke all ancient ties with Wilson Cary Nicholas indeed with all who were prominent in his favor at the election and has taken into favor all those who opposed him for President."[38]

Since 1792 the United States had been engaged in a commercial war with Great Britain. Few Americans saw it in this light and on the other side of the Atlantic Anglo-American relations were often obscured in the welter of the titanic struggle between England and France. Yet the "cold war" between England and the United States sometimes surfaced for the more discerning to see. British policy makers were alarmed at the appearance of a new maritime power on the western horizon—a power not in terms of naval arms but of commerce. More than one British measure against American trade was explicable not in terms of the defeat of France but in the context of stifling American competition. How else explain, for example, why Britain instituted a licensing system which permitted British vessels to trade with the Continent while denying such trade to American vessels? It was this as much as the Orders in Council which Madison's policy was designed to alleviate in 1810 and 1811.

In this commercial war Samuel Smith consistently urged more stringent American retaliation. Only in the case of the embargo did he feel that Jefferson and Madison had adopted a policy strong enough to exert real pressure. As a businessman, he believed that only by forcing recognition of American rights could a real future for commercial interests be assured. For this reason he deplored the halfway measures represented by the Non-Intercourse Act and Macon's Bill, even though Smith and Buchanan had profited from their lax enforcement.[39] He had a businessman's patriotic belligerence, and he enjoyed being known as "the General"; but it was more than vanity. He consistently advocated stronger military and naval forces, for he was willing to back American demands with threat of force. In Sam Smith, as in other statesmen of his time, there was an emotional patriotism that bordered on chauvinism. He never developed any fondness for Henry Clay but he welcomed the descent of the "War Hawks" on Congress in 1811, for their spirit seemed to breathe new vigor into a pusillanimous Congress and a vacillating administration. "No doubt shall remain to distant times, of our determination and our ability to have continued resistance," he had said in 1808. He still meant it.

Reaction to the war in Baltimore was immediate. A Federalist editor, Alexander Hanson, published a blistering attack on the President, intimating that he was in the pay of Napoleon. A Republican mob attacked Hanson and some of his Federalist colleagues with such severity that one, General James Lingan, was killed and another, General "Light-Horse Harry" Lee, was crippled for the rest of his life. Reaction to such terrorist tactics aroused Federalist denunciation of the "Jacobin" Republicans to such a pitch that in 1812 they gained a majority in the legislature and elected a Federalist governor, Levin Winder, although Maryland presidential electors cast their votes for Madison. This put the final touch upon Smith's loss of influence, for it insured his displacement in the Senate when he came up for reelection in 1814.[40]

He returned to Washington late in 1812 for what he knew was probably his last session in the Senate. Although the realities of the war did not as yet touch the capital, the atmosphere was far from cheerful. The first American military offensive, an attack on Canada via Lake Erie, met with defeat; and William Hull, the American general, surrendered his army and Detroit to the British. Additional defeats at Queenstown Heights in Upper Canada and the futile efforts of other American forces in the northeast to coordinate the advance showed the pitiful state of American preparation and the complete lack of capable leaders.

The seriousness of the American situation served to quell opposition to the administration. Bills were quickly passed to increase the army and navy, to authorize the issuance of letters of marque, and to provide for necessary appropriations. Smith and the other insurgents in the Senate offered no opposition save on two occasions. One was against the bill which was passed providing that none but American citizens be employed on American ships after the end of the war. This was to effect an offer which Monroe had made to Great Britain in the previous summer that American ships would not employ British seamen.[41] The bill passed as did the other measure which Smith opposed, providing for additional regiments of infantry for the army. Smith's opposition was based on the fact that the bill provided for one year enlistments. No veteran of the Revolution could forget the numbers of soldiers who had gone home at the end of enlistment terms, often at the very time when they were most needed. After attempting to make the term five years, then three, and finally, eighteen months, Smith voted against the bill.[42]

When Congress convened for the special session of May, 1813 the "Invisibles" could not resist one more fling at their old enemy, Albert Gallatin. Russia had offered her services as mediator in the dispute between England and the United States and Madison sent to the Senate the names of Albert Gallatin and James A. Bayard to cooperate with John Quincy Adams, then the United States minister in Russia. Smith and other anti-administration Senators rejected Gallatin's nomination by one vote, declaring that the duties of Secretary of the Treasury and special envoy were too important to be handled by one man and that Gallatin's duty was to the Treasury.[43] Otherwise, Smith loyally backed the administration in its measures for the prosecution of the war. And the war was going badly.

The summer and fall of 1813 were in general marked by failures for American fighting forces. The British had blockaded the Delaware and Chesapeake Bays, and the Indians were again raiding in the West. The campaign against Canada had ground to a complete halt with the American defeat at Stony Point, where the American commander, William Winder, was captured. Offsetting these events were two successes, Oliver Perry's victory on Lake Erie, followed by that of General William Henry Harrison against the British and Indians at the Battle of the Thames.

By this time Senator Smith's appearances in Washington were brief and fitful, for now he had another job on his hands. To him as commanding general of the Third Division of the Maryland Militia was entrusted the defense of Baltimore.[44] Baltimore—third largest port in the United States, nest of those cocky privateersmen who had driven the British Navy nearly frantic for a year, the town that had been Sam Smith's home for over half a century. The merchant with the Midas touch, the veteran of twenty years of political warfare, must call up the half-remembered lessons learned in the bitter defeats of Brooklyn Heights, White Plains, the Brandywine, and Fort Mifflin.

8

"When Free Men Shall Stand"

"THE FOE'S HAUGHTY HOST," as Francis Scott Key later described the British, entered the Chesapeake Bay in February, 1813. Admiral Sir George Cockburn, commanding a squadron of three ships-of-the-line and seven other vessels, blockaded the mouth of the bay at the Capes. His purpose was to clear the bay of every vessel capable of penetrating the blockade and, if possible, to destroy naval vessels being built at Washington, Norfolk and Baltimore. But because of the limited number of soldiers and marines at his disposal Cockburn at first contented himself with making forays and demonstrations here and there along the coast.[1]

At Baltimore General Smith had already made a small beginning in his preparations for the defense of the city. He had begun repairs on Fort McHenry, guarding the harbor entrance, as soon as war had been declared.[2] Division personnel were organized and weekly drills instituted. Now that the British were actually in the bay he increased his activities. And Smith the soldier was as talented as Smith the politician.

Despite the fact that he was dealing with a Federalist state administration headed by Governor Levin Winder, he secured authorization from Annapolis for 1,000 muskets.[3] So successful was he at arming and equipping the three thousand militiamen under his command that he was able to write the War Department early in the spring of 1813 that he had had no part in the request "of certain gentlemen" who had written Secretary of War John Armstrong requesting "additional arms for Baltimore."[4] But he did not allow himself to be lulled into complacency. Coastwatchers and scouts established by General Smith in cooperation with the governor's council constantly reported the movements of the enemy. Cockburn moved up the bay in the spring of 1813 and took possession of the islands at the mouth of the Susquehanna. British raiding parties were soon scouring the shores of the Potomac, the Patuxent and the Eastern shore seizing food stores, destroying foundries and mills, smashing small shore defense installations, and carrying off guns and ammunition. White Hall, Elk Landing, Havre de Grace and St. Michaels suffered from lightning-like incursions of the British.[5]

Neither General Smith nor, indeed, anyone could resist the amphibious enemy who took full advantage of his control of the water which gave him greater mobility. The British met only token resistance and moved from place to place with such rapidity that Smith decided to concentrate on building the defenses of the place where the attack was, sooner or later, sure to come—Baltimore.

No doubt could have existed in the mind of the commanding general, or indeed of any of the citizens of Baltimore, that the city was earmarked for destruction. A member of the House of Commons had solemnly pronounced it "the great depository of the hostile spirit of the United States against England," and a London newspaper had asserted that "the truculent inhabitants of Baltimore must be tamed with the weapons which shook the turrets of Copenhagen." And if these assurances were not enough, Admiral Cockburn himself "swore he would never rest until he had burned every house in it."[6]

Nor could General Smith and his fellow-townsmen expect much sympathy from nearby areas. Hezekiah Niles, editor of the *Weekly Register* quoted "a Philadelphia paper" as saying, "The people of the *Swindling city of Baltimore* are now much alarmed and apprehensive of suffering great injury from that nation whose enmity they, in part, causelessly brought upon the country.... *Who would pity such a city? ... Baltimore has brought the curse of Heaven upon itself ... let it make the best of its own situation....*" And even in the surrounding countryside the agricultural interests, which were the hotbed of Federalism, had exerted themselves to such an extent, said Niles, that "internal foes of the city, cooperating with the enemy, alarm those accustomed to deal with us from the interior, and destroy the whole trade and curtail the supplies for the subsistence of the people...."[7]

The principal attack, when it came, would certainly involve an assault on the harbor entrance. Smith's main concern therefore was the defense of Fort McHenry. He began adding to the armament of the fort by removing twelve forty-two pounders from a French frigate which had been abandoned in Baltimore after being badly damaged in a storm off the Capes. He added a supporting battery at Forts Covington and Babcock which were set farther up the entrance toward the city. Opposite Fort McHenry on the mainland to the north a battery was mounted on Lazaretto Point. In addition a number of hulks were secured and kept anchored in position to be sunk in the main channel.[8]

The first real threat to the city came in the middle of April. On the 16th Cockburn's squadron appeared off Baltimore some five miles down the Patapsco. "It was astonishing," reported the *Weekly Register*, "to perceive the animation of the people on the firing of the alarm gun. There was no fear except the fear of being late on duty. . . ." Cockburn no doubt learned of those forty-two pounders whose long snouts looked down the channel from Fort McHenry and whose gunners were, thanks to the disciplined training of the commanding general, well-grounded in the art of laying a piece. In any case the Admiral decided not to risk his small force against a defensive position such as that at Baltimore. The alarm served one useful purpose. It showed General Smith that he had done a good job. Defenses were manned and troops assembled "in decency and order."[9]

Meanwhile the state government was appealing to Washington for help. "We . . .deem it our duty to represent that other parts of the state are . . .defenceless and unprotected," wrote the governor, "and in many quarters incursions of the enemy and depredations to a considerable extent may be made. . . . we must repeat our anxiety to be informed what protection . . .may be expected from the general government."[14] But no help was forthcoming. Was it that the government had no troops to send? Or was the administration punishing its political enemies? "Virginia has but to ask," said one editor, "and she receives; but Maryland, for her late political disobedience, is denied those means of defense which she has a right, by the Constitution of the United States, to demand."[10]

As though to add insult to injury the state council was ordered by the War Department to detach from General Smith's command 63 officers and 1250 men. These orders came on the 23rd of April, with Cockburn's squadron barely out of sight. To compensate for this loss the state council authorized Smith to enlist the services of 250 seamen.[11] In the battle for the possession of Baltimore, these men, experienced in ship and boat handling and familiar with naval guns, would be valuable.

On the 1st of June Admiral Sir John Warren appeared in the Chesapeake with a large force to reinforce Cockburn. The enemy in the Bay now had at its disposal eight ships-of-the-line, ten frigates and a considerable number of smaller vessels. On the 27th of August this fleet stood up the bay, and a detachment of three ships-of-the-line and five frigates, accompanied by two schooners and a number of smaller vessels appeared before the city. The commanding general promptly ordered out his forces. Fort McHenry was manned, and General Smith sent the Baltimore County Brigade of 700 men to cover North Point, the most probable spot where the enemy might attempt a landing. On the heights east of the city and facing the North Point approach, General Smith had placed forty pieces of field artillery ranging from eighteen to four pounders. He had also constructed a few light earthworks. The British commander, however, had no sizable force of troops with which to attempt a landing, and contented himself with demonstrating in front of the city before retiring once more down the bay.[12]

The remainder of 1813 and the spring of 1814 passed with the British continuing their raids on the shores of Virginia and Maryland. Distressing as this was to the people of the state, General Smith confined his activities to keeping close watch on the enemy fleet in cooperation with the forces around Annapolis. On two occasions he obtained from British deserters signal codes which he forwarded to the War Department. His diligence inspired such confidence in him among the people of the city that they raised a loan of $500,000 for necessary expenses. Young Isaac McKim, aide-de-camp to the General and son of one of the wealthiest merchants in Baltimore, contributed $50,000. A bill to allow the citizens of Baltimore to tax themselves was introduced in the House of Delegates, but passed only after the Federalist bloc insisted on attaching a provision for the payment of damages resulting from the riot of 1812.[13]

The spring of 1814 brought with it the news that Napoleon had been defeated. While many Americans were pleased with this news, none could ignore its implications. Wellington's veterans would now be released from duty on the continent and would be available for service against the United States. The American army had resumed its offensive under a renovated command and had won initial successes at Fort Erie and had fought the British to a standstill at Lundy's Lane. But Sir George Prevost, with twelve thousand of Wellington's veterans, was on his way from Canada. Five thousand more, under Major-General Robert Ross, were on their way to the Chesapeake. The British intended to supplement their Canadian campaign with a thrust at the Chesapeake, including Baltimore and Washington, which would have far more effect than Cockburn's scattered raids. To meet this threat the President appointed Brigadier General William H. Winder, lately exchanged after his capture by the British at Stony

Point, to command and organize the defenses of the Tenth Military district which included the bay area.[14]

General Smith, in compliance with standby orders of April 27 from Washington, had for some time been holding Brigadier General Tobias Stansbury's 11th Brigade and two battalions from the 2nd and 9th Brigades ready "to march at a moment's notice." But not until the 16th of July did the President call for 6,000 Maryland troops to march to the defense of Washington. General Smith had his allotment of 2,000 men on the road in less than a week. He had become more than a little concerned over the competence of the administration and especially of the capabilities of Secretary of War Armstrong. On July 14th, two days before the call for troops, Smith wrote to Armstrong in a burst of indignation:

> You are certainly the boldest men I have known at the head of a government. To us at this distance there appears to be a danger approaching and very nigh at hand. Where will it strike? at Washington and Baltimore if the Enemy are well informed we must presume that they are. What force have you to meet an Enemy of 5,000 men? I know of none preparing at any one point capable of encountering 1500 or even half that number . . . I really envy you the tranquillity which I am told prevails at Washington . . . I am hourly censured for not calling out the 2,000 men ordered the 27 April. Would to God I had the power.

And even after the troops were called from Baltimore he wrote, though in a more conciliatory tone: "In the spirit of friendship I ask why are not more troops ordered for the defense of the capital?"[15]

Besides the force which left Baltimore on the 21st under the command of General Stansbury, there was also at hand to aid Winder a battalion of Baltimore seamen under the command of Commodore Joshua Barney. This force was part of the regular navy which had been commissioned by the government in the summer of 1813 to utilize a flotilla of small gun boats in harassing the enemy in the Bay area. Barney had rendered a good account of himself, fighting a series of hit-and-run actions until he had been ordered to abandon his boats and join Winder.[16]

Smith's fears about getting troops in the field in time to meet the enemy were unfounded. The two forces from Baltimore arrived at Bladensburg and joined the army which Winder had assembled there in advance of the enemy's appearance.

Meanwhile, the British fleet entered the Patuxent river and sailed upstream to Benedict where, on August 19, it debarked 4,200 British soldiers under the command of Major General Robert Ross, veteran of the Spanish peninsular campaign. Ross proceeded by leisurely marches north and west to the crossing of the East Branch of the Potomac at Bladensburg. Winder disposed his troops astride the two roads which led from the village towards the capital. What followed was called by some wits "The Bladensburg Races."[17] Badly led by a general who was himself bewildered and bedeviled by everyone from the Secretary of State down to some well-meaning but stupid gentlemen who had come out to see the fun, the American forces broke and melted away before the onslaught of the English veterans. A few hours later the British marched almost unopposed into Washington and, at the command of Admiral Cochrane, set fire to the public buildings. Until they withdrew from the national capital some days later, the President of the United States was a fugitive, riding the country roads of northern Virginia on horseback.[18]

Bad as the news was to Sam Smith in Baltimore, when the details filtered in, two notable phases of the battle were distinctly encouraging to him. The first of these was the gallant behavior of the Fifth Regiment of Baltimore Infantry, commanded by Lieutenant Colonel Joseph Sterrett. Placed in a bad position by orders of the Secretary of State, Colonel James Monroe, they made an admirable advance against the British right and, although in the open and facing a concealed enemy, they held their ground unsupported until ordered to retreat by General Winder. Then, caught up in the infectious fear that pervaded neighboring troops, they ran.

The other phase of the battle was even more heartening. Joshua Barney's flotillamen and their guns had been placed astride the southernmost of the two roads leading westward from Bladensburg. While the rest of the army broke or retreated in confusion, Barney and his Baltimore sailors fought coolly and gallantly until many of them were surrounded and captured.[19] But some escaped and returned to Baltimore.

It showed what discipline could do. Barney's flotillamen were old hands. They had been fighting the British off and on for more than a year. They were expected to stand firm. But Joe Sterrett's 5th Regiment had never been under fire before. They were raw militia that had never seen a red coat until that ghastly day at Bladensburg. A little more discipline, more earthworks to give them cover—Sam Smith was hopeful. He ordered more drill, "from Reveille to 8 o'clock and from 5 to 7 o'clock."

Meanwhile more encouraging news arrived. Commodore John Rodgers and a force of 500 seamen were on their way to Baltimore. These, like Barney's men from Bladensburg, would provide him with veteran artillerymen. Smith also received notice that General William

Winder and the remnant of his army were on their way. This from Colonel Monroe, who had lately succeeded Armstrong as Secretary of the War Department, in addition to his duties as Secretary of State. Further additions were three companies from Pennsylvania, one from Hagerstown, and a Virginia brigade under General Hugh Douglass. A squadron of U. S. Dragoons arrived from Washington. These, combined with the 7,000 men of the 3rd Division, plus sailors, marines and regulars already in the city, brought General Smith's total to about 11,000 men.[20]

To gain time and to attempt to reduce in some degree the odds against the threatened city, a naval expedition was sent out to trap a British squadron which had captured and exacted ransom from Alexandria on the upper Potomac. And there were some redoubtable leaders for this expedition—no less personages than Oliver Hazard Perry, David Porter, and John Rodgers. By placing batteries on the shore of the river at several points Rodgers, commanding the operation, hoped to prevent the British force, commanded by Captain James Gordon, from escaping down the Potomac and rejoining the main fleet. A battery under Perry was stationed at Indian Head, another under Porter at White House, and Rodgers himself took a small flotilla of boats to cut out H.M.S. *Devastation,* which had gone aground near Alexandria. But the news that preceded the expedition's return was as sickening as it was astounding. Porter failed. Perry failed. Rodgers failed. The British squadron, with its twenty-one confiscated ships, escaped down the river and rejoined the main fleet.[21]

It was bad news but it did not stop the commanding general at Baltimore. Sam Smith's iron-gray head stayed erect. Despite his sixty-two years he seemed to be everywhere. Problems came, not one by one, but in a devastating avalanche that threatened to engulf him. But, whatever the complaints against his imperiousness or his judgment, he was not guilty of either idleness or bewilderment.

There are two battles which every commander must fight before he even catches sight of the enemy. The first is the battle of supply, the second is the battle of discipline—of putting men where they should be, showing them what their job is and insuring as far as possible that they carry out their job. But Smith had a third battle. This was the battle for command.

Smith's adversary in this third battle was William Winder. If any blame for the rout at Bladensburg rests on his shoulders, it must be shared by others—officious civilian authorities, an inefficient government, well-meaning busybodies. Winder had been ordered with his troops to Baltimore, but the new Secretary of War, James Monroe, had said nothing as to his place in the matter of command. Winder was quite naturally eager to retrieve his reputation and, since he was a regular army officer and nominally still commanding the bay area, he expected to receive the command at Baltimore. But Sam Smith was equally determined not to trust the city to Winder's questionable judgment after his own careful preparations and Winder's fiasco at Bladensburg.

Several circumstances worked in Smith's favor. First, and most important, was military law which stated that regular army officers took precedence over militia officers only if they were of the same grade. This clearly entitled Smith, a major-general, to command over Brigadier General Winder. Secondly, his rank of major general had been confirmed by the War Department on a volunteer basis. "By request of the President of the United States of the tenth of July last, one Major-General is requested of this State. In compliance to which you have been selected," so the governor of Maryland had informed Smith on August 26th. This meant that Smith, for the duration of the emergency in the Tenth Military District, was a volunteer and under the orders of the War Department.[22]

Finally, and of paramount importance politically, the citizens of Baltimore had requested that the defense of the city be entrusted to General Smith. A group from the Committee of Safety headed by Smith's old political enemy, Colonel John Eager Howard, had called upon the General and formally requested that he assume complete command.

On Winder's side was the fact that he was a regular army man and it was well known that, in disputes of this kind, Washington was inclined to favor regulars. If Winder could secure a temporary or brevet appointment as major-general he would be able to supersede Smith. Also the fact that the governor of Maryland, Levin Winder, was General Winder's uncle assured him of support from that quarter. An indication of these circumstances was the letter which Smith received, dated August 27th, written by Governor Winder and forwarded to Smith by General Winder:

> Yesterday I received a letter from Mr. [Edward] Johnson [Mayor of Baltimore] stating that they wished Gen. Smith to take command of the militia of Baltimore . . . I returned answer that it was proper for Genl. Smith to take command of the militia and make arrangements for the defense of the place, but that I could not invest him with powers that he did not already possess except . . . That according to the requisition of the United States for one Major-Genl. he had been selected . . . But certainly this information was not contemplated to give Genl. Smith command,

nor neither could have effect in any respect, until operation was given
to it by the Genl. Government.[23]

No help could be expected from this double talk of William Winder's Federalist uncle. Smith's only recourse was to the War Department—now presided over by James Monroe under the direction of
President Madison. Sam Smith was asking confirmation from two
men whom he had fought politically tooth and nail less than two
years ago. The result was as gratifying to Smith as Governor Winder's
letter had been to his nephew: the War Department reiterated the
military law by which the officer of the highest rank, whether regular
or volunteer, took precedence. But Washington did more than that.
For Winder now asked the War Department for a promotion, stating
that "the immediate and peremptory decision of the Government
which can only give me necessary support to enable me to act with
effect, is absolutely necessary. . . . the readiest mode of avoiding all
difficulty will be giving me rank to overreach the possible danger
of conflict with any militia officer."

Winder's hopes were dashed by Monroe's reply. "The course
which under pressure here is thought advisable, is that you return
to this place with the regular infantry as soon as possible." Shortly
after came the letter from Monroe that General Smith had been waiting for: ". . .General Winder will unite with your forces such of those
under his command as may afford the most efficient aid to the protection of Baltimore. . . ." This was somewhat vague but it strongly implied
that the War Department assumed that Smith was in command. Winder nevertheless persisted in his efforts to supersede Smith until the
very day before the British attack. But Bladensburg had made a profound impression on James Monroe. In a confidential letter to Winder
he stated firmly: "there can be but one Commander in every quarter
for which any particular force is intended. The Force at Baltimore
being relied on for the protection of that place . . . being under General
Smith, the movement of troops must be under his command."[24]

Winder, then, was Smith's subordinate. He must fit him in to
the little team of officers, some of whom he could trust, others whom
he had to trust because there were no others available. To Winder
he gave, as that worthy complained to Monroe, "a patched up" brigade
from troops of "other Brigadiers who have gone away" and assigned
to him the southwestern portion of the city.[25]

For the rest, General Smith was fortunate. He had a considerable
amount of talent to choose from although some were not quite fitted
for the task at hand. The senior naval officer, Commodore John

Rodgers, was present with 1200 seamen, many of whom had fought on the *Guerriere* and the *President*. John Rodgers, veteran of four highly successful cruises against the British in the Atlantic, was a good man to have. He was muscular and vigorous, capable of strenuous energy, his tanned and wind-burned face surmounted by a shock of coal-black hair. His seamen were perhaps not as suited to solid ground as to a heaving deck, but an eighteen pounder was an eighteen pounder whether it was on the gun deck of the *President* or behind an earthwork on Loudenslager's Hill (also called Hampstead Hill). Rodgers was everywhere, helping at the fort, building earthworks, planting batteries, drilling seamen.[26]

For the important post of commander of Fort McHenry General Smith had Major George Armistead. A regular army officer and scion of a prominent Virginia family, his distinguished conduct at Fort George on the northern frontier qualified him for his job. Though weakened by sickness he was to prove himself cool and courageous in the midst of the most adverse conditions. Assisting Armistead at the fort and in charge of ammunition for the entire command was Colonel Decius Wadsworth, a regular army ordnance officer.

Fresh from the rout at Bladensburg came Tobias Stansbury. The brigadier of the 11th was a Revolutionary veteran and, while his movements in the early phases of the Bladensburg campaign had been subject to some question, after the battle commenced he had done all that a man could do who was harassed alike by the vacillations of William Winder and the military pretensions of Colonel Monroe. It was his Fifth Regiment, under Colonel Sterrett, who had stood up to "Wellington's Invincibles".

Then there was Brigadier General John Stricker. John Stricker and General Smith were neighbors and friends. Stricker's father had been in the mud of Gowanus Marsh with Smith when they had retreated from the British attack on Long Island in 1776. Young Stricker himself had been an artilleryman in the Revolution. Seven years younger than Sam, it was he who had spoken up in the Committee of Safety proposing Smith for the supreme command. John Stricker, sometime Continental gunner, was to be Samuel Smith's chief lieutenant.

There were others less important. Oliver Hazard Perry was in town to take command of a new ship, the *Java,* now building in Baltimore. But Perry was sick. Commodore David Porter, formerly captain of the *Essex* and scourge of British shipping in the pacific, commanded a battalion of seamen under Rodgers.[27]

These were the men whom Smith must use to fight his battle.

They were proud men, good fighters, most of them with records of more experience than the volunteer general. But they were not small men. Except for Winder's protests, there is no record of any quarrel over command, of any lack of cooperation between army and navy or between regulars and militia.

A thousand petty details plagued the commanding general. Lieutenant Cook had drawn his sword on his captain. Lieutenant Cook was placed under arrest. Two men drafted for service sued out writs of *habeas corpus*. Writs denied. Wadsworth must prepare ammunition for five thousand men. "I will not touch [it] until the Enemy appears," said General Smith. Armistead needed more men at the fort. Hughes' and Berry's companies were sent. The food was bad. Army contractors had changed little since 1777. "The Baker told the Contractor's clerk that it was impossible to make bread out of the flour supplied, that it was as hard as chalk and he was compelled to cut it with an ax.... It is believed that the Beef has been salted for three years...." From the tangle of red tape in the War Department came a month-old order to return some artillery which belonged to the defenses at Washington. Although three weeks had passed since the battle of Bladensburg General Smith did not argue with the army bureaucracy. He simply confused it. The guns did, indeed, belong in the capital, he replied, but the gun *carriages* were the property of the city of Baltimore. If the War Department would send proper carriages....

Should the eighteen pounders have grape and canister made up for them? Smith and Armistead thought so, but left the final decision to Wadsworth. Captain Mason reported that the sentries were lax, that he could not even locate the officer of the guard. The commanding general was forced to issue an order against "the unsoldierly discharge of muskets" in the city. Barracks were scarce. Smith called on the Committee of Safety to build sheds. Still there was not enough room. The General seized the rope-walk and converted it into a barracks, turning a deaf ear to the protests of the owners. The sick had to be cared for. The commanding general appropriated the hospital on Loudenslager's Hill.[28]

And in the midst of this maze of detail Sam Smith was forced to think of the major question. What would the British do? They would oppose him with both fleet and army. How would they dispose their forces? What would be their line of attack? Would it be by land or by sea? Or both?

Meanwhile Major W. B. Barney, younger brother of Joshua, was sending in constant reports from his scouts. The statement of a British deserter listed some 6,300 men under General Ross, including artillerists, marines, and engineers as well as a brigade of sailors to be used in landing operations. There was no doubt that the British would attack the city, for General Ross was heard to say that Baltimore was the next objective.[29]

Sam Smith probably considered his problem as much from the point of view of a merchant and businessman as from that of a general. What price would the British be willing to pay for the reduction of Baltimore? Could he make his defense so formidable that the risk would not be worth that price?

The British helped Sam Smith to determine his defensive strategy. The geography, as shown in the map,[30] was also a determining factor. The rest was shrewd guesswork. When the British withdrew from Washington and reembarked all their forces at Benedict, Smith realized that the enemy did not plan a simultaneous flank assault from the south and west to coordinate with their attack from the sea. This narrowed his problem to a choice of spots where a landing force, using the fleet as a base, could successfully launch an offensive.

The only feasible approach from the west or southwest to the city was by a circuitous march around several arms of the bay and would also entail crossing the Patapsco River. An army thus separated from its base, the fleet, might easily be flanked and cut off from its supplies even if it were not annihilated. There remained the possibility of a direct naval assault up the Patapsco or a landing force expedition from the east or northeast, or both.

The Patapsco flows into the Chesapeake Bay just south and east of Baltimore. Directly south of Baltimore, and before it reaches the bay proper, the river widens and becomes almost an arm of it. This arm forms the harbor for Baltimore and it spreads southeast from the town toward the Chesapeake. Whetstone Point divides the upper part of the inlet into two branches. To the north is the Northwest Branch, which is the main ship channel, and at the head of it are the docks and the ship basin. On the south side lies the Middle or Ferry Branch. On the tip of Whetstone, where the two branches meet, lies Fort McHenry. Opposite the fort to the east is a jut of land called the Lazaretto, and it is here that the ship channel is narrowest. Below Fort McHenry the southwestern bank of the Patapsco is pierced by a number of creeks and inlets; in 1814 the ground was low and marshy. The northwestern shore is a peninsula separated from the mainland on the north by Back River. At the end of the peninsula is North Point, and down the length of the peninsula runs Long Log Lane.

In 1814, the main road leading out of Baltimore to the east was the Philadelphia turnpike. About three miles east of the city this road was intersected by Long Log Lane, which led off from it at right angles. Half way down the peninsula, Long Log Lane was intersected by the Trappe Road, which ran west and then north, intersecting the Philadelphia pike about a mile east of the city. These roads, then, formed a rough parallelogram, the Philadelphia turnpike forming the northern side, the Trappe Road forming the western and southern sides, and Long Log Lane forming the eastern side.

General Smith, making his decision as to the best disposition of his forces, took all these things into consideration. Only one circumstance of which he was ignorant may have influenced the British movement. This was the disagreement between the members of the British high command as to the feasibility of attacking Baltimore.

Admiral Sir Alexander Cochrane, Commander of the British North American Station who had succeeded Admiral Warren as senior naval officer, was of the opinion that there was no more to be gained by operations in the Chesapeake. The principal factor influencing this decision was the condition of the troops. "The worst enemy that we have to contend with is the climate—this obliges us to proceed northward. By possessing Rhode Island we will draw the enemy's attention to that quarter...." General Ross, despite his being in favor of an attack on Baltimore earlier, seems to have concurred in this opinion. But Cockburn was extremely anxious to attack the city and his enthusiasm must have won over the other two commanders.[31] Such differences of opinion raise the question, always present in such circumstances, as to whether the attack would be pressed with vigor and decision when the senior army and naval officers were not enthusiastic as to the wisdom of the expedition.

After weighing the various courses open to him, General Smith decided to place his forces and make his plans upon the assumption that the British would try an attack by land, disembarking at North Point, against the eastern approaches to the city and that they would combine with this an assault, either in strength or as a diversion, on the harbor defenses.

This decision meant that the commanding general must dispose his force so as to make his defense by land cover and complement the defense of Fort McHenry. Likewise, Fort McHenry must be used to complement his land defenses. There was no way of establishing a line that would be in direct communication with the fort. But by choosing a position on the eastern side of the city blocking the approaches from North Point, he could anchor his right flank on the waterfront and so render his line almost invulnerable to a turning movement from the enemy's naval forces. In other words, if an attacking force attempted to land to the south on the waterfront behind his line in cooperation with a frontal assault against the city from the east, it would first have to pass under the guns of Fort McHenry.

This decision enabled Smith to take advantage of the heights on the eastern side of Baltimore. He planned a line of defense along the crest of Loudenslager's Hill so that the enemy would have to attack across Harris Creek at the foot of the hill and then advance up the slope. But raw militia would have to have more help than this. General Smith decided to dig.

The whole city turned out. The Committee of Safety was called upon to ransack the city for shovels and wheelbarrows. From Captain Babcock of the U. S. Army Engineers came suggestions: a fourteen-foot high earthwork; materials suitable for throwing a barricade across roads at a moment's notice; a redoubt at Camp Lookout and another nearer the main line. Baltimore began digging for its life. Every person capable of wielding a pick or shovel was urgently summoned by the proclamation of Mayor Johnson. "The owners of slaves are requested to send them to work on the days assigned, in the several districts. . . . Such of our patriotic citizens of the country . . . as are disposed to aid in the common defense, are invited to partake in the duties now required." Young Sam Smith, the General's nephew, aged twelve, disappeared from home. He was found some hours later digging furiously in the trenches of Loudenslager's Hill.[32]

Assembly of the Troops—Battle of Baltimore
painting by Ruckle

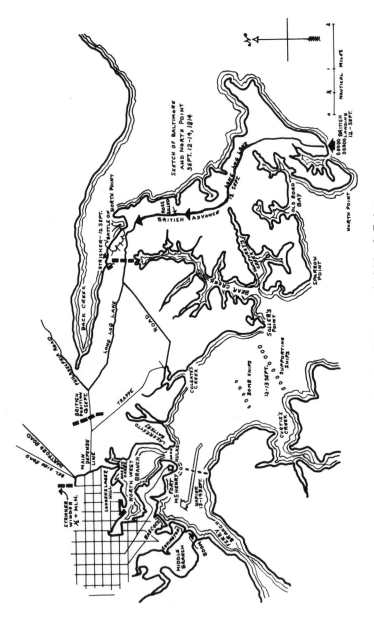

Sketch of Baltimore and North Point
September 12–14, 1814—Battle of Baltimore

Bombardment of Fort McHenry
painting by Alfred Jacob Miller

9

"By the Dawn's Early Light"

EARLY ON SUNDAY, SEPTEMBER 11, 1814, General Smith received the report that the enemy had appeared at the mouth of the Patapsco just off North Point and was making preparations to disembark troops. His calculations concerning Ross, Cochrane, Cockburn and Company had been right. General Smith disposed his forces behind the entrenchments and walls of the forts, and Samuel Smith, merchant, decided to exact a down payment before he started to bargain directly. For the task he chose John Stricker. To him Smith assigned some 3,000 men of the 5th, 27th, 39th Union Artillery, 6th and 4th Regiments. He sent Stricker and his command down Long Log Lane below its intersection with Trappe Road to fight a delaying action against the head of the British column as it advanced up the peninsula.[1] The spot Stricker chose for the defense was a neck of land less than a mile wide where the peninsula was almost cut in two by indentations of Bear Creek on the western side and Bread and Cheese Creek on the eastern. Placing his guns astride the road Stricker anchored his right flank on Bear Creek and his left on a marsh which extended to the bank of Back River.[2]

On Monday morning, September 12, the British, having passed the night on the lower end of the peninsula, began a somewhat leisurely advance up Long Log Lane. About two and a half miles below the point where Stricker had established his line, the head of the British column suddenly made contact with a small force of cavalry and infantry which Stricker had sent out on reconnaissance. The meeting was so unexpected that the British advance guard was momentarily thrown back in confusion. Support for it was somewhat slow in coming up. General Ross, riding forward to examine the ground and direct the recovery of the advance guard in person, was killed by American sharpshooters. The American advance guard soon fell back to the main line and awaited the British attack. The enemy force consisted of slightly more than 4,000 men of the 4th, 21st, 44th and 85th Regiments; the 2nd and 3rd Battalions of the Royal Marines; detachments of the Royal Artillery and Royal Marine Artillery; a brigade of seamen; and the colonial Negro Marines with six field pieces and two howitzers.[3]

The British artillery opened the battle about two o'clock. For some time they shelled the American line with shrapnel and rockets and then the entire force advanced. The 51st Maryland, holding the American left, broke and carried with it part of the 39th, which was next in line to the right of the 51st. But the British regiment which attacked on that flank pursued the broken 51st instead of rolling the American left back on the center. The main line was thus able to stand firm against the British assault "until about four o'clock," according to the American commander. Then Stricker ordered a retreat to the northern side of Bread and Cheese Creek where a reserve regiment, the 6th, was waiting. Here he formed a new line and waited pursuit until sundown. At this point, however, the senior colonel of the British force, Arthur Brooke, who took command after Ross fell, decided to halt his advance.[4]

British reports—and both American and British history—have characterized the American retirement as a rout.[5] Neither takes into account the fact that the British did not follow up the "rout" and that the American forces formed a new line and remained in the second position until nightfall. Nor do the accounts take into consideration the nature of Stricker's orders. Historians have examined Winder's orders at Bladensburg and even the tangle of controversy over the command at Baltimore. But they have made no effort to understand Stricker's orders for the expedition to North Point. John Stricker understood those orders and he obeyed them to the letter. He was to establish contact with the enemy and fight a delaying action. But he was not to make any last ditch stand. The commanding general was relying on Stricker's troops, more than one-fourth of his entire command, to supplement his main defense where Smith had planned to make his principal stand—in prepared defenses on Loudenslager's Hill.[6]

And John Stricker had exacted his down payment. In return for twenty-four men killed, 139 wounded, and fifty captured he had killed or incapacitated 290 of the enemy including the commanding general and sixteen officers. When the British column resumed its march the next morning, one brigade, one regiment, three battalions and a number of companies were under new commanding officers.[7] Whatever the reports—or history—might say, Stricker had done what Sam Smith wanted him to do.

British tactics in the Baltimore campaign called for an attack by naval forces against the harbor defenses in coordination with the land force. To meet this attack General Smith and Colonel Armistead had erected a series of defenses centering around Fort McHenry. A four-gun battery was placed on Lazaretto Point opposite the fort on the north side of the main channel. Blocking this channel was a line of hulks. About halfway between Fort McHenry and the base of Whetstone Point, on the Ferry Branch side, were Forts Covington and Babcock. Another line of sunken hulks blocked the mouth of the Ferry Branch.[8]

Fort McHenry itself was a star-shaped work with three of its redoubts facing down the channel. Its defenses consisted of three tiers: the fort itself with its five bastions containing twenty-two guns; an open work between the fort and the tip of Whetstone manned by infantry to repel a landing of enemy troops; a third tier consisting of a low earthwork at the very edge of the water behind which were mounted the Water Battery containing fifteen forty-two pounders and a number of twenty-four and eighteen pounders.[9]

On the morning of the 13th, the day after the battle of North Point, while the British army moved leisurely up Long Log Lane, Admiral Cochrane dispatched his frigates and bomb ships against this defense. The frigates anchored downstream from the inner arc—the smaller bomb ships *Aetna, Meteor, Terror, Devastation,* and *Volcano,* and the rocket ship *Erebus.* These lay some two miles below Fort McHenry. The bomb ships were small, blunt-nosed vessels mounting only two guns. But those guns fired a thirteen-inch, two hundred pound shell, and the ships were well inside their maximum effective range. But four thousand yards was beyond the range of Armistead's forty-two pounders and after a futile effort to reach the anchored ships—an effort which dismounted three of his guns because of overloaded powder charges—Armistead gave the order to cease fire. The fort settled down to the hardest task that ever falls to a soldier. They took the enemy's fire without being able to reply.[10]

Soon the rocket ship *Erebus* was in action, firing rockets whose war heads were packed solid with powder, saltpeter, pitch and sulphur. The rockets were less harmful because less accurate, but the mortars crashed around the fort every three or four minutes. Armistead moved his reserve ammunition out of the magazines, whose covers were not shell-proof, and scattered it upon the open ground behind the fort where it would be less likely to spread destruction if it were hit.[11]

The commanding general could only watch and keep constant communication with Armistead by couriers "dashing in full speed ... amidst a shower of Bombs and rockets ... to & fro from the Fort. ..."

The bombing continued for nine long and weary hours. About two o'clock in the afternoon one of the twenty-four pounders in the Water Battery was hit and one member of the gun crew killed and others wounded. The "bustle necessarily produced by the removing of the wounded" evidently caused Admiral Cochrane to believe that the defense of the fort was now sufficiently weakened to order his frigates into action. Five of them, supporting the bomb ships, advanced within range. The reaction showed Cochrane his mistake. Shot from forty guns churned the waters of the Patapsco. The ships once more withdrew out of range and the bomb ships continued their bombardment.[12]

While the fort was under this continuous and galling fire Sam Smith had been busy. He had managed to dig into two long curving lines of breastworks running north from Fell's Point at the waterfronts to a spot just beyond where the Philadelphia road entered the city at its northeast corner. Here the earthworks turned west, but only for a short distance—not far enough to cover the junction of the three northern roads leading to York, Harford, and Bel Air. Into this line he had thrown most of his forces except a token regiment in the southwestern section of the city and the men assigned to the fort. Also outside the earthworks were Stricker's Brigade and a force of regulars, General Hugh Douglass's Virginia brigade, under Winder's command. These mobile units provided protection to his exposed left flank and were supported by Stansbury's brigade which occupied the extreme left of the entrenchments. South of Stansbury, holding the center was Forman's brigade. On the right, where the slope toward the harbor and the ground around the mouth of Harris creek was not so steep, and therefore easier for an enemy advance, Smith posted John Rodgers with his seamen and their guns.[13]

Meanwhile Colonel Arthur Brooke was having his troubles. General Stricker, when he had retreated the previous evening, had felled trees across the road and these impeded Brooke's advance to a considerable degree. Upon reaching the Philadelphia road, some three miles east of the city, Brooke made his headquarters in the Kell House. Rain, which had been falling half the previous night, somewhat dampened the spirits of his troops. But what the British saw before them dampened their spirits even more. Here was a height crowned by strong defenses and, said the British Lieutenant Robert Gleig, manned by "the grand army, consisting of 20,000 men." Smith had already won a preliminary victory. He had persuaded the British nearly to double the force which opposed them, for his total concentration on the eastern and northeastern sides of the city was not more than 11,000 men.[14]

Colonel Brooke did what a good commander should do. He decided to test the American left along the Bel Air Road. General Smith did what a good defending commander should do. He sat tight and ordered Stricker and Winder to swing their brigades so that the left flank was refused and all three of the northern roads were covered. The whole operation would be endangered if Winder should blunder now or was dilatory in his execution, . . . but William Winder and John Stricker executed the movement "with great skill and judgment." Therefore when Brooke formed his order of battle along the Bel Air road he found two brigades facing him and a third, Stansbury's, held in reserve behind entrenched works. Brooke tried again. About two o'clock in the afternoon he withdrew to his original position along the Philadelphia road and began a demonstration to test the practicability of storming the heights by frontal assault. He concentrated his largest force on his right where the Philadelphia road entered the angle at the northern end of the earthworks. This was the closest the British came to a concerted land and sea attack, for it was at this time that the naval vessels in the harbor made their movement against the fort.

Again Smith matched the British maneuver. He swung Stricker and Winder back in toward the Philadelphia road so that as Brooke advanced he found his heaviest concentration of troops moving into a deadly obtuse angle formed by Winder and Stricker to his right and the face of the fortified ridge in front. Again Stricker and Winder had moved smoothly and with precision. (Winder, if he could not command, was certainly demonstrating an ability to execute.) The American commander refused to leave his entrenched position. The British advance halted and then retired. Brooke then decided that the only hope of success was a night attack in cooperation with an attack, or at least a diversion, by the fleet.[15]

General Smith could take the utmost satisfaction in the results of the day. Armistead had demonstrated that Fort McHenry and the harbor defenses could hold firm against the most powerful siege weapons that the British fleet possessed. Of the fort's defenders, four had been killed and twenty-six wounded. Admiral Cochrane was faced, not with a tactical setback, but with "disastrous" repulse. The reason so frequently assigned for the failure of the British fleet is that the depth of the channel and obstructions in it prevented the British ships from coming alongside the fort and shelling it and its dependent works. The reason is not valid. While the heavier ships-of-the-line could not get in range, the larger frigates and other vessels could certainly maneuver in waters that permitted the entrance of the USS *Constellation* and would accommodate the exit of the *Java*, which the British themselves rated as a line-of-battle ship misrepresented as a frigate. And there was not a single sunken hulk below Fort McHenry. The reason for Cochrane's failure was that, after nine hours of continuous bombardment by weapons designed specifically for such work as this, the fort was virtually intact. The bomb ketches and the rocket ship employed by Cochrane represented two-thirds of the entire siege weapons of the British fleet. The mortars fired a two-hundred pound shell which had nearly five times the weight and almost twice the range of the heaviest gun on a British ship-of-the-line.[16]

Sam Smith could also take satisfaction in the fact that he had maneuvered so skillfully that the veteran British army had not even risked an attack. He had repulsed the best fighting machine in the world without even being compelled to beat off a direct assault.

In the darkness of the night the British tried once more. Brooke decided to mass his column and crash through the northeast angle toward which his second demonstration of the day had been directed. Here he would hold on until daylight and then roll up the American defense by fighting straight south toward the water front. Only one obstacle appeared to jeopardize this plan. Rodgers' bastion at the extreme right of the American line was well armed with heavy ordnance and protected by the angle formed by Fell's Point. It was manned by experienced fighters and might well serve as a rallying point which would break the British attack. It must therefore be knocked out or attacked vigorously from the harbor side. This would serve the double purpose of diverting American attention to that point about the time Brooke launched his storming column, and of neutralizing the bastion so that its guns could not be fully effective once he renewed his attack at daylight.[17]

But Brooke's plan was based on inadequate information concerning Cochrane's failure to dent the defenses of Fort McHenry. The bomb ships would have to come within a mile or perhaps less of Whetstone Point in order to reach Rodger's bastion. This would bring them under the guns of the fort. The only other possibility was a small-boat attack which, even if it escaped detection from the fort, would be rendered extremely hazardous by the obstructions in the channel and by a flotilla of gun boats which lay in the main channel protected by the battery on Lazaretto Point. Cochrane, upon hearing of Brooke's plan, decided to create a diversion by a small-boat attack at a more vulnerable spot.[18]

General Smith had thoughts of his own about a night attack. Or rather his subordinates did. But he silenced the importunists who urged him to attack the enemy. "Yes . . . but when you fight our citizens against British regulars you are staking dollars against cents." Smith's job was to defend Baltimore, not destroy the British army. There was nothing to be gained, and everything to be lost, in launching a difficult night maneuver with raw militia against British veterans.[19]

The man chosen by Cochrane to lead the diversion was Captain Charles Napier. With eleven boats and somewhat less than two hundred men he slipped past Fort McHenry and up the Ferry Branch where he attempted a surprise attack against Forts Covington and Babcock. Had some of his boats not gone astray in the darkness or had the garrisons of the two forts been less alert and steady, Napier might have converted his attack into a real threat. But Covington was manned by eighty of Rodger's tough seamen and Babcock by the remnants of Barney's flotillamen under Sailing-Master John Webster. Webster spotted Napier's force and opened fire with telling effect. As they fought savagely in the darkness the thunder of the American guns was soon joined by fire from Fort McHenry and even from the Lazaretto. Napier was repulsed but he accomplished his purpose. Armistead believed that a major attack was developing in his rear. John Rodgers in his bastion on Fell's Point believed the same thing. Probably Sam Smith did too. The only man who was not convinced was Colonel Arthur Brooke. Even though the bomb ships were shaking the very buildings of Baltimore, even though the rockets soared and crashed, even though every gun on Whetstone and Lazaretto Points that could be brought to bear was thundering at Napier in the Ferry Branch, Brooke was convinced that "all things went not prosperously." Toward three o'clock Brooke faced his column about and, leaving a ring of blazing campfires to disguise his movement, he retreated toward North Point. Thus ended the invasion. "Not merely empty," says the British writer, William James, "but considering what had been lost by it, a highly disastrous 'demonstration.' "[20]

At dawn on the 14th Samuel Smith gazed out on the field before him and saw only the smouldering campfires left by the British army. He was not aware of the retreat until daylight disclosed it to him. He sent a force under the command of General Winder in pursuit, but the British rear guard occupied some abandoned American works above North Point. They had no difficulty in checking the few pursuers who arrived before their embarkation was complete. Even without this advantage it is doubtful whether the untrained American militia, exhausted from standing to arms for three days, could have mustered enough troops and overtaken an enemy, which had three hours start, in time to hamper them to any degree.[21]

Wellington's Invincibles carried their commanding officer and 290 other casualties back aboard their ships. Those ships, victors of Trafalgar and Cape St. Vincent and scourge of cities and forts along the entire coast of Europe, set their sails and disappeared down the Chesapeake. General Smith's citizen-soldiers, his batteries and earthworks, and the guns of Fort McHenry, when confronted by a part of the greatest fighting machine in the world, had stopped it cold. History has deprecated his achievement. But Smith did in Baltimore what Madison, Monroe, Armstrong, and Winder had been unable to do at Bladensburg just thirty miles away.

Word of the British retirement from Baltimore, together with the news of the defeat of the British invasion from Canada at Plattsburg, reached the anxious American Peace Commission at Ghent a month later. Said James A. Bayard, one of the American commissioners, "[The British] certainly did expect that the force sent to America would . . . strike a blow which would prostrate the nation at her feet. . . . The Capture of Washington was a source of great triumph and exultation and inspired a belief that their troops could not be defeated. This error was sadly corrected by the repulse in the attack on Baltimore, by the destruction of their fleet on Lake Champlain and by the retreat of Prevost from Plattsburg." Bayard's colleague, Henry Clay, proudly declared that "the issue of the last campaign has demonstrated, in the repulse before Baltimore, the retreat from Plattsburg, the hard fought action on the Niagara frontier . . . that we have always possessed the finest elements of military composition. . . ."[22]

While the bombs still burst over Fort McHenry, out in the bay aboard the British cartel ship, Francis Scott Key paced anxiously up and down the deck. He knew "by the dawn's early light" that Fort McHenry had not fallen and that the city was saved. Mr. Key did not get home until September 15th when all the British forces were back on board their ships and the fleet was ready to weigh anchor. He had gone aboard the ship to secure the release of Dr. William Beanes, a friend of his who had been captured by the British on their way back from Washington. Mr. Key came ashore, not only with Dr. Beanes, but with a few notes scribbled on the back of an envelope. A few days later "The Star-Spangled Banner" had been sung for the first time. The young republic had a battle hymn.[23]

Everyone remembers Francis Scott Key. Few remember the men who saved a city and provided the inspiration for a national anthem—John Stricker, Decius Wadsworth, George Armistead, Sailing-Master John Webster, and the merchant-senator-soldier, Samuel Smith.

It is the only time in the nation's history that an American city has been defended by its citizens.

10

The House Revisited
and the Panic of 1819

F OR THE FIRST TIME in twenty-two years Sam Smith lost an election. The victory at Baltimore and the attendant acclaim won by him came just too late to aid him in the rescue of his political fortunes. Only a few weeks before the British attack the Federalist majority in the legislature in August, 1814 had voted Smith out of the Senate and replaced him with Robert Goodloe Harper. But in Baltimore Republicanism was still dominant and its citizens returned him to the House of Representatives when Nicholas Moore, member from Baltimore, resigned in 1815. Late January of 1816 found Smith in Washington as Congress met for its first post-war session.[1]

Smith found many old acquaintances in the House but their ideas and alignments were new. The nation had seemingly turned its back upon Europe almost in the instant after the Peace of Ghent. The old "War Hawks" led by Clay, Calhoun, and Lowndes were now the advocates of a new nationalism which urged that the central government take the lead in fostering industry, transportation, and improvements in the framework of the country's economic system. The Federalists, already dying as a party because of their unsuccessful opposition to the war, were joined by a small minority of strict constructionists led by John Randolph. These dissenters could only oppose and obstruct for, with the Republican conversion to nationalism, the Federalist reason for existence had virtually ceased. It was in this setting that Smith resumed his political career.

President Madison's message to the opening session of the Fourteenth Congress embodied four principal proposals. Two of these were the outgrowth of conditions which had existed before the war and which the war itself had accentuated. No one was surprised, therefore, when the President asked for additional appropriations to increase the standing army and navy and for a renewal of the charter of the Bank of the United States. In addition, he proposed effective protection for manufactures and new national roads and canals.[2]

The proposal for a Bank charter placed Smith and many other politicians in a curious position. In 1811 Smith had led the fight against the Bank in the Senate and had been supported by Henry Clay. But the war had shown that efforts to obtain a sound medium of exchange, to secure money for the government by bond issues, and to keep new issues of Treasury notes in circulation were all futile without a National Bank to establish uniform currency and regulate its distribution.

Proponents of the Bank had attempted to recharter it in January, 1815. Smith had voted for the recharter at that time but had sustained the Presidential veto which did not approve the system which was then proposed. Under the auspices of the new Secretary of the Treasury, Alexander J. Dallas, whom Madison had chosen to succeed George W. Campbell, a new plan for recharter had already been submitted to Congress when Smith arrived and took his seat. The charter's most powerful spokesman was John C. Calhoun of South Carolina, whom John Quincy Adams two years later described as a man who "thinks for himself... with sound judgment, quick discrimination and keen observation. He supports his opinions, too, with powerful eloquence." Calhoun carried along with him a large part of the factional strife of pre-war years. General Smith virtually admitted the complete reversal of his stand in 1811. He believed, like Calhoun, that "the establishment of a Bank of the United States would contribute better than any other measure to the restoration of a general medium of circulation of uniform value.[3]

Principal opposition to the bank came from two quarters, the strict-construction Republicans, led by Randolph, and the Federalists, led by Daniel Webster. Randolph believed that the evils arising from the emission of fluctuating currency by the state banks could be eliminated without the establishment of a national bank. Webster and the Federalists opposed, not so much the idea of the Bank itself, as the increased amount of capitalization for which the bill called. Randolph found almost no supporters for his contentions but the Federalists made a strong impression by comparing the $35,000,000 capitalization which Secretary Dallas requested to the $10,000,000 capitalization of the old Bank. General Smith replied to this contention by saying that "ten millions bore a larger proportion to the uses of that day than thirty-five million did to this. ..." He thought it impossible that any man could suppose that $10,000,000 was sufficient for the present, "particularly since the Government has spread taxes over the whole surface of the country, and made the services of this institution more extensively necessary. ... With a reduced capital the operations of the Bank would be so circumscribed, that it could afford little aid to merchants. Here Smith was trying to prevent what he had considered the basic fault of the old Bank, that it had not extended its services to an extent which justified its existence. The efforts of Clay, Calhoun, Smith, and other proponents of the Bank were successful. They refuted objections to Presidential appointment of directors, to the government holding Bank stock, and other less important points; and the second Bank of the United States was chartered in 1816 for a twenty year period.[4]

General Smith was following a trend of other Republican leaders toward the theory of a strong central government which chose to go beyond the limits of strict Constitutional interpretation. The Federalists, on the other hand, were driven to defend the Constitution, to cry out against the extension of government powers which included "control and influence over a great banking institution."

Accenting the Republican trend was another request which Madison made of Congress in his message. "In adjusting the duties on imports, to the objects of revenue, the influence of tariff on manufactures will necessarily present itself for consideration." The tariff, then, was to be for revenue, but if it should operate for the protection of home industry, so much the better. Here was a chief point in Hamilton's nationalism which the Jeffersonians had attacked so bitterly twenty years ago. Small wonder that John Randolph observed "... if a writ were to issue against that old party [Republican]... it would be impossible for a constable with a search warrant to find it." But in the America whose frontier was at last open for expansion and exploitation, and whose commerce was freed from the tyranny of Europe, nascent industrial capitalism was straining to be let loose.[5]

The tariff was also very important as a source of revenue. Dallas and Madison wished to relieve the country of internal taxes occasioned by the war, and it was to make up for the deficit thus created that the tariff bill was introduced. Only Randolph clearly perceived that the protective feature would eventually be detrimental to the South, but none of his supporters backed his argument. Calhoun and other Southern Republicans believed that the South would share in the benefits of the nation's rising industry.[6]

Samuel Smith represented in his own person several conflicting interests. As a merchant, although not now a very active one, his inclination was to oppose all tariffs as detrimental to that interest, just as Webster fought it as a representative of commercial New England. But Smith acknowledged what Webster did not, that manufactures would soon play a tremendously important part in the economic life of the country, as his early interest in and profits from iron manufactures had demonstrated to him.

A third side of the man was drawn, both by economic interest and by sentiment, to the South. His brother-in-law, Wilson Cary Nicholas, was one of the largest planters in Virginia and Smith himself had large land holdings in the South. Although Smith could not be called a planter, in a few years his son, John, would be farming Montebello and would own an interest in a Louisiana sugar plantation.[7]

These various conflicts were reflected in Smith's part in the debate when the committee, headed by William Lowndes of South Carolina, reported the tariff bill. Lowndes himself was much more moderate in his views than the rest of the committee, and he had been able to influence the other members to reduce several of the rates which Dallas had proposed in his resolution to the committee. When the bill was introduced Clay immediately proposed increases of duties "to try the sense of the House as to the extent to which it was willing to go in protecting domestic manufactures." General Smith replied to Clay and, says the Gales and Seaton reporter, "took a very wide view of the subject; discussing fully and separately the effect which would be produced by the proposed duties on commerce, on manufactures, on agriculture, and on revenue. . . . He was in favor of protecting domestic fabrics but differed from Mr. Clay as to the extent of that protection." Like many other representatives, Smith could not resist the temptation to take a somewhat narrower view where his own section and interests were concerned. He proposed and secured the passage of an amendment which raised the duty on iron manufactures from the $1.50 proposed in the bill to $2.50 per hundredweight, and secured the lowering of the duty on imported raw iron from seventy-five to forty-five cents per hundredweight.[8]

The chief battle on the tariff bill was over the duty on cotton cloth. The South, dependent on Great Britain for her market of raw cotton, opposed high duties because she relied chiefly on England for cheap cotton clothing for her slaves and farmers. John Randolph put his finger on the root of Southern opposition when he stated: "On whom do your important duties bear? . . . On poor men and on slaveholders." On the other hand the growing manufacturing interests in Pennsylvania and the North were anxious to protect their products from the growing stream of British goods even now beginning to glut the American market. In this they were aided by the nationalism of Clay and Calhoun.

General Smith's position reflected the middle ground. He would protect home industry but not to the extent advocated by Clay. When the latter proposed to raise the *ad valorem* duty on cottons from the 20 percent provided in the committee's bill to 33⅓ percent, Smith exerted his keen knowledge of commerce to show that this figure represented far less than the actual advantage to American goods. Such items as insurance, freight, and commissions would, when added to the proposed high duty, give the domestic manufacturer an actual advantage of 47½ percent over cost. The final compromise provided a twenty-five percent *ad valorem* duty until 1819 when the rate would be lowered to 20 percent.

The debate was not concluded without desperate and bitter efforts on the part of the opposition. John Randolph moved a postponement until the following session. General Smith immediately objected that if some schedule were not enacted merchants would be thrown into confusion because they would be forced to act "without knowing how to shape their conduct or form their calculations, uncertain of the policy which might then be adopted." The motion for postponement was lost.

Another tactic adopted by the opposition was a resolution introduced by Robert Wright of Maryland, to exclude from voting anyone "being a proprietor or having any share in any factory of cotton or cotton yarn." Such pettiness brought forth a sharp rebuke from General Smith and the resolution was withdrawn. The amended bill was sent to the Senate where it passed with virtually no opposition.[9]

In the protective sense the tariff of 1816 was not very effective. There were several reasons for this. The protective policy as such was favored only by a few men as a long range economic policy. The fact that the duties on the most important of the young industries, cotton manufactures, was limited to a definite period indicated that the majority of the members did not have a permanent protective policy in mind. There were also a number of members, Smith among them, who favored high duties only where their own local interests were concerned, otherwise favoring a mild protective policy. Remembering that this was the first real protective tariff undertaken by the government and that commercial interests were still a potent factor, it is understandable that the policy as a whole was cautious. Times were prosperous and the full effect of British "dumping" had not been felt. It remained for the pressure of hard times in the early twenties to give impetus to the doctrine of a strong protective tariff.

1816 was a presidential election year and throughout the country Secretary of State Monroe was generally conceded to be the popular choice to succeed Madison. But this unanimity did not extend to the Congressional leaders in Washington who would meet in caucus to choose the Republican ticket. There was still a remnant of the old Smith "Invisibles" who had favored Clinton in 1811, although it is not known what part General Smith himself took in the anti-Monroe movement of 1816. There was also a good deal of dissatisfaction with Monroe in Virginia besides the usual objections to the continuation of the "Virginia Dynasty." Daniel Tompkins, governor of New York, an able and honest man, represented the hopes of the powerful New York wing but was not well enough known nationally to command the anti-Monroe groups south of the Potomac. The two forces were united on William H. Crawford, a man of brilliant abilities who had gained a high reputation as Georgia's representative in Congress both before and since the war. However, Crawford became aware in the last stages of maneuvering just before the caucus that Monroe was probably too strong for him. He decided that he could strengthen himself with the party and, since he was only forty-three years of age at this time, set himself up as Monroe's heir-apparent by instructing his supporters to vote for Monroe. Thus did Crawford attempt to become the ally rather than the rival of the "Virginia Dynasty."

But when General Smith in the middle of March, 1816 called a caucus to nominate the Republican ticket, Crawford's plan somehow miscarried. The meeting opened with the election of Smith as chairman and Henry Clay offered a resolution for postponement which was negatived. Then, to the surprise of many of the members, Crawford's name was presented in opposition to Monroe and the former's friends gave him fifty-four of the one hundred and nineteen votes cast. Monroe's nomination was salvaged only by the desperate efforts of his friends, notably Calhoun. A sharp reaction to the already unpopular caucus was felt throughout the country. Many people felt that they had been nearly cheated of the popular favorite, Monroe, by the intrigues of a few Washington politicos. It is not known how Smith voted in the caucus, but these events in 1816 were to have an important bearing on Crawford's campaign for election in 1824 and General Smith's part in it.[10]

Madison's last address as President was to the expiring Fourteenth Congress which met in December, 1816. He referred the Congress to the need for internal improvements but, with an eye to the constitutional scruples expressed in his message of 1815, said only: "I particularly invite again their attention to the expediency of exercising their existing powers, and where necessary, of resorting to the prescribed mode of enlarging them...."[11] This reference to "prescribed modes" was a suggestion for a constitutional amendment.

It was not until February, 1817 that the debate on internal improvements got under way. Calhoun opened for the bill, citing not only its need in the military sense, but unfolding the vision of a nation which would be "a perfect unity in every part, in feeling and in sentiments.... Let us then bind the Republic together with a system of roads and canals. Let us conquer space."

The method which the bill proposed for effecting this system was the allocation of an annual sum of $650,000 drawn from the bonus from the Bank charter and the interest on the stock which the government held in the Bank. This sum was to be distributed to the states and the improvements were to be carried out by the state governments. This method was put forward to overcome the constitutional objections which had previously arisen as to the power of the central government to carry out such projects.

Samuel Smith objected strongly to this feature of the bill. To the principle of internal improvements he was entirely favorable. He took pains to point out that he had given his personal efforts as well as his votes in Congress to such programs. "But, sir, I never had considered it my duty to vote for the application of large sums of money to be frittered away and applied to objects of small importance." Herein lay the burden of Smith's objection. To apply the funds to a great national project such as the Erie Canal or to a crossing of the Appalachians to the Ohio was something which the national government might undertake with profit. But to apportion money, leaving its disposition in the hands of the states, and expect any real benefit to arise therefrom was to ignore realities. In particular he objected to the amendment which would allocate funds on the basis of representation in Congress, which would be revised from time to time. Maryland, New Hampshire, Delaware, Rhode Island, Connecticut, New Jersey and South Carolina would never increase their representation. "By this bill the stationary states are making themselves completely tributary to those which may be the increasing states."

Citing the smallness of the sum in comparison to the needs of the various states he added, "The sum proposed for Maryland, as already stated, is $32,000, not enough for four miles of good turnpike road." And finally he gave the pork barrel a resounding kick: "Sir, what a time we shall have ... you are about to throw the apple of discord into this House—one that will never decay. Instead of members attending to public business they will be constantly engaged in bargaining, trucking, buying, and selling.... Sir, I look with disgust at the picture before my eyes that will result from this bill."

Smith's appeal was neither to crude prejudices, constitutional objections, nor lofty sentiments. Practical criticism backed by statistical proof was the General's favorite form of argument and he used it now. He showed that the bill, without meeting the needs which it sought, would curtail the reduction of the national debt as proposed by the Ways and Means Committee of which he was second-ranking member.

> Sir ... the great objects of Congress, I thought, on its meeting, were to establish the means to pay off the national debt, to lessen the public expenditures, and, if we had the means to spare, to repeal such internal taxes as are obnoxious and unequal—such as the stamp act and the tax on licenses.... My opinion is ... that those taxes ought to be repealed before we apply so large a sum as $650,000 per annum to a new and untried object.[12]

The time for adjournment was drawing near and such was the anxiety of the proponents of the bill that on this day, February 6, 1817, motion after motion for adjournment was lost. Daniel Sheffey of Virginia defended the bill's constitutionality. John B. Yates of New York pleaded for aid for the Erie Canal. Philip P. Barbour of Virginia attacked the bill's constitutionality and Robert Wright of Maryland supported his colleague, General Smith. It was four o'clock in the morning before the weary delegates stumbled to their beds.

The debate continued through the 7th and 8th with Sheffey, Randolph, Smith, and Wright again speaking against the bill and Calhoun closing with a final appeal for its passage. The "Yeas" were eighty-six and the "Nays," eighty-four. The Senate passed the bill with minor amendments. But to the surprise of all and to the mortification of its proponents, particularly Calhoun, Madison vetoed the bill on his last day in office. Whether the President had had his constitutional scruples all along or whether the close vote in the House had changed his mind, Madison's veto was based on the strict construction theory that "such power is not expressly given by the Constitution."[13]

The close of the session found Smith definitely aligned with the new Republican nationalism, though not to the extreme represented by Clay and Calhoun. He approved the moderate protection of the tariff bill of 1816 but future proposals for increased rates would find him in opposition. The Bank of the United States had found in him an able supporter. He approved of the principle of government aid for internal improvements but had refused to support the bill for that purpose because he found practical objections to it.

Smith returned to Baltimore where he passed most of the summer of 1817 at Montebello. Business conditions were not quite so good but no one was seriously worried about them. Two notable visitors came to the city during the summer. President James Monroe visited the city in June on his tour through the country. General Smith, with Generals Stricker and Winder, escorted him on a tour of Fort McHenry and the North Point battleground. Later in the summer John Quincy Adams visited in Baltimore. The newly-appointed Secretary of State passed the evening with General and Mrs. Smith.[14]

Monroe had selected the remainder of his cabinet with care. His appointment of Adams had been partly to avoid any appearance that "the citizens of Virga., holding the Presidency have made appointments in that dept. to secure the succession." Crawford remained as head of the Treasury. Monroe offered the War Department to Henry Clay but he declined it. Clay wanted the Secretaryship of State or nothing at all. His eye, even then, was on the presidency and he felt that he deserved the top cabinet post which would probably provide him the stepping stone. It was this circumstance, along with others, which made Clay "the gadfly on his [Monroe's] flank," in the following sessions of Congress.[15] Monroe's refusal was based on his wish to give neither Clay nor Crawford the advantage in the campaign of 1824. To the young "War Hawk" from South Carolina, John C. Calhoun, went the post of Secretary of War. Benjamin W. Crowninshield of Massachusetts headed the Navy Department and William Wirt of Virginia was picked as Attorney-General.

Two clashes between General Smith and Henry Clay marked an otherwise uneventful session of Congress which met during the winter and spring of 1817–1818. Clay was anxious to repeal the Neutrality Act of 1817 which was aimed at curbing the fitting out of privateers in the United States. Such ships were used by the Latin American countries in their war for independence to harass Spanish commerce. The administration was endeavoring to steer a course of strict neutrality until it could determine the merit and good faith of the cause of South American independence. When Clay introduced his resolution for repeal of the law he justified his action by saying that the United States was imposing upon itself restrictions far beyond those which were warranted by international law.

Smith, although not cool to South American independence,

wished to allow the administration to pursue its own course without Congressional interference. He opposed Clay on the ground that such activities, if permitted, could result in justifiable protest and retaliation from Spain. The possible result might be war. "I want to know," jeered the General, "if, with the powers the Speaker can bring into action on such subjects, he would not rouse the feelings of every man in the House to resent the injury.... What, he would say, shall we stand by and see our commerce plundered and our merchants robbed?" The Speaker's resolution was negatived by a majority of two votes.

Still attempting to further the cause of South American independence, Clay next moved an addition to the appropriation bill which would provide $18,000 for sending a minister to Buenos Aires. General Smith again opposed the Speaker. "This course of conduct on the part of Congress would be novel and wholly unprecedented. The Constitution has given Congress legislative powers—the President the direction of our intercourse in foreign affairs."

Two days later Mr. Clay recommended that "the gentleman from Maryland ... confine himself to the operation of commerce, rather than undertake to expound the questions of public law; for he could assure that gentleman that, although he might make some figure with his practical knowledge, in one case, he would not, in the other." Sam Smith waited only for the Speaker to resume his seat before he retorted that Mr. Clay had "with a politeness peculiar to himself advised—nay, sir, almost forbade—me to speak on his peculiar province, to wit: the law of nations." He had perhaps forgotten "that I have been twenty-five years in Congress, in which time the law of nations had been frequently discussed.... But, Mr. Chairman, I quoted not from the law of nations; I confined myself to the laws of common sense (which I recommend to the Speaker for his perusal.)" When the debate was concluded the House again decided against the Speaker, preferring to await the recommendations of the President. As for the rest of the session, the repeal of internal war taxes, a useless debate on internal improvements, and an ineffective effort to establish a universal bankruptcy law consumed most of the remaining time.[16]

The summer of 1818 passed quietly. News from his son-in-law John Mansfield, informed the General that "the number of your grandchildren was yesterday increased by the arrival of a young lady." There was immediate speculation at Montebello as to a fitting name. "Susan was not a pretty name," Sam observed to Molly B., "yet you must call it Susan. Sidney wished it to be called for her and said you had promised but ... it must be called for Mrs. Mansfield."

Sam and his wife felt the loneliness of parents whose children were growing up and one by one leaving home. "I bought General Miller's little place . . . near Montebello for Sidney but the Gypsy will not accept it," he complained to his daughter in England. "Her residence there would have been convenient to us . . . we [are] compelled to live alone. . . ."

Politics lacked the factional bitterness of pre-war days. Smith wrote to his son-in-law, " . . . the newspapers keep up a party war but for them animosities would soon cease among us." Business, however, seemed to be falling off somewhat. United States Bank stock had fallen but there were no large sales. He was of the opinion that the price would soon rise and dividends would increase.[17]

General Smith's optimism was shared by the whole country. Western and Southern farmers were getting top prices for their crops and buying more land, also at top prices, on credit granted either by the government or by the "wildcat" western banks. These in turn were indebted to the Bank of the United States or to the Eastern capitalists who were themselves investing heavily in new manufacturing ventures far in excess of the country's needs. This merry-go-round was kept going by a wave of frenzied speculation which swept the entire country. The Bank itself, which might have been pursuing a more conservative policy and curbing inflation, was second to none in the scramble for wealth, and branches in all parts of the country discounted loans with reckless abandon.[18]

There were several warnings that the Bank was getting into difficulties. The amount of specie was very meager and the location of its loans was out of proportion. In October, 1817 Baltimore and Philadelphia alone had discounted $21,000,000 out of the total of $33,000,000 discounted at all twelve offices. Most of this was due to blind ignorance on the part of President William Jones, whose conception of management was essentially unsound. He did not think it necessary to fix the capital of each branch nor did he require them to settle their accounts periodically or to furnish funds when they issued bank notes or sold drafts. In short, there was a "perfect want of system." Moreover, the directors at most of the branches, particularly in the South and West, were both ignorant and disobedient. Loans were over-extended, stock was accepted as security in advance of its value, and the attempt to establish Bank currency at uniform value—in the face of depreciated state bank currency and the constant drain of specie—resulted in further inflation rather than levelling off.[19] Added to this was the widespread speculation in Bank stock which characterized the boom period following the war, as well as rampant speculation in Western lands.

When the Baltimore branch of the Bank was organized, a large part of the stock was subscribed to by a relatively small number of persons, although this was expressly forbidden by the charter. About fifteen individuals, purchasing through dummy subscribers and posing as "attorneys" for the supposed owners, controlled three-fourths of the stock, and therefore that percentage of the votes of the Baltimore branch. James Buchanan, General Smith's partner in the merchant house of Smith and Buchanan, was elected president. Assisted by the incapacity of Jones, the Baltimore group was soon engaged in manipulating large blocks of stock so as to regulate its price in the open market. Their success is measured by the fact that the price of Bank stock rose from 118 in April, 1817, to 154 in December of the same year.[20]

But Buchanan did not confine himself to simple buying and selling. He formed a partnership which consisted of the firm of Smith and Buchanan, George Williams, a director both at Baltimore and Philadelphia, and James McCulloch, cashier of the Baltimore branch. Sam Smith, who had not been actively associated with the company for several years, probably knew nothing of this arrangement. Buchanan and his associates determined to manipulate prices for their own benefit by controlling the movement of large blocks of stock. Their success seemed assured because they not only controlled the Baltimore branch but Williams and Buchanan were both directors of the parent Bank. At one time the partners owned over $6,300,000 in stock purchases.

Naturally, such activities demanded large supplies of ready cash. To obtain it the partners borrowed heavily in Philadelphia and Baltimore, giving their stock purchases as collateral. When this was not sufficient, they simply loaned funds to themselves and endorsed each other's notes, giving no security at all. To inquiring members of the board of directors at Baltimore, they said that they had authority from Philadelphia to make such loans without the interference or consent on the part of the local board. This, of course, was false.

With the assumption of this power, the partners discounted to themselves a total of over $1,400,000 in unsecured notes which were constantly renewed without payment of interest. When the price of stock went down and its security value was lowered, they simply increased their unsecured loans.[21]

Says the historian of the Bank, R. C. Catterall, "By arrogating to themselves the sole right to discount loans ... by indorsing each other, by lying to the local board of directors, by false entries in the books ... by false reports to the bank at Philadelphia, the speculation was kept going." That Smith was ignorant of this state of affairs seems certain in view of the fact that it was at this very time that he was writing to this daughter and son-in-law advising them to invest in Bank stock. In the autumn of 1818 when the first stages of the panic began, the parent Bank demanded lists of stock loans at all branches, including the names of parties holding the loans and the precise nature of the stock which secured them. The partners twisted and squirmed but the result was inevitable. In May, 1819 the crash came. "The house of Smith and Buchanan," wrote John Quincy Adams, when he heard the news, "which has been these thirty years one of the greatest commercial establishments in the United States, broke ... with a crash that staggered the whole city of Baltimore and will extend no one knows how far. . . . The moral, political and commercial character of the city of Baltimore has for twenty-five years been formed, controlled and modified almost entirely by this house of Smith and Buchanan. . . ."[22]

The General was bankrupt. But it was the collapse of Smith and Buchanan, involving as it did the peculations of James Buchanan, which came as such a fearful shock. Samuel Smith was of that older breed of American businessman who did not separate business and personal ethics. To see the great mercantile house in disgrace as well as in collapse was almost too much for him, and during the summer of 1819 his family feared for his health and even his sanity. But by autumn the tough old man had rallied and began to salvage the wreck.

He wrote to one of his creditors, "Circumstances ... have so embarrassed my house of S. Smith and Buchanan that it has become necessary to mortgage my real estate for the security of my creditors. These creditors will require the relinquishment of Mrs. Smith's right of dower. . . ." Smith persuaded the Bank directors to place the affairs of the company in his hands. The committee of the Bank board was convinced that General Smith was not implicated in the fraud and showed him every consideration, even exempting his personal property from the claims of his creditors.[23]

But years of stringent economy would be necessary before the loss was liquidated. Mrs. Smith had "an interest on the sum of $9,000 which will aid in buying our House if it does not go at too high a price [at auction] but prudence would direct us to buy a smaller House. Pride or what you will induce us to wish to keep our own if possible. I am selling my Wine and your mother has sold ... her china," Smith wrote to his daughter. "General Smith's fine house and the extravagant mode of living he introduced into Baltimore caused the ruin of half the people of that place," observed Betsy Patterson Bonaparte. Whether the remark was justified or not, the old life was gone. "We live at very little cost," Smith wrote to Molly, "My pension pays all our expenses in [Washington] and we live with John during the summer months."[24]

John Spear Smith was a loyal son. Knowing his father's attachment for Montebello, he purchased the summer home; but in order to keep it the young man who had shown such promise as a diplomat and politician was now reduced to dairy farming. Nor did the change prove unsuccessful. "John is getting Montebello in order," his father reported to the Mansfields, "and clears by his cows about $2000 p. ann. which ought to support him and his family." As for the other children, "Sidney is quite delighted with Bagatelle which Mr. P. [gives] them free of rent. Her income is about $1200 which nearly pays their expenses. Edward's health is not strong, his temperance will probably restore him." And for Laura and Christopher Hughes, "It is not expected that old Mr. Hughes can live long. He has made his will and given to Christopher one half of his property, which will pay his debts and leave something for his family."[25]

To his friends Sam exhibited an outward philosophical calm but privately he admitted to Mrs. Mansfield that "you would find misery and poverty in all your connections . . . you would find me wretched, without spirits, without appetite, without employment. . . ."

General Smith grimly persisted, however, in his efforts to satisfy his creditors and so well did he succeed that by 1822 the debts of Smith and Buchanan were satisfied and by 1826 Smith himself had been released by all his creditors.[26]

It seems certain that General Smith was not implicated in the jobbing of Buchanan. Crawford wrote him in June of 1819 that there had been "no whisper" against him in Washington. To Gallatin Crawford wrote, "It is proper to observe that General Smith is acquitted of all the disgraceful acts which have covered Buchanan and McCullough. . . ." As for the attitude of the people of Baltimore, Smith was able to write in 1822, "I have been reelected to Congress and shall probably be Senator in lieu of Mr. Pinkney. I have lost nothing in the opinion of the people and the nation."[27]

11

Crawford for President

"SAMUEL SMITH," wrote John Quincy Adams in the spring of 1820, "in the midst of stupendous ruin of reputation and fortune as a merchant, maintains yet his consideration and influence as a politician, or at least struggles to maintain it. . . ."[1] These were difficult times for an influential politician. The extinction of the Federalist influence left the way open for new political alignments. Although there appeared to be no opposition to Monroe's reelection in 1820, ambitious men were already looking ahead to 1824. One of these was Secretary of the Treasury Crawford, and it was to him that Smith decided to throw his support.

William Harris Crawford was a Virginian by birth. He had moved to South Carolina and then to Georgia at an early age where his family had settled in Columbia County. He was elected to the Georgia legislature in 1803 and became associated with James Jackson, one of the political leaders of the state, and with the party which successively bore the name of Jackson, Crawford, and Troup party. Its membership was composed principally of the planter and merchant class and was distinguished chiefly by its persistent advocacy of conservative financial policies. The party was opposed by the Clark group, more nearly indentified with the debtor classes and the frontier. This opposition was led by John Clark, a soft-money man who opposed the Bank of the United States and who hated not only Crawford's policies but Crawford himself.

The temporarily triumphant Jackson party elected Crawford to the Senate in 1807. Here his independent views led him into strange alliances, for in Washington William H. Crawford was no man's man. He stood with John Randolph in the latter's denunciation of the Yazoo frauds. In his "Delphic Oracle" speech he had supported General Smith and the "Invisibles" in denouncing Madison's ambiguous message of 1810, but he fought hard for the Bank recharter in 1811. Upon the death of Vice-President Clinton he was elected President pro-tempore of the Senate. He refused Madison's offer of the War Department in 1812, served as minister to France during the war, accepted the War Department when it was again offered to him in 1816, but was soon afterward made Secretary of the Treasury.

Crawford was a man of huge physical stature. His wide, mobile mouth and jutting jaw somewhat marred an otherwise handsome face. His affable personality rendered him one of the most likable men in Washington and his keen, clear judgment gained him a vast respect among friends and enemies. "The most obvious feature in Crawford's character is decision," wrote John Quincy Adams.[2] These qualities, with his record of services and achievement, had gained him a large following in Congress. In the early stages of the race for President he was clearly the favorite. This was the man upon whom Sam Smith pinned his political hopes and it was with an eye to the election of 1824 that Smith steered his course during the next four years.

Another aspirant for the Presidency was John Quincy Adams. Favored by holding the office which had provided the stepping stone for the members of the Virginia Dynasty, the Secretary of State possessed a record of service equal if not superior to that of Crawford. Adams did not represent fully the characteristics of New England for he stood neither for the democracy of the interior nor the commercial Federalism of the coast. From the viewpoint of mentality, training, and his wide experience abroad which had given him sound views on comparative government, he was probably the most able candidate in the field. But he had inherited the unpopularity as well as the fame of his father and he had touched life so broadly that he perhaps did not have enough provincialism for his countrymen's taste. He was a man of meticulous methods and tireless work. He believed in himself and was impatient when lesser minds failed to keep pace with his clarity and astuteness. This led to a tendency for overbearing tactlessness marked by neither appeasement nor attempts to conciliate those who opposed him. He was a man almost universally respected and almost universally unloved. "I am," he wrote, "a man of reserved, cold, austere, and forbidding manners."[3] Thus did the Puritan talent for self-criticism depict the unlovely man who was pitted against the most engaging personalities of the period.

Two of the candidates represented the new nationalism and the frontier. Henry Clay, spokesman for the American system, had already established himself as a national figure. He had desired and expected the appointment as Secretary of State under Monroe and his disappointment, along with other considerations, led him into opposition to the administration. A man of engaging personality, brilliant in debate, commanding the respect of all and the admiration of many members of Congress, Henry Clay was a force to be reckoned.

John C. Calhoun, the Secretary of War, also entered the field. His mental powers were exceptional and he possessed a consistent record of nationalism with his leadership in the Bank recharter, the tariff bill of 1816, and the Congressional attempts at internal improvements. The brilliant logic and the incisive brain which later produced the theory of nullification and the doctrine of concurrent majority was not yet fully matured but, as a contemporary observer noted, "the lightning glance of his mind, and the rapidity with which he analyzes, never fail to furnish him with all that may be necessary for his immediate purposes." But for all his keen mind and ability "he was a child in party tactics."[4] He became a candidate more to defeat Crawford, whom he hated, than for any real expectations of success.

Andrew Jackson was not yet an avowed candidate in 1820. The hero of New Orleans was the oldest of the candidates and was probably more well-known to the country as a whole. Brief and scattered appearances in Congress and his administrative experience in the army were the limit of his training for office, but his appeal to the people was tremendous, particularly in the West where his military victories had been decisive in opening the frontier and curbing the Indian troubles. Five years later General Smith remarked of him, "Genl. Jackson is an amiable man in private society, hospitable, charitable and beloved by those who best know him."[5] But in 1820 Smith and the rest of the Washington politicos knew Jackson only from his reputation as a soldier. But this was 1820 and Jackson's great advantage lay in the fact that, even after he became a candidate, his opponents grossly underestimated his chances and directed very little of their efforts toward checkmating him. By the time they realized his tremendous popular appeal, the Jackson movement had become too great to halt.

Two candidates of less importance also entered the field. William Lowndes, brilliant and beloved South Carolinian, was early nominated by the legislature of his native state in 1821 but ill-health and finally death removed him from the scene. De Witt Clinton, governor of New York, entertained hopes of success in 1824, but few people outside the state took his candidacy seriously.

Among these candidates Crawford's distinct and obvious advantage lay in the fact that he controlled the more important newspapers and exerted considerable control of the party machinery through his Treasury Department patronage. Complete control of the party machinery, if it could be achieved, meant control of Congress and it was in this respect that General Smith rendered his principal service to Crawford. From the time of the convening of the Sixteenth Congress in December, 1819 Smith began to campaign to seize control of the House for Crawford and use it to strengthen his campaign and weaken that of his opponents.

The Crawford platform, somewhat nebulous and indefinite in 1820, gradually became an appeal for the return to the old Jeffersonian tenets of democracy, economy in government, strict construction and states' rights. Crawford's record and Treasury Department tenure forced him to except the National Bank and moderate tariff protection from these principles as indeed he would be forced to do in any case were he to expect to carry Pennsylvania and New York. But this return to the Virginia school, which eventually earned the Crawford forces the name of "Radicals," enabled him to make an appeal to Virginia and the South and at the same time covertly to snipe at the administration's leanings toward nationalism.

General Smith was drawn into the Crawford ranks both by principle and for personal reasons. The radical program suited him. Like Crawford he had favored the Bank recharter in 1816 and had advocated moderate protection, but he did not wish to see the latter policy carried to the extent advocated by Calhoun and Clay. The recent panic and his own financial misfortunes had made him an advocate of conservatism and economy where public finance was concerned. Smith was equally influenced by personal reasons. Essentially a man of practical affairs rather than a statesman of wide vision, he was convinced of Crawford's administrative ability. The Secretary's stout defense of his character in the recent Baltimore Bank debacle coupled with Smith's own strong liking for the man were of undoubted influence. In a campaign in which political issues were confused and personality meant much, Smith's choice was natural.

Other Crawford leaders included Smith's colleague in the House, Stevenson Archer, lately judge in the Mississippi Territory and recently returned to Maryland where he had been chosen to Congress from Annapolis. In New York Martin Van Buren, just risen to national fame as a politician, was soon to throw the weight of the "Albany Regency" behind the Crawford candidacy. A manipulator of consummate skill and political daring, Van Buren was to learn a lesson at

Crawford's expense that he never forgot when he was Jackson's champion; the most powerful political machine can be wrecked by popular indignation.

In Virginia John Randolph, representative of extreme Southern dissent to the new nationalism, lent his able voice. But Virginia did not look to him as in former days for the keen incisiveness of his brilliant mind was badly impaired and his stinging invective lacked the clear reason of former days. George Troup, Tidewater aristocrat who was heir to the Crawford party in Georgia, had been defeated in the gubernatorial campaign of 1819 by his arch-rival, John Clark. The margin of defeat was narrow and Crawford supporters believed that Troup was certain to return to office at the next election. From the new state of Maine John Chandler enlisted his aid for Crawford. A veteran of both wars and a pioneer in the Territory, Chandler had been a strong advocate of the separation of Maine from Massachusetts, and when the new state was admitted he was rewarded with a seat in the Senate. Finally, there was Albert Gallatin, Crawford's close friend and Smith's old enemy. Gallatin was in France as United States minister and so, temporarily, out of the picture. But his place in the estimation of his countrymen was only slightly less than that of Jefferson and Madison and the old Republicanism which he represented made it inevitable that sooner. or later Crawford would call on him for support.[6]

The assembling of the Sixteenth Congress was the setting for the opening skirmishes. Henry Clay was elected Speaker and, despite his previous clashes with General Smith, recognized his influence and ability by appointing him to the chairmanship of the powerful Ways and Means Committee. Thus Clay's immense personal popularity in the House was partly offset by one of Crawford's chief lieutenants securing the second position. The new Congress inherited from its predecessor the question of the admission of the new state of Missouri. The petition for admission had been received in the last days of the Fifteenth Congress at which time General James Tallmadge of New York presented a resolution to restrict slavery as a condition for Missouri's entrance into the Union. After a brief but rather bitter debate, not only on Missouri, but on the whole question of slavery in the territories, the retiring members decided to postpone action until after the next Congress had assembled.[7]

At this period the slavery debate was not primarily based on moral issues, but upon the sectional question of political power in Congress. Should Missouri be admitted as a free state it, together with Maine which was at this time applying for admission as a free state, would create a majority of thirteen free as opposed to eleven slave states in the Senate. In the Missouri issue, then, was embodied the struggle for sectional domination, and it included as well the problem of the future of slavery in the territories which would eventually form the new states in the West.

The House sent up to the Senate a bill for the admission of Maine and then swung into a bitter fight over Missouri. The restrictionists were in the majority but they received a sharp check when the Senate, which contained a bare Southern majority, sent the Maine bill back with a rider attached declaring for the unrestricted admission of Missouri, and exclusion of slavery from the remainder of the Louisiana Territory north of 36° 30'. The Northern majority in the House refused to accept it. A compromise committee was appointed which included both Speaker Clay and General Smith and on the basis of its report the Senate compromise was accepted. Maine entered as a free state, Missouri as a slave state, and slavery was forbidden in the Louisiana Purchase Territory north of 36° 30'.[8]

The Missouri Compromise controversy worked to the disadvantage of all the leading candidates. Smith represented the attitude of the Crawford party in the part which he played in the House debate. He made only one brief speech in which he admitted the power of Congress over the territories but denied its right to control the states on this subject after their admission.[9] His service on the compromise committee probably had little influence one way or the other except as it enhanced his reputation as a Congressional leader.

Crawford himself was wary when the issue was presented to the cabinet. William Plumer, Jr. reported that "Mr. Crawford [was] of course against doing anything on the subject whatever."[10] His course was to keep out of the controversy as much as possible, for "it is apparent that Crawford is already aware how his canvass for the Presidency may be crossed by this slavery contest."[11] Crawford may well have missed an opportunity of gaining the solid support of the Southern slave holders by not taking a stronger stand on this issue. But the Radicals were still angling for Pennsylvania and New York support. In view of Crawford's clear ascendency at this early stage it is not surprising that he took as neutral and nebulous a course as possible.

Henry Clay received a large share of the credit for the Missouri Compromise and thereby lost support in both the South and North. The North knew that he would never stand with them on slavery restriction and the South resented the fact that he had given ground after being the leader of the opposition to exclusion in the House.[12]

John Quincy Adams likewise failed to take full advantage of the issue. As the sole candidate from the North he might well have gained solid support from the anti-slavery elements. His position, however, was somewhat equivocal. William Plumer, Jr. of New Hampshire thought that "Mr. Adams declared himself at first in favor of the Restriction [in Missouri]. This was pretty generally understood to be his opinion to the end—But it is not correct. He said that he had not the least doubt of the Constitutional power of Congress to impose the restriction; but he was satisfied that we could not enforce it in this case . . . he was therefore in favor of the compromise—I was sorry to hear these opinions from him so I took care not to make them known where they could do any harm."[13]

As the Missouri issue reached its climax and subsided, the Crawford forces moved to strengthen their position. Their first move was to pass a bill of which Crawford was the author, providing that certain civil and military officers, mostly those controlled by the Treasury Department, should be subject to reappointment every four years. The purpose of this act was to increase the efficiency of governmental officers who handled large sums of money by making them put their accounts in order every four years and it also gave to the administration a means of dismissing aged or inefficient officers without the stigma usually attached to such dismissals. Crawford's opponents, particularly John Quincy Adams, immediately saw in this bill a means whereby Crawford could make use of patronage to create a well-oiled machine which would elect him in 1824.

Whether Crawford intended to use his powers in this manner or whether, as the evidence seems to point, he was sincerely interested in increasing efficiency in the government's many and often far-flung agencies, the belief persisted that he intended to do so. In such states as Georgia, New York, and South Carolina, where state government patronage was regularly used to bolster the party in power, office seekers and their friends were inclined to climb aboard or stay within jumping distance of such a "band-wagon."[14]

In addition to these measures General Smith led an attack on Secretary of War Calhoun. In line with the Radical program of economy in government and Secretary Crawford's financial retrenchments, the Ways and Means Committee slashed the War Department appropriation bill which Calhoun presented in 1819 by one-third. The allowance for army clothing was cut and the funds for coastal fortifications were halved. Chief targets of this latter cut were what Smith deemed useless forts at Dauphin Island and Mobile Bay. When the committee's report was offered on the floor of the House, some members of the Radical bloc asked for still further reduction in the military appropriations; Smith opposed them both from a desire to stand by his report and from a sincere wish not to reduce the defenses of the country to a ridiculously low point merely to spite Calhoun. His report was accepted and subsequently passed by the Senate.[15]

General Smith figured prominently in another step to promote the Crawford drive which revolved around the caucus of 1820. No one supposed that any serious opposition to Monroe's reelection would develop, but there was considerable question as to Vice-President Daniel Tompkins. Tompkins, backed by Van Buren and the Albany Regency, was running for governor of New York in an effort to prevent the reelection of De Witt Clinton in 1820. This movement, if successful, would force Tompkins to withdraw his Vice-Presidential candidacy. But it would be a distinct advantage to Crawford in several ways. First, it would place the Crawford party in control in New York. Secondly, it would leave the Vice-Presidency vacant. Smith hoped that he could engineer the nomination of Henry Clay to the Vice-Presidency by a caucus which would thus leave the speakership vacant. As the second ranking member of the House it seemed almost certain that Smith could secure election as Speaker and thus strengthen the position of the Crawford forces in the House.[16]

This last factor, control of Congress, was considered of the utmost importance. "It has already been foreseen by . . . Crawford . . . and [his] partisans, that the most probable result of the next Presidential election will be no position majority in the Electoral College for any candidate, so that the choice will fall to the House of Representatives," noted John Quincy Adams.[17] If Clay could be nominated for the Vice-Presidency the double purpose of "burying" him in that office and clearing the Speaker's chair for Smith would be achieved, and the Crawford forces would be in a better position to seize control of the House by 1824.

The only fault in the plan lay in the unpopularity of caucus nominations. The 1816 caucus in which Crawford had almost succeeded in beating Monroe had aroused a great deal of indignation, for Monroe had been the overwhelming choice in the country. Many people were afraid that the intrigue and vote-trading of the Congressional caucus might result in the thwarting of the real wishes of the electorate. Aware of this growing public sentiment, Senators and Representatives in many cases failed to answer the call for a Congressional caucus which was issued in the spring of 1820. Only about forty members attended and, having elected General Smith as Chairman, immediately passed the resolution introduced by Colonel Richard

M. Johnson of Kentucky that it was inexpedient at that time to make any nominations for the offices of President and Vice-President.[18]

This check to Smith's fight for the leadership of the House was offset by the fact that Clay announced his withdrawal as a candidate for speaker in the next session of Congress. Clay, like Smith, had suffered financial reverses, which made it necessary for him to practice law while he attended the Congressional sessions in Washington. Whether, as Clay himself said, these losses resulted from his endorsement of a friend who had subsequently failed, or as rumor and John Quincy Adams seemed to think, "he has more than once won and lost an affluent fortune at the gaming tables [and the] winter was an unlucky one for him,"[19] the way was opened for Smith's hopes to be realized. During the summer of 1820 Smith spent his time in covert campaigning and careful examination of the situation. Crawford contributed his advice and views. "Much depends on your being taken up by the Pennsylvania representatives," wrote the Secretary. ". . . Mr. Lowry [Walter Lowrie, of Pennsylvania] was decidedly for your election. As you are a native of that state, with proper precaution I think it will be induced to give you general support." Smith possessed the additional advantage of being from a middle state, for it was known that the President did not favor a Virginian or even a Southerner. Monroe was anxious to keep all sections mollified but "probably will not interfere directly."[20]

When the Congress reconvened in November, 1820 it was apparent that Smith and his adherents had underestimated the force of the Missouri question. Although Monroe lacked only one electoral vote of being reelected unanimously, John W. Taylor of New York, who had led the anti-slavery debate in the House, was supported for the Speakership by the Northern and Western representatives while the Southern support was divided between Lowndes and Smith. The balloting for speaker began on the 13th of November and lasted through three days and twenty-two ballots. Lowndes took an early lead, but Smith, probably because he had taken little part in the Missouri debate and was a compromise candidate, took the lead on the twelfth ballot. But the twenty-second ballot gave seventy-six votes for Taylor, forty-four for Lowndes, and twenty-seven for General Smith, and Taylor was elected.[21]

General Smith was again appointed chairman of the Ways and Means Committee. The Radicals continued their sniping at Calhoun's military appropriations but General Smith was not so eager for the measures proposed by extremists of his own Crawford faction. Time after time he rose to protest at the drastic reductions which were espoused by several members of the House who had allowed their enthusiasm for crucifying Calhoun to get the best of their judgment. John Cocke of Tennessee objected to an amendment by Smith to retain a large part of the topographical engineers who rendered peacetime service. "He [Cocke] wished it to be seen that, on this occasion, there was something like discipline in their ranks, and that they would not be decoyed from their object by amendments." Smith replied sharply that he had "never heard so broad a declaration as this in the House—that the friends of reduction were to rally round a bill, right or wrong, good or bad." He was a friend of the bill for reduction but he desired "to make the organization as perfect as possible."[22]

The admission of Missouri was again questioned and a series of debates and resolutions were presented by members of the House. The new dissension arose over the provision in Missouri's Constitution which she had submitted to the Congress for approval which, in effect, forbade the entrance of free Negroes into the state. Smith followed his previous course, saying virtually nothing in the debates, voting with the Southerners in all cases and voting for what came to be called the Little Missouri Compromise. This provided that Missouri must never construe the objectionable clause to exclude citizens of any of the states from the enjoyment of any privileges and immunities to which they were entitled under the Constitution. Thus Northern sentiments were assuaged and Missouri was admitted to the Union.

The debate showed that the Northern anti-slavery bloc could control the House whereas the South remained in control of the Senate. More important for the immediate future it greatly enhanced Clay's reputation. His wisdom in engineering this second compromise led William Plumer, Jr. to remark, "no other man could have effected it. . . ."[23] Later when the Presidential aspirations were more evident, he noted: "They [the people of Missouri] are not a little indebted to him for their admission to the Union upon terms which they consider more favourable than the north was willing to allow."[24]

The summer of 1821 brought the Crawfordites bad news from Georgia. Here the Clark faction had triumphed again in the election for governor, defeating George M. Troup, the Crawford candidate. Crawford's inability to control his own state did not aid his prospects as a presidential candidate. Governor Clark was already making an effort to undermine Crawford's strength by attempting to get General Andrew Jackson appointed to the commission for an Indian treaty which would secure additional lands for Georgia. This was a direct thrust at Crawford "whose deadly enmity with Jackson is now perfectly notorious and to whom is attributed the whole persecution of Jackson during the Seminole war. Crawford would take no satisfaction in the success of Clark or of Jackson, in rendering important and acceptable service to the people of Georgia."[25]

Although Jackson was not yet an avowed candidate, his name had been mentioned in connection with the election of 1824. He himself was known to be willing to "support the Devil" before Crawford.[26] Monroe recognized that Jackson's tempestuous nature was ill-suited for diplomacy, particularly where the Indian Nations were concerned, and he refused Clark's suggestion. But the incident showed that, as John Quincy Adams noted, "the personal enemy . . . is a vice . . . that shows itself in every form of Government."[27] As the candidates maneuvered for position, it was evident that relations in the Cabinet were becoming more and more strained. Adams became convinced that the various factions were depending on the failure of Monroe's administration to enhance their prospects. "The worst of it is that this applies more forcibly to Crawford, a leading member of the Administration, than to any other. Crawford has been a worm preying upon the vitals of the Administration within its own body. He was the instigator and animating spirit of the whole movement . . . against Jackson and the Administration. In all the vicissitudes of the Spanish negotiations, wherever there has been difficulty or prospect of failure, he has been felt where he could not be seen; and all the attacks against the War Department during the Congress have been stimulated by him and promoted by his partisans."[28]

With such a spirit prevailing, the new Seventeenth Congress opened its first session in December, 1821. The assemblage soon deteriorated into a battleground of personal conflicts and became an arena for mud-slinging. John Cocke of Tennessee, who later came out for Jackson, attacked the appropriation bill which Smith had reported from the Ways and Means Committee. Cocke proposed amendment after amendment to reduce items of the bill and General Smith conducted a tireless defense of his report. The whole debate was nothing more than an attempt on Cocke's part to show Crawford's inefficiency and hamstring the Treasury. Smith struck back by securing amendments to the military appropriation bill which reduced funds suggested by the Secretary of War for fortifications in the Mobile area and northern Maine.[29]

In the President's cabinet, dissension among the three candidates was rife. "It is now nothing but a system of mining and countermining between Crawford and Calhoun to blow up each other," wrote John Quincy Adams, "and a continual underhanded working of both, jointly against me, which has been the more effective because I have neither creature nor champion in either House or Senate. Of this game Crawford is a much superior artist to Calhoun."[30] Adams did not mention that his own instructions to Albert Gallatin to remain in Paris against the wishes of the latter to return home, were well calculated to keep that venerable radical abroad where his influence in favor of Crawford would not be felt. Such incidents as the publication of letters by Jonathan Russell in which he accused Adams of being willing to give up the right of navigation of the Mississippi in the negotiations at Ghent in 1814 were not calculated to improve the strained relations. Jonathan Elliot, editor of the pro-Crawford *Washington Gazette,* accused Calhoun of instigating the publication of the letters but Adams himself thought "it was the hand behind the curtain—Crawford."[31]

Monroe, seeking always to remain neutral, said nothing, but he was seriously disturbed. By the summer of 1822 rumors were thick that Monroe was about to demand Crawford's resignation because he had consistently opposed some of the administration's measures. It was also said that Crawford had denounced Monroe as betraying the old Jeffersonian doctrines by his nationalistic leanings. Of this Crawford took note and seemed to feel that "it will not be injurious to me to remain in this state, or even to be removed from office."[32] Finally, in a bitter correspondence with the President in which he was accused of openly criticizing the Monroe views, Crawford denied the charge and satisfied Monroe at least to the extent that the latter asked him to remain in the cabinet. But relations between the two remained strained, for Crawford was bitter that he could not secure the open endorsement of the Virginia Dynasty.[33]

The summer and fall of 1822 saw the formal entrance of the principal candidates into the field. The death of William Lowndes, who had been the South Carolina legislature's nominee, brought forth an endorsement from that state for John C. Calhoun. In the summer of 1822 the Tennessee legislature, under the influence of the Nashville junto, elected General Jackson to the Senate and nominated him for the presidency. The Nashville junto, which was composed of a number of Tennessee politicians, ex-soldiers and newspaper editors, formed the nucleus around which the Jackson movement started. Realizing the impossibility of controlling the party machinery or securing any large fraction of press support, they determined to turn these very disadvantages into issues which would make the "Old Hero" the people's choice, the frontier fighter who was leading the masses against an unrepresentative and undemocratic party machine.[34] The last of the 1822 nominees was Henry Clay, who was nominated by the Kentucky legislature on November 18.

12

The Election of 1824

IN BALTIMORE GENERAL SMITH passed the summer and fall quietly. The strain of getting the affairs of Smith and Buchanan in order and his ceaseless political activity were getting to be too much for a man of seventy. "I am often afflicted with boils and feel a want of appetite." Mrs. Smith was also not well. "[She] is afflicted with a chronic rheumatism yet she goes about and is fat."[1] John Spear Smith, despite the financial troubles occasioned by his father's failure, was becoming a prominent citizen. He had been elected to the Maryland legislature and had received an appointment as brigadier general in the Maryland militia. To supplement his income from Montebello he invested in a sugar plantation which his cousin, Robert Carter Nicholas, had purchased in Louisiana, later to prove highly successful.[2]

The second session of the 17th Congress found General Smith resuming his old seat in the Senate. The death of William Pinkney had created the vacancy which the Maryland legislature, now dominated by a Republican majority, filled by electing General Smith. As a senator Smith would undoubtedly exert less influence than as Chairman of the Ways and Means Committee of the House. His decision to accept the appointment was influenced by a desire to relieve the strain involved in his former job and because of the heavy burden of work induced by his financial distress. His income was only slightly more than a thousand dollars a year and he still had unsatisfied creditors.[3]

Smith took very little part in the debates in the Senate during the spring of 1823. "I have only let off a speech now and then, going late into the Senate," he wrote in March.[4] One of these speeches was in favor of a bill introduced to appropriate money for repairs to the Cumberland Road. Such a bill had been introduced in the last session but Monroe had vetoed it on his old constitutional scruples.

When the question was again brought up in February, 1823 Smith felt obliged to support it, despite the fact that it was an embodiment of government spending which Clay advocated and to which Crawford was opposed. Maryland, however, had built many feeder roads which connected with the national road and its existence had done much to benefit Maryland trade. Smith felt that his duty to his constituents outweighed his duty to Crawford in this case and he spoke and voted in favor of the repair appropriation.[5]

Smith's inactivity in the Senate was compensated for by his vigorous efforts to promote the Crawford candidacy. He was ceaseless in his correspondence with party leaders throughout the country through whom he kept a constant check on Crawford's position in the various states. During the summer of 1823 a constant stream of letters went to Van Buren in New York, Chandler in Maine, Jesse B. Thomas in Illinois, Stevenson Archer in Eastern Maryland and many others.[6] In the midst of this activity Smith made a last effort to secure an outright endorsement of Crawford from the aged Jefferson. To General Smith came the reply:

> I learn with great satisfaction that wholesome economies have found [sic], sufficient to relieve us from the ruinous necessity of adding annually to our debt by new loans. The deviser of so salutary a relief deserves well of his country....
>
> On the question of the next Presidential election, I am a mere looker on. I never permit myself to express an opinion or to feel a wish on the subject. I indulge a single hope only, that the choice may fall on one who will be a friend of peace, of economy, of the republican principles of our Constitution, and of the salutary distribution of powers made by that between the general and local governments; to this I ever add sincere prayers for your happiness and prosperity.[7]

Although this was somewhat disappointing as an outright blessing, it nevertheless allowed the Radicals to link their party with the magic name of Jefferson without fear of being denied. As the spring of 1823 passed, Crawford seemed to be well ahead of his rivals.

Although the election was over a year away, the press now began an all-out fight in support of the various candidates. In Washington Crawford's control of the *National Intelligencer* and the *Washington Gazette* was rivaled by Calhoun's *Washington Republican*. In nearby Baltimore where several prominent newspapers flourished, none was strongly for Crawford, though the *American* seemed to lean toward him. Hezekiah Niles, editor of the *Register* who had government printing contracts, was carefully on the fence. Said Jonathan Elliot, of the *Washington Gazette:* "A portion of the Baltimore presses is held by *hope* and by *ties* to the cause of the Secretary of State . . . the *pure* Hezekiah, of the *Weakly*, . . . having pocketed to the tune of a few thousand, carries on the work of enlightening the people in favor of the Adams family in rare style. . . . The Weekly Register breaks down the fences of democracy, the Patriot [anti-Crawford] enters, frisks, and throws up its heels at the Republican party, and the *American* looks complacently on."[8]

In other states, too, Crawford had a wide following among the editors. Thomas Ritchie's powerful Richmond *Enquirer,* in Virginia, the Philadelphia *Democratic Press,* the Albany *Argus,* in New York, and the *Raleigh Register* in North Carolina were a few of the many newspapers which strongly favored the Georgian.

Crawford's strength was demonstrated by the action of his enemies who concentrated their attacks on him rather than against each other. "It is a curious fact," noted the Baltimore *American,* "that Mr. Crawford is assailed by the friends of Mr. Adams, Mr. Clay, and Mr. Calhoun. All their efforts are to put down Mr. Crawford—the reason is obvious: they know that if the election was to take place immediately that Mr. Crawford would have two votes for one. . . ."[9]

The *Baltimore Patriot* and the *Washington Republican* were particularly vicious in their denunication not only of Crawford but of those who supported him. General Smith came in for his share of criticism. The *Republican* baldly accused him of being a Crawford supporter, as though this in itself constituted a crime. Elliot's *Gazette* quickly replied: " . . . we suppose the fact must be so. . . . What, then, is the ground for complaint? Why, the oldest, and most intelligent, and most republican . . . are inclined to the election of the Secretary of the Treasury."[10]

Chief grounds for the attacks against Crawford were his independence in the 1807–1811 period when he had sometimes opposed Jefferson and Madison and the consequent imputations that he was more Federalist than Republican. General Smith, writing under the signature of "A Friend to Truth," replied vigorously. Crawford had voted against the embargo, but so did many good Republicans. "Mr. Crawford gave a decided and uniform support to the embargo [after its passage] and to every measure judged necessary to make it efficacious." His support of the Bank of the United States had been justified by subsequent events. "A gallant General" (probably Robert Goodloe Harper) assigned Crawford's "Delphic Oracle" speech, delivered in 1810, to the period just prior to the War of 1812 and thereby inferred Crawford's opposition to the war. "It was necessary to his purpose to confound these dates," replied General Smith, "for he asserts that

Mr. Crawford voted against war.... This assertation ... is false.... But I ask his pardon for supposing him to be a moral agent in this case. Perhaps he has received a *military order* fixing the date, and was as indifferent as his chief is known to be of the truth of his statements."[11]

To Adams "A Friend of Truth" now directed the charge of Federalism, for he recognized that Adams was a stronger force to be reckoned with than either Clay or Calhoun:

> It has been asserted by some eastern papers that Mr. Adams was elected in opposition to Mr. Pickering.... It is, however, a fact that they were both elected by the same Legislature and the journals of the Senate will show the kind of support given by him to Mr. Jefferson. Upon the bill authorizing Mr. Jefferson to take possession of Louisiana ... all acts relative to Louisiana ... except that for paying for it ... were opposed by his votes, in conjunction with every Federalist in the Senate ... The proceedings of the Senate upon the impeachment of Judge Pickering and Judge Chase show almost conclusively his federal bias ... I mean not to impeach Mr. Adams's motives. I take his acts to shew that until 1807, he was a consistent federalist. If he chooses to insist that federalists acted upon principles of faction, I shall not defend them.[12]

To the Jackson candidacy the Crawford press acted with more circumspection for they did not yet dare to defy Jackson's popularity with the people as the hero of New Orleans. "The character of General Jackson is that of a brave and determined soldier," said the *Gazette*. "It does not follow, however, that he has any fair claim to the Presidency.... If it were possible to elect General Jackson President, we should be in perpetual danger of having the country embroiled with some foreign power."[13]

While the Crawford press in and near the capitol alternately defended him and attacked his rivals, a far more important struggle was going on in the states. In Virginia Thomas Ritchie and the other members of the pro-Crawford Richmond junto were exercising their influence to stay the pretensions of rival candidates, particularly Adams and Jackson. Ritchie was dismayed at the apparent disintegration in the Republican party and was anxious that it unite on one candidate. He at first advocated a national nominating convention but was soon convinced that this was impractical. Ritchie, as well as Andrew Stevenson, John Taylor of Caroline, and other Virginians, were somewhat perturbed at the nationalistic leanings of Monroe. They saw in Crawford a man who fitted their conception of a proper Republican.

The Richmond junto decided that if they could enlist the aid of Van Buren, who had control of the "Albany Regency" and had just been successful in the last election against the Clintonians, they could not only secure the election of Crawford but recreate the old New York-Virginia alliance and thus induce, in a large measure, the party regularity which Ritchie so desired. When, therefore, "Little Van" visited Richmond in the early part of 1823, the alliance was sealed and Van Buren returned to New York openly and definitely committed to Crawford.[14]

Van Buren had been biding his time because he realized that New York might well be the key to the election. With three sections represented among the five leading candidates, Van Buren and the "Regency" wished to keep their state noncommittal until the late stages of the campaign. Despite the fact that the "Regency" candidate, Joseph C. Yates, had defeated De Witt Clinton in the recent gubernatorial election in New York, Van Buren was having his troubles. Yates proved to be hard to handle and Clinton, from his retirement, was sniping away in the newspapers. When Van Buren began his canvass for Crawford, a popular movement centering around the Clintonians protested against the choice of presidential electors by the legislature; but the Regency continued in control of the Senate. Van Buren made a show of conceding to the popular demand but insisted that all reform be postponed until after election time. He was confident of Crawford's success and as late as the summer of 1824 wrote to General Smith "that New York will support the nomination [of Crawford] at Washington . . . is not to be doubted."[15]

As to the situation in the other states, General Smith had by the middle of 1823 formed an estimate based on opinions of members of Congress and letters from his numerous correspondents throughout the country. Adams, he thought, would not get a vote south of the Potomac. Crawford would control the middle states plus Georgia and possibly Tennessee. Clay was impregnable in the West and Southwest and Calhoun's nationalism would give him Pennsylvania together with his native state. Jackson, so thought the optimistic General, would get votes only from Mississippi, Alabama, and Tennessee.[16] Like most other politicians, Smith's calculations of Jackson's strength were badly in error. Indeed, one of the many smart political moves which Jackson's managers made, consciously or not, was to delay the movement in his favor until late in the game so that the wave of popular enthusiasm for "Old Hickory" did not subside before the election.

In Maryland General Smith made little headway. Despite his personal influence, economic interests did not favor the Crawford program. The strong commercial interests of Baltimore were balanced by a growing industry which peopled the city with ever-growing numbers of artisans and mechanics. Five and a half million dollars were invested in manufacturing in Maryland. This was only half a million less than Pennsylvania and only the latter in addition to New York and Massachusetts exceeded Maryland in manufacturing capital. These interests wanted strong protection and internal improvements. In addition, the panic of 1819 had created a considerable debtor class which did not favor the Radical conservatism in national finance. So strong, in fact, was the opposition between Smith's views and those of the dominant interests in the state that he was forced to moderate his stand on some issues because of pressure from his constituents.[17]

Two important states seemed likely to swing in Crawford's favor. In Georgia the Troup party had finally ousted Governor John Clark, although by a small margin. The latter ruined himself and his party by publishing an attack on Crawford that totally discredited its author by its libelous nature and bad taste.[18] In December, 1823 the Georgia legislature formally nominated Crawford for President.

The key to the election and the plum for which all the candidates strove was Pennsylvania. Its twenty-eight votes was the largest single block except for that of New York. In an effort to secure support in Pennsylvania, as well as to align himself intimately with the old Republican party, Crawford requested Albert Gallatin to run for Vice-President on the Radical ticket. It was a wise choice, for the venerable Gallatin embodied in his long and distinguished career all that the Radical program proclaimed. In the spring of 1823 he requested permission to return home. Adams replied that the situation in Europe was such that he could not spare Gallatin from his post. Gallatin did not "perceive any reason connected with the public service for protracting my stay in this country."[19] Crawford thought he saw another reason for Adams's desire to keep Gallatin abroad. "Some of the little people who buzz about the government have . . . been very busy in the expression of their opinion that the change of relations between France and Spain renders [it] highly important that you should remain. The people have had their cue and repeat their lessons by rote. . . . The reason, then, assigned . . . is not the true one. That must be sought, not in Paris, but in the United States. . . . Your presence in the United States during the present year may not suit the views and projects of certain gentlemen. . . ." Crawford had his wish and Gallatin returned to the United States early in the summer of 1823 to run for Vice-President on the Crawford ticket.

The old rift between General Smith and Gallatin might have

posed something of a problem. But the two elder statesmen had no difficulty in effecting a reconciliation. Political issues had changed and there were few differences to prevent a meeting of minds. Gallatin spent the winter of 1823–24 in Baltimore and resumed relations with General Smith, "not," says Henry Adams, "perhaps, so cordial as in the early days, but at least externally friendly."[20]

General Smith's estimate of Crawford's chances in the summer of 1823 was undoubtedly optimistic. Yet he was as well-informed as any politician of his day through his proximity to Washington and his extensive correspondence. There can be no doubt that Crawford was the leading candidate. There were numerous factors against him. Clay and Jackson precluded any possibility of Crawford support in the West save in Illinois where Jesse B. Thomas, a pro-Crawford Senator, exerted considerable influence. Nor was Crawford as well known to the people as either Jackson or Clay and his conservative financial policies would certainly not endear him to soft money men in the West and Southwest. Finally, Crawford had to contend with the growing unpopularity of the caucus, for as the party regular he ought to receive the caucus nomination.

Grave as these disadvantages were, they were outweighed by the distinct gains which Crawford had made. He, as much as anyone, controlled the party machinery and, consciously or not, wielded a vast amount of influence through Treasury Department patronage. He was the champion of the slave-holding South, where the memory of the Missouri Compromise was still fresh. While not enjoying the outright endorsement of the Virginia Dynasty, no one could doubt, from the expressions that emanated from Monticello, that it leaned strongly toward him. His record of public service was an enviable one; and if he shared the blame for the panic of 1819, he likewise shared the credit for the recovery of the early twenties. With Van Buren and the "Regency" behind him in New York and Gallatin's influence in Pennsylvania, he was making, in 1823, a stronger bid for votes outside the section which he represented than any other candidate, with the possible exception of Jackson. Moreover, he alone enjoyed the advantage of having a name and a platform. When opponents tagged his supporters with the name of Radicals, it was gladly accepted. Said the *National Intelligencer:*

> They believe that the existing revenues, with necessary modifications, are adequate to all exigencies of the government. They are friends of an *efficient and adequate Navy*—a small but well-organized Army . . . it is their duty to manage [public money] prudently and spend it economically; to ferret out drones and abolish sinecures. . . .

Adding its advocacy of abolition of internal taxes, moderate protection and economy in government, the *Intelligencer* continued:

> To whom are we to ascribe the reduction of the army? The Radicals. To whom the specific and limited appropriations for fortifications? The Radicals. To whom a just and economical system of collecting revenues? The Radicals. To whom the withholding of salaries of officers until their accounts are settled? The Radicals. To whom, in fine, nine millions in the Treasury? The Radicals. And yet those Prodigals who would fix on us this term as a term of reproach, have the audacity to arrogate to themselves all the honor for our economy and prosperity.[21]

General Smith did not escape the wrath of the anti-Crawford press. "It is not long since the Washington Republican in this city . . . denounced Mr. Smith, the venerable senator from Maryland, one of the patriarchs of the party. . . . The work of denunciation goes bravely on . . . and suffers the characters of six or eight Democrats at a time to be butchered." Smith was not deterred. "I have been drawn into the contest," he wrote his daughter, "and I shall probably sink my popularity, for Maryland is against Crawford. But I know them all and think him the best man in every point of view and under this opinion I act, and must abide the consequences."

From the highwater mark of the summer of 1823, Crawford's fortunes began to decline. The first and perhaps the most serious blow to his campaign came in the autumn of 1823. Crawford was struck down by a paralytic attack which, his friend Joseph B. Cobb said, "deprived him for a time of his speech, his sight, and the use of some of his limbs, and which so shocked his whole nervous system as to seriously impair his memory and to obscure his intellect."[22] The news of this attack greatly depressed the spirits of his friends and, of course, was secretly welcomed among some of the anti-Crawford people, although his friends strove to keep the seriousness of his illness a secret. Crawford was forced to give up his duties at the Treasury and, in fact, to retire completely for a time. It was not until the following April that he was able to return to his offices at the Treasury Department.[23]

General Smith and the Radicals were in the position of supporting a candidate who could not even make a public appearance when Congress assembled in December, 1823. The President pro-tempore of the Senate, John Gaillard, appointed Smith chairman of the Finance Committee in recognition of his preeminence as a veteran legislator and manager of public financial policy. His position gave the Radicals a commanding position in demonstrating their economic policies, which were the principal plank of Crawford's platform.

It was inevitable that the tariff question should be introduced in the 1823–24 session. Not only were manufacturing interets clamoring for further protection but it was important as revealing the stand of the various Presidential candidates. And no one was watched more closely than the newly elected Senator from Tennessee, Andrew Jackson. The triumphant return of Henry Clay to the Speaker's chair was the signal, and almost at once an avowedly protectionist bill was introduced in the lower House. It proposed an increase of duty upon iron, hemp, cottons, cotton bagging, woolens and other less important articles to between 25 percent and 50 percent *ad valorem*. The debate in the Senate did not begin in earnest until April. When the House bill was presented, Smith and the Radicals joined forces with other anti-protectionists to revise the duties downward. The House bill proposed an increase in the duty on raw wool to 25 percent in 1824 and then a yearly increase to 50 percent in 1830. Smith spoke and voted for a maximum of 30 percent, which was carried. Other revisions, many of which Smith introduced, were carried out. The duties on raw iron, hemp and distilled spirits were struck from the bill. Duties on cotton bagging and silks were lowered. The motion to eliminate the principle of charging duty on cotton manufactures at a minimum *ad valorem* figure, regardless of actual cost, was lost by one vote.[24]

Despite these alterations a sharp increase of duties from the 25 percent of 1816 to about 33⅓ percent *ad valorem* made the bill repugnant to Smith. He made the final speech for the opponents to its passage. A memorial from his Baltimore constituents urging his support of protection, which was triumphantly produced by the Chairman of the Commerce Committee, did not deter him. "... the signers of that memorial are highly respectable—some of them my relatives—most of them my friends," said the General. "They will wish to know my reasons for the vote I am about to give. There must, Mr. President, be some point at which to stop." He pointed out that the tariff bill as reported from the House would, in reality, amount to a tax of $5,000,000 on the people. "I do not speak at random, Mr. President. No sir; my calculation is bottomed on a report of ... the Register of the Treasury, which was submitted to the Senate...." In a sneering thrust at the protectionist majority in the House, he added, "Had this document been before the House, it might possibly have had an effect; I say possibly—I cannot say probably—for the cabalistic word 'Tariff' was superior to all discretion or reason."

Then Smith launched the main theme of his attack:

I call it a tax because the new duties are imposed on articles indispensable to the people, many of which cannot be made in this country for years, and some of them never; and wholly unnecessary to the protection asked for by the manufacturer. If the articles which required protection had been selected and a rational protection granted, the bill would probably have been acceptable to many of its opposers—certainly to me. As the bill stands now, it affords very little protection, and imposes a heavy tax on the people, at a time when they are distressed, and when we do not want revenue; . . . It is true that the people will not be sensible to the tax they are paying; they do not know that the duties now proposed impose a tax on 50 per cent of all their consumption . . . . Let us suppose, Mr. President, that a direct tax and internal duties were proposed to the extent of three or four millions annually, as a bounty to the manufacturers to enable them to compete with the British—how many advocates would it have? And yet it would be a fairer mode—those taxes would fall on the whole; whereas the tax by this bill will be most severely felt by the South and Southwest.

He then proceeded to prove his allegations by an array of facts and figures which showed how thoroughly he understood the working of the bill. In discussing the duties on silk, he did not hesitate to deride his protectionist opponents:

Have we any such manufacture? . . . Will we ever have it? Then why lay it on? On whom does it fall? On the ladies. . . . I call on the Chairman; I call on the other bachelors of the Senate; where is their gallantry? Does it sleep? Will they oppress their countrywomen with this heavy imposition on their dresses? . . . Had these recreants lived in the time of chivalry, they would never have broken a lance in honor of beauty and bright eyes.

He concluded his argument by reiterating the taxation principle behind the bill. The benefits to the country were not enough "to induce the Senate to vote a perpetual tax of $3,500,000 per annum on the people." But the appeal was in vain. The bill as amended passed by four votes, and Senator Jackson's vote was recorded in favor.[25]

The delicate question of internal improvements was again introduced in the form of a proposal for an appropriation for surveying proposed routes for roads and canals. Maryland, perhaps more than any other state, needed internal improvements, for her trade was not increasing in the same proportion as that of the other eastern states, particularly New York with its route to the West via the Erie Canal. Baltimore was in desperate need of a route to the Ohio if she were to keep her commercial standing. Yet such a bill was in direct opposition to the program of strict construction and economy in government advocated by the Radicals.

In the previous Congress Smith had made an unsuccessful effort to meet the problem by introducing a Constitutional amendment giving Congress the power to aid internal improvements.[26] When the Survey Bill came before the Senate he proposed an amendment to it which would preclude it from being construed to grant Congress "on their own authority, to make roads and canals in any State of the Union." In support of the amendment he said that he feared such a bill "would be considered as an entering wedge to the great system of improvements, the power to adopt which, he for one was not disposed to admit." Van Buren, Chandler, Taylor of Virginia and the other Radicals supported him but the amendment was lost. Smith voted for the final passage of the bill. It was noted that Senator Jackson likewise voted for the bill.[27]

Equally embarrassing from General Smith's point of view was the bill for an annual appropriation of $425,000 to be used in building additional naval vessels. The Radicals had already proclaimed their advocacy of a small but efficient Navy, but General Smith's record ever since 1798 had favored a strong Navy and he had not hesitated to go against his party on this issue in the past. He objected to the present bill on the ground that the finances of the country could not withstand so large an appropriation. Though he advocated additions to the fleet he preferred that the additions proceed gradually lest the ships be built and the Navy Department would find that there was neither sufficient money for their upkeep nor experienced personnel to man them.[28]

The newly appointed Senator from South Carolina, Robert Y. Hayne, rose to defend the bill. His eloquence and brilliant logic, even at this early stage of his career, were powerful. One by one he attacked the arguments against the bill and answered General Smith, "a gentleman entitled to the highest respect, as well from his situation, as the guardian of our finances, as from his great experience," by pointing out that the protection of our commerce by a strong Navy would "outweigh the real value of money locked in the Treasury. . . . A navy contains more of the elements of strength, and is in every way superior to money, as it contributes more to the character of the nation abroad, and its dignity at home. . . ."[29]

General Smith had too much sense to try to answer eloquence with eloquence. His reply was down to earth and coldly factual. There was no one, he pointed out, who objected to a Navy, or to an increase in the size of the present force. "It requires no eloquence to speak of its usefulness. It is a self-evident proposition. It might be thought, from some of the remarks that have fallen from the gentleman, that

I was opposed to a navy. Sir, I have always been in favor of a navy." His own wish, continued Smith, was to spread the cost over a period of years so as to allow suitable time for the purchase of proper materials and training of sufficient personnel, as well as to relieve undue strain on the Treasury. His argument was successful and the Senate voted to appropriate $250,000 for the first year and $200,000 annually for the next three years.[30] Thus Smith was able to achieve economy without being forced into the position of opposing national defense.

While carrying on their program in Congress the Radicals moved to secure for Crawford the Congressional caucus nomination which would label him the Republican party candidate. Considerable opposition to the caucus method of nomination had been growing and this opposition was encouraged by Crawford's rivals, particularly the Jackson partisans. The anti-Crawford newspapers took up the cry against "King Caucus." Said "A Jeffersonian of '98' in the *Baltimore Patriot:* "Here is a democrat recommending a resort to conspiracies and caballing for the purpose of EVADING THE CONSTITUTION!!! Is this democracy? Is this Republicanism?" As the long-time leader of the Congressional caucus Smith received a great deal of criticism. Hezekiah Niles commented: "Several letters from Washington say that the 'commander-in-chief' intends to issue his 'general orders' for an attack upon the people by caucus, about the middle of next month...." And a week later he pointedly observed: "The fact is, the people of Maryland are, almost one and all, opposed to a caucus. In the great city of Baltimore... I am doubtful if there are one hundred persons in all, who are friendly to such a proceeding at this time." To which the *Washington Gazette* replied: "It is not to the press alone that we can appeal for the truth... that Mr. Crawford is the genuine Republican candidate for President. We can refer to men... whose opinions are not to be bought or biased by anything or anybody: We can refer to the names of JEFFERSON, of MADISON, of GALLATIN, of MACON, of SMITH, of LLOYD and a host of others...."[31]

But Niles was right in his assertion that Smith's support of the caucus was against the wishes of his constituents. On the 18th day of December the Maryland legislature passed a resolution which stated, "The legislature of Maryland will view with concern any attempt to control the election of president and vice-president of the United States, by means of a Congressional caucus." In Baltimore a mass meeting of citizens was held to protest against a caucus nomination.[32]

Smith and the other Radicals felt that they should respect the wishes of their constituents when acting in their official capacity as legislators, but that their participation in a caucus was in the capacity of private citizens and they were therefore justified in ignoring the instructions of the legislature.[33]

On the 7th of February, 1824, an invitation appeared in Washington newspapers summoning the Republican members of Congress to a meeting for the purpose of nominating a President and Vice-President. On the appointed evening, February 14, a disappointingly small crowd of Senators and Representatives, only 66 out of 216 Republican members, filed into the brilliantly lighted House chamber. Although the turnout of members was small, over a thousand spectators packed the galleries to cheer or heckle, as their sympathies dictated. Philip P. Barbour of Virginia called the meeting to order and Benjamin Ruggles of Ohio was chosen chairman. After Ruggles had announced the purpose of the meeting, a short pause ensued. Then, from the galleries came cries of "Adjourn! Adjourn!" but other spectators countered with "Proceed! Proceed!" When order was restored, Philip S. Markley of Pennsylvania moved to postpone the nominations. The motion was defeated and the members cast their votes. Crawford and Gallatin were chosen almost unanimously with one or two votes going to Adams and Jackson. General Smith, along with several others, secured courtesy votes for Vice-President. When the teller announced the results, a voice from the galleries cried: "Long live King Caucus!" This was greeted with a chorus of hisses and catcalls. Again order was restored and after publishing a resolution endorsing the views of the candidates, the last presidential caucus of Congress ever held in the United States adjourned.[34]

Try as they might to disguise the fact, the Radicals knew that the caucus was a dismal failure. They were committed to it and they had to go through with it, but Crawford had been hurt as much as he had been helped by the proceedings of the 14th. Said the *Baltimore Patriot:* "It is an insult to the good sense of the people to say, that the voice of LESS THAN ONE FOURTH of the members of Congress shall be taken as the voice of *the members of Congress,* or as the voice of the majority.... The proceeding as a whole may be considered as the greatest abortion ever recorded in the political history of this country."[35] Nor did Samuel Smith escape censure for his part in the caucus. "A Native of Maryland," writing in the *Patriot,* said: "One of the Senators from Maryland signs the invitation for a caucus... while the other it is understood holds the same sentiments.... The senators are appointed by the legislature of the state; and the members of the legislature have requested them to use their influence against a proceeding fraught with so much evil to the community...."[36]

The controversy over the caucus did not end here. In the Senate several bills were introduced to change the method of presidential elections so as to make the process more democratic. In general, these were directed toward taking the choice of electors from the state legislatures and having the people vote for them directly. Under cover of debating this question, senator Rufus King, the Federalist patriarch from New York, lashed out in a biting condemnation of the caucus and the members of Congress who had participated in it. On March 18, he said:

> Members of Congress belonging to this central power, and moreover possessing great talents, learning, and experience, will obtain influence with the Executive departments which must impair the just influence of others, not possessing the same power . . . . the members of the central power have influence and advantages in making laws, as well as in securing appointments of all sorts, and, above all, in promoting the election of such candidate for President as they may select and nominate. The members of the central power will, under such circumstances, devote more of their time . . . arranging, combining, and extending the means to effect the election of their candidate than will be bestowed on the ordinary and regular business of Congress . . . .

The next day General Smith took up King's ill-mannered challenge:

> I regret that the honorable gentleman from New York (Mr. King) should have deemed it proper to introduce this subject. It is true that he qualified it by a new name—"central power" . . . his meaning was perfectly understood, but I wish to give it the known name—I wish to call a spade a spade. . . . That gentleman was a leading chief in the Federal party, and he, no doubt, thinks, what I know and believe, that, owing to the caucus system, his party was prostrated, and the Republican party brought into power; by which change, I believe, and every Republican does believe, that the nation has greatly benefited. . . . The caucus system has heretofore been approved. I attended several, was president at one—and consistency of conduct called imperiously on me to attend that lately held, and which has met with the disapprobation of the gentleman. It appears also to have met with the displeasure of several gentlemen with whom I have served in caucus more than once. Well, sir, they have their reasons, such as are satisfactory to them, with which I have nothing to do. That of being conscientiously against it, they cannot offer.[37]

Even though Smith and the rest of the Crawford party may not have realized it, their candidate was virtually defeated by the spring of 1824. Crawford's slow recovery from his illness had convinced many people that he was not physically able to serve, although his friends had been at some pains to conceal the seriousness of his condition. If further proof of his frailty were needed it was provided by the pitiful attempt which Crawford made to demonstrate that he was a well man. He had not attended the *soirees* and drawing room festivities that marked the season in Washington when Congress was in session. But a few days before adjournment he went to the capitol, where he stayed several hours renewing acquaintances. William Plumer, Jr. described the sick man: "His situation is such as to satisfy me that, if there is no other objection, he ought never to think of being President. He has lost entirely the use of one eye—& sees so imperfectly with the other, as not to know any person whose name is not announced to him.... I do not believe that he will be five months hence."[38]

The beginning of the end occurred in Pennsylvania. Senator Jackson had lost some ground by his vote for internal improvements and the tariff but his stand had endeared him to the hearts of Pennsylvanians in the east and he needed no help in the frontier west. At the Harrisburg Convention, despite the influence of Gallatin, Pennsylvania went "Jackson-mad." For Vice-President she chose John C. Calhoun, who had by this time given up hope of attaining the Presidency and had thrown his support to the old hero.[39]

By the summer of 1824 Samuel Smith was thoroughly discouraged. He seemed almost to lose interest, and the loss of two of his grandchildren did nothing to improve his spirits. To Molly he wrote: "Sidney has lost a fine Baby and my dear little prattler Dorcas about 4 weeks past both in one year.... I am kept busy at our President-making—a silly business with which, if I had common sense, I would have nothing to do."[40] In October Baltimore received a visit from General Lafayette, who was making a grand tour of the country. General Smith, now the city's leading elder citizen, welcomed the "Hero of Two Worlds" at Fort McHenry and that night there was a grand ball in his honor. To Mrs. Mansfield Sam recounted the details of the festivities and the part the Smiths had played in the entertainment of Lafayette. "Your mother gave an evening party. His reception in this city exceeded anything I had ever seen for *Taste, Brilliance, Order* and *Decorum*. Above 100,000 assembled, no riot, not a drunken man...."[41]

But the social round of Baltimore could not disguise the failing hopes for the giant Georgian. In New York, a state which the Radicals had considered as certain, Van Burenites so antagonized the People's Party that the state was finally lost. During Van Buren's absence in Washington, Governor Yates secured the consent of the legislature to dismiss De Witt Clinton as commissioner of the Erie Canal, a position in which he was serving without pay. This, coupled with the high-handed action of the state senate in refusing to pass the new electoral law in the face of an overwhelming majority in the lower house, caused such a wave of indignation against Van Buren and the "Regency" that Crawford was overwhelmingly defeated. Van Buren wrote Smith just before the New York State election returns were in: "We have been substantially defeated ... by the unyielding opposition of Mr. Clay's friends."[42]

A second though less severe stroke further weakened Crawford's precarious health. Again he made a desperate effort to conceal his condition by appearing in public. But, said a witness of the scene, Joseph Cobb, "Those with whom he shook hands ... were observed to leave him with a grave face, and with all the signs and tokens of a melancholy interview."[43] A letter which General Smith received from Crawford in early November seemed a mute testimony of the hopelessness of his cause. The pen had scrawled shaky, child-like characters, the lines were uneven, and huge blobs of spilled ink showed where the almost helpless hand had been unable to control the pen at all. Smith knew then that all was lost. He wrote to Molly that he thought Jackson would win. "He was brought forward to subserve the interest of Mr. Adams by divesting the interest of Crawford in the South."[44] Smith seemed incapable of appreciating the popular force behind the clever manipulations of Jackson's lieutenants.

At the same time he wrote, perhaps a little wearily, to his grandson in England: "We are all engaged in electing a King for 4 years, alias a President, there are four candidates all tolerable good yet if we believe the newspapers they are the very worst of men. The Election of a Chief Magistrate, whether King, Doge, or President is the rock on which all Republics are split."[45]

Last ditch efforts were made to repair the crumbling hopes of Crawford. Gallatin withdrew as Vice-Presidential candidate in an effort to save some sections who might vote for a Crawford-Calhoun ticket, since the latter was now virtually conceded the Vice-Presidency. In Georgia the legislature nominated Van Buren for Vice-President in a desperate attempt to save New York. But all this was of no avail. Nor did Van Buren's last minute appeal to Clay for a coalition meet with any favorable response.[46] The Electoral College which met December 1 gave to General Jackson 99 votes, to Adams 84, to Crawford 41, and to Clay 37. Crawford carried only Georgia, Virginia and Delaware. In New York the "Regency" was repudiated completely with the election of Clinton as governor, and Crawford secured only five of New York's thirty-six electoral votes. In Sam Smith's own state he received a single vote. Since no candidate had a majority of electoral votes, the choice was thrown into the House of Representatives, the top three candidates only being eligible for election.

There remained for Mr. Clay only the problem of which of the three candidates he would support. Crawford followers attempted to woo him to their cause again, but even a combined Clay-Crawford vote would probably still leave Crawford trailing. "Harry of the West" was not inclined to back a sure loser. Jackson's election would stand in the way of his hopes for ultimate election since it would be difficult for the West to elect two Presidents in succession. To the man who had called the American System into being, John Quincy Adams appeared the most likely man to carry it into effect. With Clay's support, on the first ballot in the House, February 9, 1825, Adams received thirteen states, Jackson seven, and Crawford four.[47]

Crawford's loss was due to a number of factors, one of which was his failure properly to estimate the popular mind. This led to serious setbacks for him because he was the choice of "King Caucus" and therefore the product of "machine politics." Similar failure to appreciate the popular movement behind General Jackson led Crawfordites to ignore him and do little to checkmate his campaign. Such an attitude accounted for Van Buren's failure in New York and the loss of Pennsylvania. But Crawford might still have triumphed had not his health been wrecked. William Plumer, Jr., said in the spring of 1824: "How monies are drawn from the Treasury nobody knows—It is not by Mr. Crawford—it is not by any other responsible person—There is a delicacy about mentioning such things publicly—but if the people knew the real state of Mr. Crawford's health, he would no longer be considered as a candidate."[48] Too many people knew by the time of the election. Finally, Crawford's early entry into the race and his position as the regular party candidate allowed enthusiasm for him to reach a peak and fall off before the election. This fault in timing is particularly highlighted when compared with the Jackson campaign, which was not pushed with vigor until early in 1823. Crawford's position also made him the target for attack from partisans of other candidates who, although divided and vague on issues, were united in their opposition to Crawford.

The Crawford campaign was Smith's last effort in partisan party politics. To his daughter in England he wrote: "My favorite was Mr. Crawford. He has retired to private life with a broken constitution, a fair character but in very narrow circumstances ... Had his health been good he would (I think) have been the President and the Republicans would have contrived to rule—as it is I consider it broken into so many factions that it can never make head again."[49] And when, in 1828, Crawford asked for his aid against Jackson, Smith, then seventy-six years old, replied:

> When your election was lost, I made a determination which I communicated verbally and by letter to some friends . . . "That I never would take an active part in any future Presidential election," to which I have rigidly adhered and from which (respect for myself and my own tranquility) I feel no inclination to depart. I am now too old to be active and am rather inclined to live quietly.[50]

13

The Elder Statesman

SAMUEL SMITH'S political career after 1824 was that of an independent statesman who kept as aloof as possible from party or factional alignments. This does not mean that he no longer took a lively interest in issues or that he failed to express his convictions when he felt called upon to do so. Although now seventy-two years old his mind was as keen as ever and the fact that he had no particular political axes to grind makes his actions and views during the administration of John Quincy Adams and the first four years of Andrew Jackson's presidency particularly interesting, as they were largely uncolored by political ambitions. In the last period of his career Smith was no longer as active as formerly, for his advancing years could not stand the strain of continued strenuous work. He therefore exerted himself only on the important issues of those stormy times. An examination of his course on the tariff, the fight for the recharter of the Bank of the United States, and the struggle for the recovery of the British West Indian trade during this later period of the Adams and Jackson administrations is valuable as an expression and summation of his political views.

The renewal of the protectionist movement in 1827 found Smith's stand in no way abated from that of 1824. Henry Clay, Secretary of State, was no longer in Congress to direct the fight, but the Adams administration favored Clay's American System. The proposal of 1827 for increased duties did not lack able advocates. The bill for increased rates on imported woollens was introduced in the House in March of that year. It provided for no change in the 33⅓ percent *ad valorem* duty but inserted a minimum plan similar to that adopted for cotton. All woolens costing less than forty cents a yard were charged as if they cost forty cents and all between forty cents and $2.50 were charged as if they cost $2.50.[1] In the Senate, General Smith attacked not only the provisions of the bill but the whole system on which it was based. After pointing out that the proposed bill would give the manufacturers a profit of 12 percent as opposed to the normal 6 percent that most businessmen were content with, he added:

> ... the bill ... ought to be called a bill to tax the poor for the benefit of the rich. The rich had their broadcloth with no addition of duty, while the poor man was to be taxed beyond sufferance for articles required by him.... We have given them [the manufacturers] our teeth and now they ask for our tongues. No concessions could satisfy them until they were allowed to put their hands into the pockets of other classes ...[2]

No decision was reached largely because the Senate felt that there was not time to debate the question fully. The bill was tabled by the deciding vote of Vice-President Calhoun.

By the time the Twentieth Congress met in the fall of 1827 the tariff issue, as in 1824, had been turned into a political issue. Andrew Jackson was determined to secure the office for which he thought he had been the people's choice in 1824. Both Jackson, who had voted for the tariff in 1824, and Adams were thought to favor a protective system. Jackson, however, refused to commit himself strongly on the subject because he feared the loss of Southern support. But such manifestations of public opinion as the Harrisburg Convention which met in the summer of 1827 to advocate increased protection could not be ignored if Jackson were to score in the industrial sections. In this dilemma the Jacksonians resorted to a scheme by which they hoped to further measurably the election of Jackson in 1828.

The Committee on Manufactures reported a bill which was high-tariff, but not merely that. The Jackson men who dominated the Committee had not only raised the duty on manufactured goods but on imported raw materials which New England manufacturers desired to remain low.[3] All of Jackson's supporters then united in their opposition to any amendments. The result they hoped would be rejection of the bill by a combination of New England, which would not accept the high duties on raw materials, and the South, which did not want any protection. Adams men would be accused of being unfriendly to a tariff, the South would be satisfied, and Jackson men could pose as friends of protection in the middle states. John Randolph remarked acidly, "The bill referred to manufactures of no sort or kind except the manufacture of a President of the United States."[4] Nor was it any wonder that Samuel Smith labeled it the "Tariff of Abominations."[5]

Although well aware of the growing protectionist sentiment in Maryland, Smith could support no such bill as this. While he favored Jackson for the Presidency he refused to sacrifice his independence or repudiate his commercial background. His voice and vote were recorded against the tariff of 1828.[6] But, to the surprise of everyone, a number of New Englanders voted for the bill and it passed.

The reaction to the "Tariff of Abominations" was immediate and violent. Nationally prominent newspapers like *The National Intelligencer* and the *New York Evening Post* became virulent in their denunciations and the expression by local editors was equally violent, particularly in the South. But far more important were local, district, and state conventions which met all over the South to register their protests against the bills. In South Carolina the protests contained thinly veiled threats of nullification. Smith was uncertain whether Calhoun was behind some of these protests. He knew that the Vice-President, looking in vain for indications that his section was profiting by the nationalistic policies which he had long advocated, had gradually modified his earlier views. But Smith did not know that Calhoun was the anonymous author of the *South Carolina Exposition and Protest* of 1828 which set forth the doctrine of nullification.

This aspect of the tariff question seriously perturbed Samuel Smith. The news of a nullification meeting held in the Colleton district of South Carolina, so Smith wrote to Calhoun, "has distressed me beyond any word that I can find.... Be assured its principles will not be sustained by Virginia, Maryland or any of the states.... It will be looked upon as little less than a counterpart of the Hartford Convention." More disturbing still was the rumor that the governor of South Carolina intended to call the legislature in session for the purpose of declaring Charleston a free port. Smith begged Calhoun, "for God's sake, for your own, for that of your friends, do your utmost to prevent any intemperate measures from being adopted."[7] Calhoun replied that South Carolina's actions had been misconstrued. But he did not hesitate to let Smith know where his feelings lay. The tariff, he said, "originated in motives of avarice on the part of great capitalists in other sections."[8]

Whatever the arguments might be, for or against the constitutionality of the protectionist theory, Smith took no part in them. During the months that followed while the constitutional question was debated Smith's position was as simple as it was plain. He was opposed to a high tariff and favored only a mild protective policy such as that embodied in the bill of 1816 or 1824. He did not, however, follow Calhoun in declaring the protectionist system unconstitutional, and he was seriously alarmed by South Carolina's threat of nullification.

At the beginning of the second session of the Twentieth Congress which met late in 1828, the anti-protectionists introduced a resolution declaring the unconstitutionality of the existing tariff. It brought forth little debate and was defeated.[9] In the next Congress Smith, as chairman of the Senate Finance Committee, introduced a bill reducing duties generally; but it was never discussed owing to the attention received by a House bill which proposed reductions all along the line. The net result was a reduction of the duties on tea, coffee, cocoa, salt and molasses.[10] In the spring of 1831 the issue was hardly touched upon, but the agitation throughout the country went on. By the beginning of the Twenty-second Congress which convened in December, 1831, a revision was generally expected and desired, not only because of the anti-protectionist sentiment but because of the fact that the public revenue had increased due to prosperous times and the debt had almost vanished. The problem of surplus revenue, chiefly derived from the tariff, had to be met. Henry Clay, now back in the Senate, proposed that the solution be found in abolishing or reducing duties on unprotected articles and retaining those articles which need protection.[11]

General Smith picked up the argument where he had left off in 1828. Attacking not only Clay's proposals but the activities of the tariff lobbyists, he said:

> Where is the difference if the people are taxed by the manufacturers or by any others? I say manufacturers—and why do I say so? When the Senate met there was a strong disposition with all parties to ameliorate the tariff of 1828; but now I see a change which makes me dispair of anything being accomplished. Even the small concessions made by the Senator from Kentucky have been reprobated by the lobby members, the agents of the manufacturers. . . . These men hang on the Committee of Manufacturers like an incubus. I say to that committee . . . discard sectional interests, and study only the common weal—act with these views—and thus relieve the oppressions of the South.

Foreseeing the danger which so appalled him, anxious to see the South at least partially mollified, he continued:

> We have arrived at a crisis. Yes, Mr. President, a crisis more appalling than a day of battle. I adjure the Committee on Manufacturers to pause—to reflect on the dissatisfaction of all the South. South Carolina has expressed itself strongly against the tariff of 1828. . . . The South—the whole Southern States—all, consider it oppressive. They have not yet spoken; but when they do speak it will be with a voice that will not implore, but will demand redress.[12]

Henry Clay, supporting the American System and bidding for protectionist votes, made a brilliant three-day reply in favor of retaining the protective duties on articles of domestic manufacture. Several times he asked the indulgence of the Senate for adjournment because of his age and ill health. When he had concluded, Smith remarked that "when the gentleman spoke to us of his age [Smith] heard a young lady near him exclaim—'Old—why I think he is mighty pretty.'"

Mr. Clay replied sharply, alleging Smith's past inconsistencies and ending:

"Old politicians chew on wisdom past,
And *totter* on in blunders to the last."

The eighty-year old Senator from Maryland was on his feet. "The last allusion is unworthy of the gentleman," he said. "Totter, sir, I totter? Though some twenty years older than the gentleman, I can yet stand firm and am yet able to correct his errors. I could take a view of the gentleman's course which would show how inconsistent he has been." "Take it, sir, take it—I dare you!" snapped Clay. Cries of "Order" rang through the Senate chamber. "No, sir, I will not take it," said General Smith. "I will not so far disregard what is due the dignity of the Senate."[13]

In the end the protectionists prevailed, although the minimum principle was abolished and the protective system was, in the main, put back where it had been in 1824. Even this modified form could not withstand the attacks of the South. Two weeks after Jackson was reelected South Carolina issued her Ordinance of Nullification declaring that the tariff acts were "unauthorized by the Constitution of the United States, and violate the true meaning and intent thereof, and are null and void, and no Law, nor binding upon this state, its officers or citizens."[14] Clay's answer was his compromise tariff of 1833 which he introduced early in February. It called for a series of annual reductions of all duties until they should reach an *ad valorem* level of 20 percent. Its appearance in the House was the signal for one of the most dramatic battles in tariff history.

The protectionists realized they were fighting for existence. The South realized that it had a victory for its free trade doctrine almost within its grasp. The controversy was also complicated by debates on Jackson's "Force Bill" by which he had determined, if necessary, to coerce South Carolina. This bill became law but, fortunately, the President did not have to invoke its provisions, for the South accepted the Clay compromise. Not so Senator Smith. He opposed the principle of the Tariff of 1833 and he fought it to the end, for "we now see them [the protectionists] crouching under the whip that has been raised over them; and the apology is, that at a future date they may be able to regain that which they have lost." He was of the opinion that Clay's bill was in no way a cure for the evils complained of by the South. The South wished to try the constitutionality of the protective system but Clay's bill was "protection from beginning to end." As to Clay's assertion that the bill would provide a permanent tariff policy, such assurances sounded very like those which had been given in 1816. Smith "had been *cheated* once and would not be *cheated* again."[15]

Smith was frankly disgusted at the accession of Calhoun and the rest of the South to the compromise. He wanted the high duties abolished at once, but he did not agree with the position of the nullifiers.

> Everybody knows that it is for protection, yet South Carolina and the South vote for the bill, which embodies the principle against which South Carolina has actually prepared for war. We are being whipped into passing a bill to gratify South Carolina with no indication that she will be conciliated at all. If she shall be satisfied with the bill, it will only show that she is easily reconciled, and makes no sacrifice to anything except principle—and, that costs no money. . . . I know, Mr. President, that no argument will have any effect on the passage of this bill. The high contracting parties have agreed.[16]

He flung the challenge in the teeth of the nullifiers and they were silent. It remained for the man who acknowledged the constitutionality of the protective system but who fought it on its merits to point out to them that the Southerners were, for all their fine words, not bold enough to stand firm for their principles. But Smith, perhaps blinded by a stubborn refusal to retreat from his belief in the principle of moderate protection, indicated a failure to recognize the seriousness of the situation which existed in South Carolina's stand as to nullification. If he had carried his point and a deadlock had occurred, President Jackson might have carried out his threat to use force against the nullifiers, with serious and far-reaching consequences. On the other hand, he may have realized that Calhoun and the nullifiers would be forced to retreat from their position and vote for the compromise, and he merely took the occasion to vent his disappointment that the actions of South Carolina had forced the constitutionalists into such a dilemma that they had to withdraw. This made the defeat of the tariff by a coalition of states rightists and men of Smith's view impossible.

Smith's tenacity and practical viewpoint were more successful in helping to effect the recovery of the British West Indian carrying trade. This problem had been harassing the nation, and particularly the commercial interests, ever since the nation had become independent. British restrictions in the West Indian trade had begun immediately after the Treaty of 1783 and had continued through succeeding years. Following the Treaty of Ghent which ended the War of 1812, American products could enter British West Indian ports only in British vessels or through such transhipping points as St. George and Hamilton in Bermuda. Before the War of 1812, however, there had been a vast difference between the spirit and the letter of the law. British governors in the West Indies had often opened their ports to American vessels by proclamation or had simply winked at their entrance, since Great Britain, busy with the European war, was unable either to supply the Islands or to enforce the regulations effectively. Samuel Smith had profited by the trade that supplied the Islands with flour, lumber and other staples which could be gotten cheaper and more conveniently from America. But after the cessation of hostilities in Europe, when England began once more to set her colonial house in order, regulations were enforced to the letter. When colonial governors were induced to open their ports to American ships they received severe reprimands from England. The American ministers at Ghent had been unable to secure any commercial agreement regarding this trade, nor did they deem it particularly important as compared to the difficulties of securing an honorable settlement on other points.[17]

After the British merchant marine had gotten on its feet, it immediately stepped in and took over the valuable triangular trade in which, by virtue of British restrictions, Americans were unable to share. Since British merchants had little market in the Islands for manufactured articles, they exported these to the United States, picked up a cargo of American produce for the West Indies, from whence they sailed to Europe with sugar, molasses and rum. This had the effect of cutting into the direct carrying trade of Americans to Europe.[18]

In 1816 the House Committee on Foreign Relations had introduced a bill, subsequently passed, which provided some retaliation by prohibiting British vessels from importing British colonial products into the United States. Against the charge that this might be considered an unfriendly act by England, Smith had replied at that time by enunciating the principle that if our vessels were admitted to the colonial ports of a foreign nation "then it becomes our duty to favor the importations therefrom, and to exclude those from countries which will not permit our vessels to enter and trade on equal terms."[19]

Since this act had little effect in curtailing the triangular trade, American merchants petitioned Congress to prohibit foreign ships from clearing American ports bound for ports where American vessels were excluded. Smith voted and spoke for this prohibition, but its enactment would have cut off exportation to the British West Indies of some $6,000,000 worth of farm products. Agricultural interests proved stronger than commercial and the bill did not pass.

In 1817 Great Britain had offered small concessions which allowed enumerated articles in single-decked American vessels to be imported into her colonies and permitted a few articles to be exported to the United States. Rather than accept this pittance, the United States rejected the offer and prepared more stringent retaliation. This took the form of prohibition of all trade in British vessels between the United States and all British West Indian colonial ports which were closed to American ships. This bill was based on the theory that while America was independent of the West Indian trade, the Islands were almost entirely dependent upon America for necessities such as grain, provisions, and lumber. The law, called the Navigation Act of 1818, was hailed as a proper measure throughout the country, particularly in the shipping centers.[20]

Great Britain promptly made concessions in the form of offers permitting the vessels of each country to trade in the same articles, and on equal terms between ports of the United States and the British West Indies. Having gained this much, however, the American ministers demanded more. Their principal contention, and one which was to plague future negotiations for years, was that Great Britain should pledge not to impose any discriminating duties whatsoever on American products. Great Britain held that she reserved the right to lay a protective duty on those imports into the West Indies from the United States which competed with similar products from British North America.[21] This difference halted the negotiations and the American ministers refused to retreat from their position.

During this time American commerce had picked up in the direct carrying trade. But the total effect of the American Navigation Act was lessened by the fact that Great Britain had opened Bermuda and Canadian ports to American vessels trading between them and the United States. British West Indian products came to these ports in British vessels and were transhipped to the United States in American vessels. Thus *entrepots* for the West Indian trade were established which gave to the British vessels most of the carrying trade. Further, Great Britain allowed additional imports of articles badly needed by West Indian planters to enter her colonies from foreign colonial ports.[22] The United States retaliated in 1820 with an act which forbade intercourse in British vessels between British colonial and American ports and prohibited all articles of the colonies unless imported directly from the colony which produced them.[23] This left as the only route for American goods to the British West Indies the foreign West Indies *entrepots* to which American vessels carried exports and there received imports from British vessels which operated as inter-island carriers. In consequence, Americans secured the greater part of the carrying trade, but the cost of transhipment produced disastrous rises in the price of colonial imports and equally disastrous drops in exports.[24]

There was a like but not as serious effect among agricultural interests in the United States, but Congress stood firm against a movement for repeal of the Act of 1820 in the spring of 1822. The Baltimore Chamber of Commerce petitioned for repeal but their representative, Samuel Smith, turned a deaf ear and voted against the motion.[25] Congress did, however, authorize the President to issue a proclamation of reciprocity to meet any action of the British Parliament which might be published during the summer.

Parliament did act in the summer of 1822 by permitting the importation into British colonies of livestock, grain, provisions, lumber, naval stores, cotton, wool and tobacco. The articles were permitted to enter colonial ports in the vessels of any country, provided the goods were produced in that country, and provided that that country reciprocated in extending like privileges to British vessels and British colonial products. A 10 percent *ad valorem* duty was levied on foreign articles which competed with similar products from her own colonies.[26]

In reply President Monroe, guided by Secretary of State Adams, issued a proclamation and the trade was reopened. But one protest to the proclamation was particularly noted by the British minister. There was a 10 percent *ad valorem* and 95c per ton alien duty on the statute books which Monroe felt that he had no authority to repeal, and he issued specific orders that it be collected from British vessels.[27] The British justly claimed that this was not reciprocity and levied similar duties against American ships entering British West Indian ports.

When Congress met in the winter of 1822–23 it drafted an act, under the guidance of Adams, to give permanent effect to the

President's proclamation. It proved satisfactory to Great Britain (although it took no notice of the alien duties) except on one point. The act provided that no discriminating duties were to be levied on American goods which were not also paid on British goods "imported into the said colonial ports from elsewhere."[28] To the Senators and Representatives this seemed to mean from any foreign port. To Adams who drafted the bill, it meant that Britain could not levy her protective duties on competing goods. Smith stated several years later: "I voted for it, believing that it met in a spirit of reciprocity the British Act of Parliament. The bill, however, contained one little word 'elsewhere' which completely defeated all our expectations. It was noted by no one. The Senator from Massachusetts (Mr. Webster) may have understood its effect. If he did so understand, he was silent."[29] This was the sole point on which agreement could not be reached and negotiations were suspended. Smith later remarked, "The cause was, that all the Administration were lawyers."[30]

Meantime, reports from the Islands indicated to Parliament that the advantages of opening the trade were not all that had been expected. American merchants were demanding less rum, sugar and molasses and were asking to be paid in cash, hard come by in an agricultural economy.[31] Already irritated by American smugness at the supposed dependence of the colonies on American produce, and also anxious to curb American competition in trading with the newly independent South American Republics, Great Britain shifted her ground. By an Act of Parliament in 1825 she opened the trade of British-American ports to almost all products and to vessels of all nations on a basis of reciprocity, if the nation had colonies, and on a most favored nation basis if it did not. January 5, 1826, was set as a deadline for nations to either accept or reject the terms after which the offer would be withdrawn.[32]

As the negotiations dragged on and the bickerings continued Samuel Smith became increasingly irritated at the "lawyers." When the latest English proposal reached the United States, Adams had become President and had appointed Henry Clay Secretary of State. Clay submitted the British offer to Smith for his opinion. Smith expressed his views in a series of exchanges with Clay and with the President. He attacked, first, the fact that the United States had made no move to remove the 10 percent *ad valorem* and 95c per ton alien duties so as to induce Great Britain to remove those on American vessels. If the latter result could be effected, said Smith, "⅔ to ¾ of this trade would be in American ships. If this can be got rid of we can compete."[33] Then, in a letter to the President, he criticized him for the stand he had taken in denying Great Britain the right to protect her own colonial products. "We complain if the British put prohibitions," he said. "Suppose G. B. should offer to revoke the prohibitions in the Schedules in the Act alluded to on condition that we in return repeal all our prohibitory duties—would we consent?—I am inclined to think that our answer would be in the negative."[34] Finally, Smith informed Clay that it was his decided opinion that we ought to accept the offer "without delay."[35]

When Congress convened in December, 1825 a petition was presented from the merchants of Baltimore, requesting Congress to remove the discriminating duties against Great Britain. This was submitted to the Committee on Commerce in the Senate which recommended that the matter be settled through executive negotiation. Smith knew that this method was preferred by Clay but he himself wanted legislative action.[36] He probably was also aware that, although the British offer had been made over a year before, Clay had as yet sent no instructions whatever to Rufus King, the American minister, on the subject.

To the report of the Committee, therefore, Smith replied:

The Committee on Commerce think it better to be done by negotiation. Others think it can be effected by an Act of Congress, which shall meet at once, and *without delay*, the very liberal offers of Great Britain. . . . On this last I most fully concur; we know what we mean when we act by law. All branches of the Government concur, and our acts go into execution without delay. Whereas, if we wait for negotiation, we know not whether instructions have yet gone, nor when negotiations will terminate.

Smith only partially carried out his point. The resolution was withdrawn and the petition was turned over to Senator Smith's Finance Committee. He reported out a bill providing that all discriminating duties on British goods be repealed and authorizing the President to suspend the act should Great Britain not act to repeal her retaliatory act. But the bill was tabled, whether, as Smith later said "for want of time," or because the administration had it shuttled aside so as not to have its negotiations hampered.[37] In any case, administration conduct was strange. If, as Clay said, the proper way to act was by negotiation, it was inexplicable that Rufus King, who had been sent to London to replace Rush, was not given some instructions. It is true that Clay had reason to believe that the British would extend the deadline until the United States gave some indication of her acceptance or rejection of the Act of 1825.[38] Smith desired to give such indication by the passage of his bill which was, in effect, an

American good-will offer to take the initial step in abolishing the discriminating duties. He feared that continual delay would cause Britain to lose patience. As late as March, 1826, two months after the deadline, Clay admitted to the British minister in Washington that he would not be able to furnish Rufus King, who had succeeded Rush, with his instructions until May. The latter became disgusted with the situation in London and returned to the United States, and his place was taken by Albert Gallatin.

In the instructions to Gallatin, Clay conceded one of Smith's points. Gallatin was told to waive American objections to Britain's right to protect her colonial products by protective duties. Had Clay also heeded Smith's urgings to accept the offer "without delay" the problem might have been settled then and there. But Gallatin, when he arrived in London, asking only what the British had offered in 1825 and no more, found the door closed. A British Order in Council of July, 1825 had withdrawn the offer and closed the British-American ports to vessels of the United States.[39]

A Boston paper summed up the situation in an attack on the administration for its dilatory conduct:

> Who, then, was right during the last winter; Mr. Tazewell, Gen. Smith, etc., or Messrs. Adams and Clay. The first wished to remove the great difficulty by law—the last by treaty. If a law had been passed, no treaty would have been necessary. Our diplomatic administration set their faces against the first, and now they cannot accomplish the last.[40]

When Adams faced Congress in December of 1826 he was far from penitent. Stating that England had no right to suspend so important a trade with the United States he concluded this phase of his message by saying, "The refusal . . . of Great Britain to negotiate, leaves the United States no other alternative than that of regulating or interdicting altogether the trade on their part . . . and with that exclusive object, I would recommend the whole subject to your calm and candid deliberation."[41]

The Senate Committee on Commerce responded with a bill which, after recounting a long list of the wrongs suffered from Britain, provided that after September 30, 1827, United States ports should be closed against any and every vessel coming from British-American ports and that British vessels could not clear ports of the United States for any British colonial ports. This act was not to go into effect, or could be suspended by the President, if Great Britain opened her trade to the United States on the terms of the Act of 1825. In this case the President could respond with a reciprocal proclamation.[42]

Senator Smith's reply to the proposal summed up his views on the matter and expressed his disgust for the administration's conduct. "All nations," he pointed out, "with very few exceptions held it right to monopolize the trade of their colonies, and I could not perceive that those nations who had no colonies had any right to complain." After reviewing the course of the negotiations and criticizing the administration's conduct, he denounced the bill now proposed as "filled with criminations and recriminations. . . . It appears to me like one of the manifestos . . . accompanied by a declaration of war." And then he grasped the hard reality of the problem:

> A trade so mutually beneficial ought not be lost, if it can be avoided; and I feel disposed to hope that a spirit of conciliation on our part may open the trade. . . . The report dwells on our great magnanimity throughout our discussions on this subject. The British also talk of theirs. Magnanimity! I see none on either side. I can only, throughout, perceive a desire to make the best bargain. It is a mere business of pounds, shillings, and pence, on one side, and dollars and cents on the other.[43]

He then proposed his alternative. The American Acts of 1823, 1820, and 1818, except as to discriminating duties on foreign vessels, were to be suspended until December 31, 1827, and after that date no other or higher duties were to be levied on British ships and goods than on American. The President, upon satisfactory evidence that Britain had revoked her suspension of American trade, might fully repeal the above acts.[44]

The difference in the two acts, as far as actual content was concerned, was very slight. The original bill held out the threat of widespread non-intercourse. Smith's bill gave no provision for reprisal save the non-repeal of the American Acts. The original aimed to save President Adams and the administration their stuffy pride. The substitute compelled them to swallow it and attempt to regain the West Indian trade. The bill was carried in the Senate but was disagreed to in the House, the latter desiring a positive assertion that if the President issued no proclamation the Acts of 1820 and 1818 should be in force, and that the section on discriminating duties should be struck out. The Senate refused to agree and Congress adjourned.[45]

After adjournment Adams, under the Act of 1823, declared in force the Acts of 1818 and 1820. Since he had, in effect, gained his point by circumventing his advisory council on foreign relations, the Senate, Smith and the other Senators were furious. Said the *Richmond Enquirer:* "The *President's Proclamation* is at length issued. The direct trade is lopt off . . . Thanks to the Diplomacy of the Administration. Gen. Smith asserts that they *duped* him into believing that they wished to regulate the matter by law."[46] Hoping to untangle the knot Clay instructed Gallatin to insist on the necessity for opening the trade again, but his overtures were met with a curt refusal. He was then instructed to withdraw to the position that would have been acceptable to the British in 1825. But British patience was exhausted. All negotiation was temporarily at an end.[47]

The situation in 1828, then, was that Americans could trade through the Canadian ports or through foreign ports in the West Indies. Since American products were allowed into Canadian ports duty free, most of it went by this route and the British ships did the bulk of the carrying. Not only was this a hardship on the merchants but it cut the market price of the agricultural products because of transhipment charges. The failure of Adams and Clay was a telling point which was vigorously played up in the 1828 election.

When Jackson was elected he placed Martin Van Buren at the head of the Department of State and appointed Louis McLane to the post in London. Although McLane, of course, received his instructions from Van Buren as to the course to pursue, he wrote to Smith asking for his advice as to what line he should take. Only a few months later McLane informed Smith that he "agreed" that the best course to pursue was to ask Great Britain for privileges instead of Adams's demand for rights. Later McLane wrote Smith that the latter's advice had been of greater assistance to him than anything else in the negotiations. It would seem reasonable to infer that Smith was in a large measure responsible for the changed attitude of American representation.[48]

McLane waived all American claims of equal rights or of demands that British ships sail directly from the colonial ports to the United States. He asserted to the British government that the election of Jackson constituted a disavowal of the policy pursued by the Adams administration. Although the British balked at the first overtures, they too had experienced a change of ministry and were faced with the problem of inviting stringent American retaliation by refusal or arousing ill-feeling among the commercial interests of British North America which were profiting by being *entrepots* between the United States and the British West Indies.

At this point Smith intervened. At his instance a bill was passed, May 29, 1830, authorizing the President to issue a proclamation of reciprocity upon receipt of satisfactory evidence of British resumption of colonial trade on the basis of the act of 1825.[49] Backed by this assurance, McLane renewed his negotiation and finally, late in the summer, secured an agreement with Great Britain by which she agreed to revoke her Order in Council of 1826 and admit American vessels to her American colonial ports. The agreement stipulated that British North American ports were to enjoy whatever privileges the United States extended to the West Indian ports, that American vessels must trade in American produce directly to the Islands, and that Great Britain reserved the right to levy protective duties on her colonial products which competed with those of the United States. In return the United States admitted British vessels carrying colonial products to American ports on a "most favored nation" basis.[50]

The Reciprocity of 1830 was one of the most solid achievements of Smith's career. It is all the more creditable since he saw the problem and its solution in a clear light from the outset. His stubborn opposition to the pretensions of Adams and his insistence that America demand only what was right had great weight in the determination of the Jacksonian policy which was finally successful. His influence in settling the outcome of the West Indian problem is attested to by Van Buren, who wrote to him shortly afterward, "You have uniformly exercised the utmost frankness in the expression of your sentiments, condemning or approving as your judgment appeared to dictate; and it is on that account, in addition to your known competency ... that I place so high a value on the favorable impression you have been pleased to express in regard to the management of our foreign relations."[51]

14

The Last Battles

THOUGH SMITH had been an administration stalwart on other questions, he fought it on the last of the three important issues of his closing years in the Senate. The charter of the Bank of the United States was due to expire in 1836. President Jackson privately expressed his animosity to the Bank before his first inauguration but, on the advice of friends, had refrained from mentioning it in the inaugural address.[1] Samuel Smith, merchant and keen student of things financial, in contrast to Jackson, saw in the Bank of the United States an institution necessary to the economic life of the country.

The President of the Bank, Nicholas Biddle, set about winning Jackson's approval of the Bank some six years before the charter was due to expire. This he hoped to achieve by convincing the President of the Bank's utility in general and, in particular, its usefulness in one of Jackson's pet policies, the payment of the public debt. But many of Jackson's followers, particularly those from the West, were raising complaints against the Bank. Biddle countered by industriously investigating all charges and forwarding his reports to the President.[2] However, in his message of 1829 Jackson openly asserted that he considered the Bank unconstitutional, inexpedient, and as having failed to establish a sound currency. But Biddle refused to take alarm.

He wrote to Smith in January, 1830 that he did not consider the President's assertions as dangerous, but rather as a mere personal opinion.[3] But he continued his industrious efforts to convince the President, particularly Jackson's objection to the soundness of the currency. To this end he sent to General Smith a report on the state of the currency. Smith's receipt of the report coincided with an investigation which his Committee of Finance was making on the condition of the currency, and the report of the Committee closely followed

Biddle's information. It stated that the currency was entirely sound and appended some statements of Biddle in reply to certain questions which Smith had asked. While the report delighted Biddle, his answer to one of the questions provided opponents with perhaps their most powerful arguments. Smith had asked Biddle whether the Bank had ever oppressed any of the state banks. The latter replied that it never had, but added that the Bank could, by an exertion of its power, destroy any state bank if it wished to do so. Opponents argued that the vesting of such power, whether exercised or not, was too great to grant to an institution not controlled by the national government.[4]

Biddle spread the Smith report and other pro-Bank propaganda all over the country. But he soon learned that, despite all his efforts, not only Jackson but Van Buren were determined to kill any attempt to recharter. As the election of 1832 approached Biddle faced a dilemma. Should he propose the recharter on the eve of election, when Jackson might hesitate to veto for fear of losing pro-Bank votes? Or should he wait until after the election when Jackson's fear of losing anti-Bank votes would have disappeared? The obvious key to the problem was to determine how deep-seated Jackson's opposition to the Bank was. He was not long in finding that, as the election drew nearer, Jackson's determination to defeat the recharter was becoming stronger. Biddle, now joined by Clay and the followers of the "American System," was determined to force the issue just before the election. Thinking that Jackson would probably, in any event, veto the Bank, Biddle hoped that fear of losing pro-Bank votes would deter him. To increase chances of success he circulated propaganda directed particularly at the state legislatures to build up a wave of pro-Bank public opinion.[5]

General Smith and other influential friends of the Bank thought the plan ill-advised. He wrote to Biddle early in December, 1831:

> I had last night a long conversation with McLane, and I am authorized by him to say, that it is his deliberate opinion and *advice* that a renewal of the charter ought not to be pressed during the present session, in which I concur *most* sincerely. . . . If [Jackson is] pressed into a *corner* immediately, neither McLane or myself will answer for the consequences. But we both feel confident of ultimate success if the time be given for the P___t to convince himself of the Error into which Opinion long formed, (prejudice if you please) has committed him.[6]

Late in December, 1831 Thomas Cadwalader, Biddle's principal agent in the bank campaign, came to Washington to sound out the pro-Bank leaders as to the final decision on the time for the recharter.

Smith, Louis McLane, now Secretary of the Treasury, Senator George M. Dallas of Pennsylvania and George McDuffie of South Carolina, chairman of the House Ways and Means Committee, met with Cadwalader. Senator Smith and McLane both urged Cadwalader to advise Biddle to postpone the Bank issue until after the election but McDuffie advised immediate action. Since Biddle placed more confidence in McDuffie's judgment, as well as that of Clay, who also urged immediate action, he decided to apply for the recharter at once.[7] His determination, as he wrote to Smith, was based on the unanimous wish of the stockholders and the desire to secure a decision on the charter in plenty of time to close up its affairs properly before the expiration of 1836, should the application for recharter be rejected.[8]

Not only did the Bank thus go against Smith's opinion but it set the eighty-year-old Senator aside as the leader in the debate over the petition for recharter when it was presented early in January. As head of the Senate Finance Committee, he was the logical choice but the petition was presented by George Dallas, Pennsylvania pro-Bank Jacksonian, a younger and more vigorous man. But Smith lent his ability to secure its passage. As the debate dragged through the winter and spring and into early summer, he was time and again on his feet lending his voice to the bank's support. His principal speech in its defense was on June 6. He pointed out that the Bank paid only 5.6 percent to its investors as compared with 6 percent return currently paid on many investments available on the market. Foreign stockholders, against whose supposed large profits anti-Bank members protested, were taking a loss of 10 percent on their dividends because of the current rate of exchange and the charges made by their agents in this country. There was, consequently, little danger of foreigners securing control of the Bank or removing any considerable amount of wealth from the country. As for the exclusive privileges granted the Bank, it had more than paid for them in the services which it had rendered the government. Finally:

> Mr. President, I entreat Senators to pause and reflect; avoid any trammels on the bank that may, in the slightest, tend to endanger its safety and security. It is a national institution of great public utility; on its punctuality and integrity depend the general credit and confidence in the circulating medium of the country. If its credit or solidity be doubted, confidence will be withdrawn.[9]

The bill passed the Senate by a vote of 28 to 20. Still certain that Jackson meant to veto, and realizing that the Senate could not muster the two-thirds vote necessary to over-ride it, Smith decided to appeal directly to Jackson. On June 17 he wrote:

The mooting of the question at the present Session was against my opinion. It will, however have the effect to cause all the Elections to be controlled on the Principle of Bank or no Bank. And if the people shall in that way determine for a renewal of the charter, Sound policy would say—Comply with their declaration.

My own private opinion is to disappoint those who have pressed the Subject, who expect and Count on your Veto, as a means to injure the Party in public Opinion. I believe it will have little effect but I should like to disappoint those gentlemen.[10]

But Jackson carried out his determination to veto. As he told Van Buren, he thought "the bank . . . . is trying to kill me, *but I will kill* it."[11] His veto message was based on the opinion that too many privileges were accorded the Bank in proportion to services rendered; that the Bank itself was unconstitutional; that Congressional investigation "discloses enough to excite suspicion and alarm."[12] The necessary two-thirds vote was not obtained and the Bank was doomed.

At the end of the 1833 Session General Smith, now eighty-one years old, retired from national politics. After forty years of continuous service the old man was feeling his years. He returned to his home in Baltimore, determined to give up public life.

Less than two years later, however, General Smith was called from his retirement by the citizens of Baltimore to defend the city once again—this time from the violence of a local mob. A riot had broken out in the city, occasioned by the failure of the Bank of Maryland. Disappointed stockholders, angry not only at their losses but by the failure of the trustees to give any satisfactory explanations or account of the conduct of the Bank's officers, formed a mob. On August 6, 1835, they attacked the home of Reverdy Johnson, former president of the Bank. Mayor Jesse Hunt managed to disperse them before much damage was done but the next day the malcontents re-formed their mob and attacked not only Johnson's home but those of several directors of the Bank as well. The mayor lost control of the situation and for three days the city was in an uproar. On the fourth day a committee of citizens appealed to General Smith. The old man promptly organized a temporary patrol which restored order. Jesse Hunt, thoroughly discredited by his incompetency, resigned as mayor. At this crisis in the city's history, people once again turned to their first citizen and elected Smith their Mayor.[13]

The passing of the next few years witnessed the sprightly old gentleman living contentedly and discharging efficiently his duties as mayor. In 1837 Sam, now eighty-five years old, wrote to his daughter, Mrs. Mansfield, whom he had not seen since her marriage in 1811:

My health is most excellent, never better. I walk well and erect—no stoop in the shoulders. I use the same glasses I did 12 years past. I perform all my duties as Mayor to the satisfaction of the good people. Never was a city of 100,000 people more quiet or peaceable than Baltimore. . . . You seem to think me an extraordinary old man. . . . I certainly feel very little of old age —You have always been temperate, say some. Not I, is the answer. I lived as other men, drank as my companions—sometimes too much but not too often. . . . I do not rise from my seat as actively as I have done. When up my walking is fast and alert. I feel no tremor whatever. My hair is grizzled not white as many much younger are.[14]

The years which he carried so lightly represented a long career of unusual and varied achievement. He had fought for his country in two wars and when people addressed him as "General" he could take some pride in the fact that he deserved the title.

His career as a merchant made him wealthy, and if he had not always abided by the strict letter of the law neither was there any of the rapacious greed which earned for a later generation of businessmen the name of "robber barons." He was no economic theorist but he instinctively resisted the practices of the new breed of entrepreneurs who saw in the Bank of the United States a check on credit and monetary expansion.

He contributed no philosophical insights to guide the early republic but at times he had a keener insight into the immediate needs of the nation than those who were called statesmen. He was not entirely unselfish, and he might have answered his critics by saying that what was good for Smith and Buchanan was good for the country. His patriotism sounded at times bombastic and fustian and he yielded to no man in his belligerent nationalism. But if he helped to push the country into war he did not, like most politicians, leave the fighting of it to others.

He was obviously gratified that the city had made him mayor—not as an honor but because an emergency required him. Yet he soon realized that the tasks of office had become too arduous for him, and late in 1838, as he was approaching his eighty-seventh year, he resigned his last public office.

On April 22, 1839, General Smith returned home after a carriage drive and stretched out on the sofa for a short nap before dinner. The servant who was sent to wake him found him dead.

Three days later one of the largest funeral processions that Baltimore ever witnessed escorted the city's first citizen through the streets. As the body left the Exchange Place residence, the President of the United States, Martin Van Buren, and his cabinet followed in its wake as a tribute to the political achievements of the man who had

Montebello

Baltimore Taken Near Whetstone Point—1835
lithograph by Benn

represented his state in the national legislature through the administrations of seven presidents. As the procession reached Baltimore Street and turned east along the waterfront, the ships in the Patapsco lowered their colors to half-mast for the merchant whose ships had known the ports of the world from Europe to China. And as the throng of citizens watched the hearse with its military escort ascend Hampstead Hill, the guns of Fort McHenry boomed a final salute.[15]

Notes

The three major Samuel Smith manuscript collections are located in the Alderman Library at the University of Virginia, the Maryland Historical Society in Baltimore, and the Library of Congress. The Alderman Library collection is contained in the Smith-Carter papers and is referred to as Smith-Carter Mss. The Library of Congress collection is referred to as the Smith Mss. The principal items in the Maryland Historical Society are the letterbooks of Smith and Buchanan, the firm which John Smith founded, and which went by various titles during Samuel Smith's lifetime. They are referred to as Smith Letterbooks. Cary Nicholas Fink made typed transcripts of all the letters in the Smith-Carter collection some years ago. Since then some of the originals have been removed, but I have not hesitated to use the copies since a check shows that Mrs. Fink was a painstaking and accurate copyist. These are designated in the notes.

The following abbreviations are used for the sake of convenience:

AHR	*The American Historical Review*
HM	*The Historical Magazine*
MHM	*The Maryland Historical Magazine*
ASP FR	*American State Papers, Foreign Relations*
DAB	*The Dictionary of American Biography*

Reference to "Smith" in the notes refers to General Samuel Smith. He is occasionally referred to as "S. Smith" to try to avoid confusion.

Chapter 1

1. Smith to his father, Dec. 16, 1772. Smith-Carter Mss. Alderman Library, University of Virginia, Charlottesville, Va.

2. Smith to his father, July 25, 1772. Smith Papers, Library of Congress, Washington, D.C. Hereafter cited as Smith Mss. Smith to his daughter, Aug. 6, 1772. Smith-Carter Mss.

3. Smith to Mildred, Roberts and Co., Sept. 26, 1772. Smith-Carter Mss. Smith to his father, Aug. 6, 26, 1772. Ibid. Same to same, Sept. 9, 1772. Ibid.

4. Smith to his father, Dec. 23, 1772. Ibid.

5. Same to same, March 26 to Dec. 30, 1773. Ibid.

6. Smith refers to this letter in his own letter to his father Dec. 20, 1773. Ibid.

7. Description of Smith based on two profiles by Fevret St. Memin,

Collection of Portraits (London, 1862), portraits of Gilbert Stuart and an unknown artist in the Maryland Historical Society and a portrait by Rembrandt Peale in The Municipal Museum in Baltimore, Md.

8. Smith to his daughter (Mrs. Mansfield), May 5, 1823. Smith-Carter Mss.

9. "Papers of General Smith," *Historical Magazine* (Hereafter cited as *HM*), 17, (Feb., 1870), 81. This account of Smith's early life and Revolutionary career is written in the third person, probably by the General himself. It was submitted by General Smith's son, John Spear Smith. This and the letter to Mrs. Mansfield quoted above are the only sources for Smith's ancestry and early life.

10. John Thomas Scharf, *Chronicles of Baltimore* (Baltimore, 1874), pp. 23–58. *passim.* Hamilton Owens, *Baltimore on the Chesapeake* (New York, 1941), p. 48.

11. Frank Roy Rutter, *The South American Trade of Baltimore*, Johns Hopkins *Studies in Historical and Political Science,* 15th series (Baltimore, 1897), pp. 381–382.

12. "Papers of General Smith," *HM*, 17, 81.

13. Charles A. Barker, *The Background of the Revolution in Maryland* (New Haven, 1940), pp. 293–308, *passim.*

14. John Thomas Scharf, *History of Maryland from its Earliest Beginnings to the Present Day* (Baltimore, 1879), 2, pp. 110–20, *passim.*

15. Merrill Jensen, *The Founding of a Nation* (New York, 1968). "Papers of General Smith," *HM,* 17, 82.

16. Facsimile of the Articles, Scharf, *Maryland,* 2, pp. 184–85. Scharf, *Baltimore,* p. 126. "Papers of General Smith," *HM,* 17, 81, 82.

17. John Smith and Sons to John Roberts and Son, Oct. 20, 1774. Smith and Co. Letterbook, Maryland Historical Society. Hereafter cited as Smith Letterbook. Barker, *Background of the Revolution in Maryland,* p. 376. John Smith and Sons to the Maryland Council of Safety, Dec. 11, 1775. Smith Letterbook.

18. Muster Roll of the Baltimore Independent Cadets, Maryland Historical Society. John Smith and Sons to B.C. Berwicke, Sept. 17, 1774. Smith Letterbook.

19. Smith and Co. to Joseph Jones and Son, Dec. 6, 1775. Smith Letterbook. "Papers of General Smith," *HM,* 17, 81. This account continues through Smith's Revolutionary career. In matters of fact it is reliable insofar as it can be checked with other primary and secondary sources. Ibid., 17, 82.

20. Ibid., 82–83. Eden was one of the few royal governors who was well-liked by the people of his colony.

21. Ibid., 83, 94. Alexander Graydon, *Memories of His Own Time* (Philadelphia, 1846), p. 180.

CHAPTER 2

1. "Papers of General Smith," *HM,* 17, 82–83. Scharf, *Maryland,* 2, p.

246. Sydney George Fisher, *The Struggle for American Independence,* (Philadelphia, 1908), 1, pp. 494–697. Douglas Southall Freeman, *George Washington, A Biography* (New York, 1950), 4, p. 166.

2. "Papers of General Smith," *HM,* 17, 83. Washington to President of Congress, Aug. 31, 1776. John C. Fitzpatrick (ed.), *The Writings of George Washington* (Washington, 1932), 5, pp. 506–508.

3. "Papers of General Smith," *HM,* 17, 83–84.

4. Ibid., 84.

5. Ibid. Samuel Smith Mss., Maryland Historical Society, Baltimore, Md. Hereafter cited as Smith Mss., MHS. The commissions are dated Dec. 10, 1776 (major), and Feb. 2, 1777 (lt. colonel).

6. Fisher, *American Independence,* 2, p. 20. Christopher Ward, *The War of the Revolution* (New York, 1952), 1, pp. 330–34. The quote is Fisher's.

7. Fisher, *American Independence,* 2, pp. 24–26. Henry Seidel Canby, *The Brandywine* (New York, 1941), pp. 179–220, *passim.* Freeman, *Washington,* 4, p. 485.

8. "Papers of General Smith," *HM,* 17, 85–86. Freeman, *Washington,* 4, pp. 479–83. Stirling had been exchanged after his capture at Long Island.

9. Washington to Baron d'Arendt and to Commodore John Hazelwood, Sept. 23, 1777. Fitzpatrick (ed.), *Washington,* 9, pp. 256, 255. Washington seems to have had a very high regard for the baron's ability although the latter had just been commissioned in the American army a short time. D'Arendt's subsequent conduct at Fort Mifflin, at least according to Smith's account, does not seem to have justified this high opinion. Washington did not again entrust a combat command to him but made him an army inspector.

10. Washington to Smith, Sept. 23, 1777. Ibid., 9, p. 260.

11. "Papers of General Smith," *HM,* 17, 86. Washington to Smith, Nov. 4, 1777. Fitzpatrick (ed.), *Washington,* 10, p. 7.

12. Fisher, *American Independence,* 2, pp. 44–45. Smith to Washington, Oct. 10 and 14, 1777. Printed along with other reports from Smith to Washington during the Fort Mifflin action in "The Defense of Fort Mifflin," *Maryland Historical Magazine* hereafter referred as *MHM,* 5 (1910), 213–15. Ward, *Revolution,* 1, pp. 376–77.

13. Smith to Washington, Sept. 26, 1777. Smith-Carter Mss. (copy).

14. "Papers of General Smith," *HM,* 17, 86.

15. Ibid. Fisher, *American Independence,* 2, p. 45. Freeman, *Washington,* 4, p. 526.

16. Fisher, *American Independence,* 2, p. 43.

17. Smith to Washington, Oct. 10, 1777. Smith-Carter Mss. (copy). "Papers of General Smith," *HM,* 17, 86.

18. "Papers of General Smith," *HM,* 17, 87. Smith to Washington, Oct. 11, 1777. "The Defense of Fort Mifflin," *MHM,* 5, 217.

19. Smith to Washington, Oct. 14, 1777. Smith-Carter Mss. (copy).

20. Same to same, Oct. 15, 1777. Ibid.

21. "Papers of General Smith," *HM,* 17, 88.

22. Washington to Smith, Oct. 18, 1777. Smith-Carter Mss. (copy).

23. Washington to D'Arendt, Oct. 18, 1777. Worthington C. Ford (ed.),

Writings of George Washington (New York, 1890), 6, p. 124. "Papers of General Smith," *HM,* 17, 88.

24. "Papers of General Smith," *HM,* 17, 88.

25. Smith to Washington, Oct. __, 1777. Smith-Carter Mss. (copy). Washington to Smith, Oct. 22, 1777. Ford (ed.), *Washington,* 6, p. 124.

26. Fisher, *American Independence,* 2, p. 47. and Gardner W. Allen, *A Naval History of the American Revolution* (Boston and New York, 1913), 1, p. 244. He lists the *Augusta* at 64 guns, the *Merlin,* 18 and the *Vigilant* 16 24-pounders; Hazelwood to Washington, Oct. 16, 1777. Jared Sparks (ed.), *The Writings of George Washington* (Boston, 1839), 5, p. 113n. Freeman, *Washington,* 4, p. 528.

27. "Papers of General Smith," *HM,* 17, 88.

28. Ibid., 17, 89. Sparks (ed.), *Washington,* 5, p. 108n.

29. Smith to Washington, Nov. 3, 1777. Smith-Carter Mss. (copy). "Papers of General Smith," *HM,* 17, 89.

30. "Papers of General Smith," *HM,* 17, 89. Fisher, *American Independence,* 2, p. 47. Smith to Washington, Nov. 9, 1777. "Defense of Fort Mifflin," *MHM,* 5, 227. Freeman, *Washington,* 4, p. 528.

31. Smith to Washington, Nov. 9, and 11, 1777. Smith-Carter Mss. (copy).

32. "Papers of General Smith," *HM,* 17, 90.

33. Sparks (ed.), *Washington,* 5, pp. 154–155n.

34. Varnum to Washington, Nov. 18, 1777. Ford (ed.), *Washington,* 6, p. 185n.

35. Fisher, *American Independence,* 2, p. 50. Freeman, *Washington,* 4, p. 551. F. Knox to Smith, May 31, 1786. Smith-Carter Mss., MHS.

CHAPTER 3

1. "Papers of General Smith," *HM,* 17, 90–92.

2. Ibid., 17, 91.

3. This was the occasion of Washington's furious reprimand to Lee for withdrawing. Fisher thinks that from all available evidence Lee was tactically correct in this order since he actually was opposed by the main British force. *American Independence,* 2, pp. 185–96, *passim.* C. H. Van Tyne takes the opposite view but his basis is the biased testimony of Hamilton. *The American Revolution* (New York, 1905), p. 245. General Anthony Wayne and General Scott, both of whom were on the ground, thought a splendid opportunity to score a victory was lost. Troops were in perfect position but no orders to attack came from Lee. Instead, the troops were withdrawn. Generals Wayne and Scott to General Washington, June 30, 1778, "Lee Papers," *Collections of the New York Historical Society,* 5, (1872), 439–40. Freeman, *Washington,* 5, pp. 28–38, concluded that Lee faced no more than 3,000 British.

4. "Papers of General Smith," *HM,* 17, 91. Fisher, *American Independence,* 2, pp. 178–85, *passim.* Ward, *Revolution,* 2, pp. 580–85.

5. The two armies, in fact, remained almost in this position with no heavy fighting by either until Washington slipped away to Yorktown in 1781. Fisher, *American Independence,* 2, pp. 206–207. "Papers of General Smith," *HM,* 17, 92.

6. Extract from the Journal of Baron de Closen, Rochambeau Papers, Library of Congress. Reprinted under the title "French Troops in Maryland," *MHM*, 5 (1910), 231.

7. "Papers of General Smith," *HM*, 17, 92.

8. Smith to Washington, May 10, 1779. Washington to Smith, May 29, 1779. Smith-Carter Mss.

9. Council of Safety to Smith, April 19, 1781; Benjamin Nicholson to Governor Thomas Sim Lee, Aug. 5, 1780. *Archives of Maryland: Journal and Correspondence of the State Council of Maryland,* edited by Bernard C. Steiner (Baltimore, 1884–1944), 45, pp. 42, 404.

10. As evidenced in correspondence of Council with Smith and others in *Archives*, Dec. 24, 1799, 43, p. 41; Council to Mr. Holker, Feb. 21, 1780, 43, p. 93; Smith to Council, Jan. 3, 1780, 43, p. 398; Smith to Governor Lee, Nov. 14, 1780, 45, p. 181.

11. Scharf, *Baltimore*, p. 241. Owens, *Baltimore on the Chesapeake,* pp. 97–117. Howard I. Chappelle, *American Sailing Ships* (New York, 1935), pp.130–75, *passim*. The latter work discusses chiefly the types of ships used and their sailing characteristics and armament.

12. Smith to Williams, July 2, 1779. Otho Holland Williams Papers, Maryland Historical Society.

13. Council to Smith, Dec. 11, 1779, *Archives*, 47, p. 35. Same to same, Dec. 30, 1780. Ibid., 45, p. 257. Same to same, Aug. 28, 1780. Ibid., 47, p. 267. Smith seems to have been handling most of the correspondence and business of John Smith and Sons, probably because his official position as a militia officer gave him more prestige when dealing with the state council.

14. Specifically mentioned in the *Archives* are the *General Wayne*, the *Cato*, the *Otho*, the *Porgie*, the *Rambler,* and the *Rover*. The *Race Horse, Statia, Fiery Dragon,* and the unnamed brig are mentioned in his letters to Williams.

15. Smith to Williams, Feb. 14, 1782; Same to same, March 14, 1781. Williams Mss.

16. Same to same, Sept. 9, 1782. Ibid.

17. Council to Smith, Oct. 8, 1779. *Archives*, 21, p. 552. Same to same, May 24 and June 6, 1780, Ibid., 47, pp. 181, 191.

18. Same to same, Nov. 30, 1780. Ibid., 45, p. 230.

19. Same to same, Jan. 27, 1781. Ibid., 45, p. 281.

20. Same to same, March 13 and 18, 1781. Ibid., 45, pp. 397, 404.

21. Remarking on what he regarded as the feeble opposition to the British, Smith wrote Williams, June ___, 1781: "Oh! Virginia, is this your boasted pride? Perhaps you eased of their riches, and deprived of their slaves, they may become useful members of society." Scharf, *Maryland*, 2, p. 450n. Smith to Council, April 23 and 25, 1781. *Archives*, 43, p. 203, 214.

22. Council to Smith, May 30, 1781. *Archives*, 45, p. 450.

23. Council to Smith, June 28, 1781. Ibid., 45, p. 490. Smith to Council, June 1, 1781. Ibid., 47, p. 266. Same to same, Aug. 1, 1781. Ibid., 43, p. 345. Philip A. Crowl, *Maryland During and After the Revolution,* Johns Hopkins *Studies in Historical and Political Science,* 61st Series (1943), p. 50.

24. John P. Kennedy, whose lecture, "Baltimore Long Ago" is quoted in Scharf, *Baltimore,* pp. 233–34. This was later revised and published in Kennedy's book, *At Home and Abroad* (San Marino, 1943), p. 180.

25. Wilson Miles Cary to "Polly" ____?, Feb. 28, 1897. Smith-Carter Mss. Robert Hunter, Jr. *Quebec to Carolina in 1785–1786,* edited by Louis B. Wright and Marion Tinling (San Marino, 1943), p. 180.

26. The name of the firm was changed several times. It was John Smith and Sons until 1784. From 1784 to 17,89 it was known as Samuel and John Smith, and in 1789 Sam and his cousin, William Buchanan, son of John Smith's old partner, reorganized under the name of Smith and Buchanan. Smith Letterbook, Maryland Historical Society.

27. Smith and Co. to Messrs. James, Bird and Co., Leghorn, July 1, 1784. Ibid.

28. Smith Letterbook, 1787–1791, *passim.* Smith and Co., Instructions to Captain James Deale, June 2, 1794. Ibid.

29. April 15, 1784. Ibid. Announcements were made to all of Smith and Company's customers.

30. Smith and Co. to Daniel Bowden & Sons, Lisbon. April 24, 1784. Ibid.

31. Same to John Noble and Co., June 7, 1784. Ibid.

32. Same to Henry von der Smissen & Son, Hamburg, May 12, 1784. Ibid.

33. Kathryn Sullivan, *Maryland and France, 1774–1789* (Philadelphia, 1936), pp. 138, 143. Samuel Flagg Bemis, *Jay's Treaty* (New York, 1923), pp. 21–30, *passim.* Smith and Co. to Oxley and Hancock, London, Dec. 29, 1783. Smith Letterbook.

34. Same to John Noble, June 7, 1784; same to John Noble & Co., Oct. 11, 1784. Smith Letterbook. Sullivan, *Maryland,* pp. 143–44. Smith and Co. to Daniel Crommlin & Son, June 28, 1786. Smith Letterbook.

35. Smith and Co. to Francis LeMee, Marseilles, Dec. 8, 1784; Smith and Co. instructions to Captain Dean, June 9, 1786; same instructions to Captain Denny of the *Louis,* July 1, 1787; same to Perkins, Burling and Perkins, July 1, 1787; same to John Noble and Co., July 28, 1786. Smith Letterbook. Smith told of the food shortage in the West Indies due to the unusual number of ship seizures in 1786 but the fact that Smith had an unusually good year would seem to indicate that few if any of his own ships were seized. "Stress of weather" was the phrase used to describe the universally accepted rule that a vessel might put into any port when bad weather endangered her safety.

36. Smith to his father, March 26 to Dec. 30, 1773. Smith Mss. Smith and Co. to Berrand & Co., March 2, 1787. Smith Letterbook.

37. Same to M.V.T. Gregory, London, April 30, 1787; same to Joseph Cates, Dec. 20, 1787 and John Ridings, March 1, 1788. Smith Letterbook.

38. Jonathan Elliott, (ed.), *Debates on the Adoption of the Federal Constitution* (Philadelphia, 1901), 5, p. 119. Bernard C. Steiner, "Maryland's Adoption of the Federal Constitution," *American Historical Review,* 5 (1899), 22–44, 207–

24, *passim.* Crowl, *Maryland During and After the Revolution,* pp. 111–63, *passim.*

39. Scharf, *Baltimore,* pp. 250–51. Smith to W. Gibbons and Co., May 16, 1789. Smith Letterbook.

40. Edward Channing, *History of the United States* (New York, 1935), 4, p. 117. For the Nootka Sound controversy see W.R. Manning, "The Nootka Sound Controversy," *Annual Reports of the American Historical Association* for 1904, 279–478, *passim.*

41. Smith and Buchanan to Rathbone and Benson, Dec. 24, 1793; same to Taylor, Ballentine and Fairlie, May 26, 1794. Smith Letterbook.

42. Same to Fenwyck, Mason and Co., June 24, 1794; Same to Taylor, Ballentine and Fairlie, May 26, 1794. Ibid.

CHAPTER 4

1. *Votes and Proceedings of the House of Delegates of the State of Maryland* (published yearly at Annapolis), Nov., 1791 session, p. 4.

2. *Maryland General Assembly Proceedings, 1791–1796* (Annapolis, 1797), 138, p. 78. Ibid., pp. 24, 95.

3. Bernard C. Steiner, *Life and Correspondence of James McHenry* (Cleveland, 1907), pp. 137–138. *Maryland Gazette* (Annapolis), Nov. 1, 1792.

4. John Adams, "A Defense of the Constitutions of the United States of America," *The Works of John Adams,* edited by Charles Francis Adams (Boston, 1851), 4, p. 290.

5. Smith, "Remarks upon the Anniversary of the Death of Thomas Jefferson," delivered at Baltimore, April 18, 1830. Smith-Carter Mss. For the origins of political parties see Noble E. Cunningham, *The Jeffersonian Republicans: The Formation of Party Organization, 1789–1801* (Chapel Hill, 1957), and Joseph Charles, *The Origins of the American Party System* (Williamsburg, 1951).

6. For a fuller discussion see Dumas Malone, *Jefferson and the Rights of Man,* Volume II of *Jefferson and His Time* (Boston, 1950), especially pp. xvi–xx; and Cecelia Kenyon, "Alexander Hamilton: Rousseau of the Right," *Political Science Quarterly,* 73 (1958), 161–178.

7. Jefferson to Thomas Mann Randolph, Jan. 7, 1793. Paul Leicester Ford (ed.), *Writings of Thomas Jefferson* (New York, 1892–99), 6, p. 157. Steiner, *McHenry,* p. 143.

8. Alexander Deconde, *Entangling Alliances: Politics and Diplomacy under George Washington* (Durham, 1958), Chaps. III and VII.

9. *Debates and Proceedings in the Congress of the United States* (Washington, 1834–1856), Third Congress, 229. Hereafter cited as *Annals.*

10. Ibid., 3rd Congress, 495.

11. Bemis, *Jay's Treaty,* pp. 194–196, *passim. Annals,* 3rd Congress, 115, 602, 849.

12. *Maryland Gazette,* Sept. 18, 1794. Scharf, *Maryland,* 2, pp. 583–87. Henry Adams, *Life of Albert Gallatin* (New York, 1943), pp. 124–50, *passim.* See also Leland Baldwin, *The Whiskey Rebellion: The Story of a Frontier Uprising* (Pittsburgh, 1939). Smith's commission as major general dated April 4, 1795. Smith Mss., MHS.

13. *Annals,* 3rd Congress. 1092.

14. Bemis, *Jay's Treaty,* pp. 257–71, *passim.*

15. John Jay, *Mr. Jay's Second Letter on Dawson's Introduction to the Federalist* (New York, 1864), p. 19. Quoted in Thomas A. Bailey, *A Diplomatic History of the American People* (New York, 1947), 66.

16. *Annals,* 4th Congress, 1st session, 1154.

17. Ibid., 4th Congress, 1st session, 623.

18. Hamilton instructed Rufus King to sound this note in a letter to the latter on April 15, 1796. John C. Hamilton (ed.), *Works of Alexander Hamilton* (New York, 1851), 6, p. 105. Irving Brant, *James Madison: Father of the Constitution* (Indianapolis, 1950), pp. 425–39.

19. James Winchester to James McHenry, April 22, 1796. Steiner, *McHenry,* p. 194. *Annals,* 4th Congress, 1st session, 1153–157.

20. Winchester to McHenry, April 22, 1796, Steiner, *McHenry,* p. 194; William Vans Murray to McHenry, "2nd day of Election," Ibid., p. 198; Charles Carroll to McHenry, Dec. 5, 1796. Ibid., p. 204.

21. William Penn Cresson, *Life of James Monroe* (New York, 1946), pp. 138–54, *passim.* Alexander DeConde, *The Quasi-War: The Politics and Diplomacy of the Undeclared War with France, 1797–1801* (New York, 1966). p. 16–18.

22. *Annals,* 4th Congress, 2nd session, 2133–136, 1981, 2093.

23. Ibid., 5th Congress, 1st session, 259–61.

24. Erroneously attributed to C. C. Pinckney. He denied it but the words are inscribed on his tombstone in Charleston. Albert Beveridge, *Life of John Marshall* (Boston, 1916), 2, pp. 272–75. DeConde, *The Quasi-War,* pp. 49–50. Bailey, *Diplomatic History,* p. 85n.

25. *Annals,* 5th Congress, 2nd session, 2740, 1772, 2006, 1865, 2178.

26. Ibid., 5th Congress, 2nd session, 1494.

27. Ibid., 5th Congress, 2nd session, 2068–2069.

28. Ibid., 5th Congress, 2nd session, debates on the Naturalization Act, 1427–630, *passim;* on the Alien Acts, 1773–2049, *passim;* on the Sedition Act, 1868–2116, *passim.*

29. Smith "To the voters of the City and County of Baltimore," Sept. 7, 1798. Smith Mss. Winchester had voted for Jefferson in 1796 but by 1798 "he comes forward and declares his intention is to support the administration." James Ash to McHenry, Aug. 24, 1798. Steiner, *McHenry,* p. 334.

30. Clipping (undated) from the Baltimore *Federal Gazette and Daily Advertiser.* Smith Mss.

31. William Hindman to McHenry, Aug. 12, 1798. McHenry Mss. Maryland Historical Society. Smith's opponent, Winchester, wrote to him indignantly, "It is notorious that freedom of Election has been greatly obstructed by the violence exercised by your friends . . . and by their parade of drums, fifes, and flags." Undated, Smith Mss.

32. George Salmon to McHenry, Aug. 12, 1798. Bernard C. Steiner, "Maryland Politics in 1798 from the Correspondence of Dr. James McHenry," *Publications of the Southern Historical Association,* 10 (1906), 106. Hindman to McHenry, Aug. 29, 1798. Steiner, *McHenry,* p. 336.

33. DeConde, *The Quasi-War,* Chap. III. Hamilton to Washington, March 8, 1794. Henry Cabot Lodge (ed.), *The Works of Alexander Hamilton* (New York, 1904), 10, p. 63. Same to same, April 14, 1794. Ibid., p. 5, 106.

34. Baltimore *Federal Gazette and Daily Advertiser,* Aug. 7, 1798. Frank Cassell, Samuel Smith: Merchant Politician, unpublished Ph.D. dissertation (Northwestern University, 1968), pp. 15–20.

35. Scharf, *Baltimore,* p. 248. Dice Robins Anderson, *William Branch Giles: A Study in the Politics of Virginia and the Nation from 1790 to 1830* (Menasha, Wis., 1914), p. 59.

36. Edward S. Delaplaine, "Luther Martin," *Dictionary of American Biography* (hereafter *DAB*), edited by Dumas Malone and Allen Johnson (New York, 1928–1944), 12, p. 344. Edward S. Corwin, "Samuel Chase," Ibid., 4, p. 36. Ellen Hart Smith, *Charles Carroll of Carrollton* (Cambridge, 1943), p. 223.

37. Smith to Wilson Cary Nicholas, Aug. 8, 1800. Smith-Carter Mss. Scharf, Baltimore, 133–134.

38. Kate Mason Rowland, *Life of Charles Carroll of Carrollton* (New York, 1898), II, p. 238–39.

39. Scharf, *Maryland,* 2, p. 602.

40. *The Federalist* (Washington, D. C.), Dec. 31, 1800.

41. Burr to Smith, Dec. 29, 1800. Smith-Carter Mss. The location of the original being unknown, I have used a copy made by Cary Nicholas Fink when she was working on her never-completed biography of General Smith at the Alderman Library in the early twenties.

42. Smith to Burr, Jan. 11, 1801. Smith-Carter Mss.

43. Hamilton, *Works,* 6, p. 506. Sedgwick to Hamilton, Jan. 10, 1801. Hamilton, *Works,* 6, p. 513.

44. J. Fairfax McLaughlin, Matthew Lyon, *The Hampden of Congress* (New York, 1900), p. 386.

45. Nathan Schachner, *Aaron Burr, A Biography* (New York, 1937), p. 192.

46. Smith to Burr, Jan. 11, 1801. Smith-Carter Mss.

47. Burr to Smith, Jan. 16, 1801. Smith Mss.

48. *Congressional Globe, Containing the Debates and Proceedings,* Appendix, 33rd Congress, 2nd session (Washington, 1856), 31, 139. The excerpts published in the *Globe* were portions of Bayard's deposition in Burr's suit against James Cheatham, editor of the *American Citizen.* (See text.) The occasion was a vindication of Bayard's conduct during the election that was entered in the *Globe* by James A. Bayard, Jr., then a member of Congress. Ogden later denied that he had "any understanding or concert with Col. Burr." Ogden to P. Irving, Nov. 24, 1802, quoted in Matthew L. Davis, *Memoirs of Aaron Burr* (New York, 1858), 2, p. 196.

49. Smith Mss. Christie stated that he had substantiated the facts by consulting with George Dent, Maryland Republican Congressman, who was also present at the meeting. I am unable to discover the exact date of the meeting between Burr and Smith but it was probably just before the balloting began

in the House. The libel suit for which the letter was used was instituted by Smith against the *Anti-Democrat* published by Charles Prentiss and John Cole. The paper accused Smith of intriguing for Burr's election but shortly published a retraction.

50. Robert Goodloe Harper in a letter "To His Constituents" gives the following tabulation for the first ballot, showing how the Federalist majority carried only six states for Burr. (*Correspondence of James A. Bayard,* edited by Elizabeth Donnan, *American Historical Association Report for 1913,* 2, p. 136.

State	Jefferson	Burr
New Hampshire	6	0
Vermont	1	1
Massachusetts	3	11
Rhode Island	0	2
Connecticut	0	7
New York	6	4
New Jersey	3	2
Pennsylvania	9	4
Delaware	0	1
Maryland	4	4
Virginia	14	5
North Carolina	6	4
South Carolina	1	4
Georgia	1	0
Kentucky	2	0
Tennessee	1	0
	51	55

However, by February 13, the Washington *National Intelligencer* showed that three North Carolina representatives, two from Virginia and one from South Carolina had switched from Burr to Jefferson.

51. Davis in his *Memoirs of Aaron Burr* presents a great deal of related source material, particularly documents and depositions from the Cheatham case (p. 11). James Parton in his *Life and Times of Aaron Burr,* (2 vols., Boston, 1884) insists that Burr would have resigned if elected and Samuel Wandell and Meade Minnegerode rely only on the December 16 letter. (*Aaron Burr,* 2 vols., New York, 1925). Mr. Schachner shows Burr as the unfortunate victim of an embarrassing situation which his enemies used to discredit him. Herbert S. Parmet and Marie B. Hecht contend that Burr played his ambivalent role in order to be available as a compromise candidate should the Republican victory threaten revolution. *Aaron Burr: Portrait of an Ambitious Man* (New York, 1967), p. 207.

52. Jefferson to Martha Jefferson Randolph, Jan. 4, 1801. Ford (ed.), *Writings,* 7, p. 479.

53. Rodney to Nicholson, Jan. 3, 1801. Nicholson Mss., Library of Congress, Washington, D. C.

54. Samuel Smith to John Spear Smith, July 19, 1804. Smith Mss.

55. Donnan (ed.) *Bayard Correspondence,* 2, pp. 128–129n.

56. *Congressional Globe,* Appendix XXXI, 138, quoting a letter from Baer to R. H. Bayard, April 19, 1830.

57. Smith to J. A. and R. H. Bayard, April 13, 1830. Smith Mss.

58. Schachner, *Burr,* p. 108.

59. A. A. Lipscomb and A. E. Bergh (eds.), *The Writings of Thomas Jefferson* (Washington, 1903), 1, p. 453 (from the "Anas").

60. Smith to the Bayards, April 30, 1830. Smith Mss. The copy of the altered draft of the deposition with Smith's marginal notes is also in the Smith Mss. (Answers by S. Smith to Interrogations in the case of James Gillespie against Abraham Smith, April 15, 1805).

CHAPTER 5

1. Quoted from "an old paper" in Scharf, *Baltimore,* p. 289. Contract of Buchanan, Spear and Co., May 20, 1794. Letterbook in Smith-Carter Mss.

2. Scharf, *Baltimore,* pp. 260, 284. Scharf, *Maryland,* 2, p. 542n. He had been appointed director of the Bank of Maryland in 1790. The internal improvement projects were the Reistertown Road Co. and the Susquehanna Canal Co. On the estimate of Cary Nicholas Fink, descendant of Wilson Cary Nicholas, apparently from account books no longer in the Smith Mss., Smith owned or had options on real estate in Maryland, Georgia, and Kentucky worth $400,000. Taking into account all of his holdings, chief of which was, of course, Smith and Buchanan, Sam must have been worth well over $1,000,000. Smith and Buchanan was clearing $200,000 a year by 1810. Smith to Mrs. Mansfield, June 8, 1810. Smith-Carter Mss. (copy).

3. From Cary Nicholas Fink notes. Smith-Carter Mss. The *Baltimore Directory* for 1832 confirms the location.

4. Lawrence Hall Fowler, "Montebello, Maryland," *Architectural Review,* Nov., 1909, 146–49. He also confirms the Exchange Place residence.

5. From a list of Smith's children, Wilson Miles Cary to "Polly", Feb. 28, 1897. Also notes of Cary Nicholas Fink for which no source is given. Smith-Carter Mss.

6. Entry by R. H. Randolph in "The Commonplace Book" of Mrs. T. J. Randolph. Ibid. Jane, another sister married John Hollis, an Englishman, and Hester, the youngest of John Smith's children married, first, Dr. George Stevens, and, after his death, Peter Carr. Their son, Dabney, was later editor of the *Baltimore American* and was appointed to a diplomatic post by President Jackson. For George Nicholas, see Thomas Perkins Abernethy, "George Nicholas," in the *DAB,* 13, 482–83. Cary Nicholas Fink notes on appointment of John Smith as attorney for Arthur Cramond and Co., June 19, 1797. Smith-Carter Mss.

7. C. C. Tansill, "Robert Smith," *American Secretaries of State and Their Diplomacy,* edited by Samuel Flagg Bemis (New York, 1927), pp. 151–52. Mary Wilhelmina Williams, "Robert Smith," *DAB,* 17, 337.

8. Jefferson to Smith, March 9, 1801. Ford (ed.), *Works,* 8, p. 13. Smith to Jefferson, March 20, 1801. Smith-Carter Mss. (copy).

9. Gallatin to Mrs. Gallatin, March 5, 1801. Adams, *Gallatin,* p. 265.

10. Gallatin to Jefferson, Jan. 1, 1803. Henry Adams (ed.), *Writings of Albert Gallatin* (Philadelphia, 1879), 1, p. 24.

11. Smith to Jefferson, March 20, 1801. Smith-Carter Mss.

12. R. W. Irwin, *The Diplomatic Relations of the United States with the Barbary Powers, 1776–1816* (Chapel Hill, 1931), pp. 103–106.

13. Jefferson to Smith, July 9, 1801. Henry Stephens Randall, *Life of Thomas Jefferson* (New York, 1871), 3, p. 630.

14. Anderson, *Giles,* p. 118.

15. Joseph Story to S. P. Fay, Feb. 13, 1808. William Story, *Life and Letters of Joseph Story* (Boston, 1851), 1, p. 159.

16. William Cabell Bruce, *John Randolph of Roanoke, 1773–1833* (New York, 1922). See for example, 2, 200–221; 1, pp. 228–32.

17. *Annals,* 7th Congress, 1st session, 312.

18. Ibid., 7th Congress, 1st session, 434–62, *passim.*

19. Ibid., 7th Congress, 1st, session, 1018, 1029, 1036. Adams, *Gallatin,* p. 295.

20. *Annals,* 7th Congress, 1st session, 1060–1061. Of the states named by Smith only Georgia and Tennessee had voted for Jefferson.

21. Ibid., 7th Congress, 1st session, 1063.

22. Ibid., 7th Congress, 1st session, 41. Henry Adams, *History of the United States During the Administrations of Thomas Jefferson and James Madison, 1801-1817* (New York, 1889–1891), 1, p. 274.

23. *Annals,* 7th Congress, 1st session, 597, 601, 605.

24. Ibid., 7th Congress, 1st session, 664.

25. Ibid., 7th Congress, 1st session, 639–41.

26. Ibid., 7th Congress, 1st session, 849–51.

27. *Maryland Gazette* (Annapolis), Nov. 18, 1802.

28. Scharf, *Maryland,* 2, pp. 609–11.

29. A. P. Whitaker, *The Mississippi Question, 1795–1803* (New York, 1934), pp. 176–214, *passim.*

30. *Messages and Papers of the Presidents,* compiled by James D. Richardson (Washington, 1899), 1, p. 343.

31. *Annals,* 7th Congress, 2nd session, 314, 316. Jefferson did, in fact, submit some unimportant documents which had already appeared in the newspapers.

32. Ibid., 7th Congress, 1st session, 324.

33. Ibid., 7th Congress, 2nd session, 357.

34. Henry Adams, *History,* 1, p. 440.

35. *Annals,* 7th Congress, 2nd session, 664.

36. C. C. Tansill, *The United States and Santo Domingo, 1798–1873* (Baltimore, 1938), p. 87ff.

37. Scharf, *Baltimore,* p. 294. Eugene L. Didier, *Life and Letters of Madam Bonaparte* (New York, 1879), pp. 1–8, *passim.*

38. Adams, *History*, 2, p. 377. William Patterson was right about Napoleon's reaction. Despite a contract drawn by Alexander Dallas and witnessed by the French consul in Baltimore, Napoleon annulled the marriage and refused to allow Betsy to enter the country with her husband in 1805. She went to England where she gave birth to a son, Jerome Napoleon. Napoleon, who had now been made Emperor, attempted to get an annulment from Pope Pius VII but was refused. Nevertheless, Jerome was made King of Westphalia and wed to Frederica Catharina of Wurtemburg. Betsy, by judicious use of the income granted her by the French government, provided her son with a Harvard education and he was later admitted to the Maryland bar. Madame Bonaparte returned to France after presiding over one of the most brilliant salons of post-war Paris. She later returned to Baltimore where she died in 1879 leaving an estate valued at over $1,000,000. Didier, *Madame Bonaparte;* New York *Herald* clippings in scrapbook, vol. 17, Smith Mss.,

39. Pichon to Talleyrand, quoted in Adams, *History* 2, p. 378. While Smith did have aspirations as minister to England, there is no indication that he ever wanted a diplomatic post in Paris.

40. John Quincy Adams, *Memoirs, Comprising Parts of His Diary from 1795 to 1848,* edited by Charles Francis Adams (Philadelphia, 1874–1877), 1, pp. 284–85. Dr. Willis was a noted English psychiatrist.

41. Wilson Cary Nicholas to Smith (undated), 1803. Nicholas to Jefferson (undated), 1803. Smith-Carter Mss.

CHAPTER 6

1. Jefferson to Gerry, March 4, 1804. Lipscomb and Bergh (eds.), *Writings,* 11, p. 16.

2. Adams, *History,* 2, pp. 218–44, *passim.* Bruce, *Randolph,* 1, p. 205 ff. *Annals,* 8th Congress, 2nd session, pp. 665–68. Smith himself voted Chase guilty on only four of the eight counts. Claude Bowers, in *Jefferson in Power* (Boston, 1936), pp. 268–93, has caught the color and drama of the trial although he is somewhat inaccurate and biased against Chase; cf. Dumas Malone, *Jefferson the President: First Term,* vol. 4 of *Jefferson and His Time* (Boston, 1970), pp. 468–80.

3. *Annals,* 9th Congress, 1st session, 9.

4. Adams, *History,* pp. 128–32.

5. Richardson (ed.), *Messages and Papers,* 1, pp. 384–85; 388–90.

6. Charles Hill, "James Madison," in Bemis, ed., *American Secretaries of State,* 3, pp. 58–62. Haitian independence was a *fait accompli* after 1804 but France did not recognize the new black republic and used every opportunity to harass and interdict its trade. For the Florida negotiations see also Herbert Bruce Fuller, *The Florida Purchase* (Cleveland, 1906), pp. 162–63.

7. *Annals,* 9th Congress, 1st session, 31–37.

8. Ibid., 9th Congress, 1st session, pp. 1215–223.

9. Bruce, *Randolph,* 1, pp. 227–31.

10. Ibid., I, 231. *Annals,* 9th Congress, 1st session, 1131.

11. Adams, *History,* 3, p. 138.

12. Hill, "Madison," *American Secretaries of State,* 3, p. 33.

13. Smith to Nicholas, March 11, 1806. Smith Mss. (copy).

14. *William Plumer's Memorandum of the Proceedings in the United States Senate, 1803–1807,* edited by Everett Somerville Brown (New York, 1923), p. 456.

15. Adams, *History,* 3, pp. 44–45. Bailey, *Diplomatic History,* pp. 108–112.

16. Bailey, *Diplomatic History,* pp. 111–12. For a fuller account see J. M. Zimmerman, *Impressment of American Seamen* (New York, 1925). He gives a statistical breakdown from available figures in ibid., pp. 259–76.

17. *Annals,* 9th Congress, 1st session, 167–81.

18. Jefferson to Monroe, March 10, 1808. Ford (ed.), *Writings,* 9, pp. 177–78.

19. Smith to Nicholas, April 8, 1806. Smith-Carter Mss. (copy).

20. Smith to Nicholas, May 16, 1806. Ibid. (copy).

21. Smith to Nicholas, May 23, 1806. Ibid. (copy).

22. Bruce, *Randolph,* 1, p. 258 ff.

23. Smith to Nicholas, April 1, 1806. Adams, *History,* 3, p. 170.

24. *Supra,* note 17.

25. The appropriation was never used. Napoleon, after his victories on the Continent in 1805–1806, so strengthened his position that he preferred to wield Florida as a club to keep the United States from opposing him. Fuller, *The Florida Purchase,* pp. 175–81.

26. Richardson, *Messages and Papers,* 1, pp. 405–10.

27. Adams, *History,* 3, pp. 346, 401.

28. Smith to Nicholas, Jan. 9, 1807. Quoted in Henry Adams, *John Randolph* (Boston, 1883), p. 208.

29. Debates for the second session on the 9th Congress are very briefly reported and from Plumer's *Journal* it is evident that most of the members were agog over the report of Burr's conspiracy. Smith introduced a resolution in the Senate suspending the writ of habeas corpus until the "rebellion" was put down. The resolution was carried in the Senate but the House rejected it. Plumer, *Journal,* pp. 587, 591.

30. This quote and previous comments of Smith on the treaty, Smith to Madison, April 3 and April 18, 1807. Smith Mss. His analysis of England's intention to cripple American commerce was sound. Lord Auckland so accused the government on February 15, 1808. *The Parliamentary Debates, published under the superintendence of Thomas Curson Hansard,* 1st Series, X (1808), pp. 467–69. James Stephens had this in mind in his famous pamphlet, *War in Disguise; or, The Frauds of the Neutral Flags* (London, 1805). Spencer Perceval, later to become prime minister, wrote to the Speaker of the House of Commons in late November, 1807: "If therefore we can accomplish our purpose, it is this,—that either those countries [neutrals and the United States, in particular] will have no trade, or they must accept it from us.... Our Orders add only this circumstance: they say to the enemy, 'If you will not take our trade, as far as we can help it you shall have none.... The only trade, cheap and untaxed, which you shall have shall either be direct from us, in our own produce and manufactures or from our allies....'" Quoted in Adams, *History,* 4, pp. 98–99.

And in 1814, at the height of the war, Wilson Cary Nicholas wrote: "G.B. seizing what she deemed a favorable opportunity to conquer or cripple us for a great length of time, has assumed new ground, the objects of the war are now entirely changed on both sides. The British do not pretend that they are now fighting for their existence, that they are fighting for the liberty of the world. . . . She now prosecutes the war not in defense of her rights under the usage of nations as a belligerent, but for the chance of conquest or at least dismemberment, to drive us from the lakes, and in certain expectation of destroying our ships public and private, our mercantile capital & cities & all hope of our ever being a commercial power." Nicholas to Jonathan Mason, Sept. 23, 1814. Smith-Carter Mss.

31. Giles to Monroe [no date], 1807. Quoted in Anderson, *Giles,* p. 108.

32. Smith to Nicholas, March 4, 1807. Smith-Carter Mss.

33. Smith to ____, Dec. 14, 1805. Ibid.

34. Scharf, *Maryland,* 2, p. 614. The Federalists won a majority in the House of Delegates in the election of 1808 and swept both houses of the legislature in 1812.

35. Evidence suggests that Nathaniel Macon may have originated the tag "Invisibles." It has become historically fashionable to deny the validity of such terms as "Invisibles," "Conway Cabal," "Essex Junto" and the like. This is usually done by carefully sifting through the documents of those thus identified and then preparing a lawyer's brief based on some such "historical principle" as innocent because not proven. The very existence of such terms arose from the necessity of giving a name to something which was difficult to identify but which nonetheless did exist, and to which contemporaries gave a name—usually in some degree of derogation. Thus Macon and others used the term "Invisibles" to identify a group which they had difficulty defining exactly. I am sure that several decades from now historians will deny the existence of President Kennedy's "Irish Mafia" simply because there is no evidence that the President or his associates ever used the term. Yet who would deny that there was a set of tough, spirited, somewhat arrogant young men who thought they had the future firmly in their grasp—and perhaps were secretly proud of the fact that their enemies feared them enough to call them the "Irish Mafia."

For the "Invisibles" see Macon to Joseph Hopper Nicholson, May 23 and June 23, 1809, and Jan. 11, 1810; Edwin Gray to Nicholson, Dec. 16, 1810. Joseph Hopper Nicholson Mss., Library of Congress.

36. Bruce, *Randolph,* 2, p. 581.

37. Nicholas to Jefferson, July 7, 1807. Nicholas Mss., Library of Congress.

38. Richmond *Enquirer,* July 21, 1807.

39. *ASP FR,* 3, p. 267; 5, p. 478; 6, p. 74.

40. Richardson (ed.), *Messages and Papers,* 1, p. 433 (Dec. 18, 1807).

41. *National Intelligencer,* Feb. 1, 1808. The quote is from Smith to ____, Jan. 30, 1806. Smith-Carter Mss.

42. Adams, *History,* 4, p. 127. Cresson, *Monroe,* p. 220ff. *Anderson, Giles,* pp. 123–24.

43. Published in the *National Intelligencer,* March 7, 1808.

44. Nicholas to Smith, ____, 1808. Nicholas Mss.

45. Richard Hildreth, *The History of the United States, 1778–1821* (New York, 1880), 6, p. 95. Scharf, *Maryland,* 2, p. 631. *Maryland Gazette,* Dec. 8, 1808.

The Maryland Federalists, stronger than at any time since 1800, disclaimed all allegiance to New England's Essex Junto, a group of pro-British Federalists whose hatred for Jefferson was so strong that, a few years before, it had led them to plot secession and alliance with England. The composition of the two parties in the two localities was almost reversed. In Maryland the Federalists were led by the old planter class consisting of such distinguished men as Carroll of Carrollton, Robert Goodloe Harper, and John Eager Howard.

In contrast to New England merchants, who were anti-embargo Federalists, Maryland merchants, particularly those in Baltimore, were pro-embargo Republicans. The exception to the foregoing statement would be, of course, those merchants who served the planter class in their tobacco trade with England.

46. *American State Papers. Documents, Legislative and Executive of the Congress of the United States.* (Washington, 1832–61), 1, p. 725.

47. Ibid., I, p. 672. Figures in the tables consulted give the values for the entire state. The above estimates are based on the assumption that trade of individual ports is in ratio to their registered shipping, the latter being listed by towns. Whether this assumption is entirely correct or not is of no great importance since the purpose for which the figures are used above is primarily to show rates of increase and decrease.

48. Ibid., 1, pp. 672, 722.

49. Ibid., 1, p. 739.

50. Baltimore *Evening Post,* June 11, 1808.

51. Baltimore *Federal Republican and Commercial Gazette,* Aug. 22, 1808.

52. Ibid., Dec. 12, 1808.

53. Ibid., Aug. 28, 1808.

54. *Evening Post,* July 5, 1808.

55. Ibid., July 6, 1808.

56. Ibid., July 13, 1808.

57. Ibid., Aug. 14, 1808.

58. *American Register* (Philadelphia, 1808–1809), 5, p. 85.

59. *Annals,* 10th Congress, 2nd session, 2239.

60. Robert Smith to Gallatin, Aug. 1, 1808. Quoted in Adams, *History,* 4, p. 261.

61. *Annals,* 10th Congress, 2nd session, 35–39.

62. Ibid., 10th Congress, 2nd session, 138–61.

63. Ibid., 10th Congress, 2nd session, 35–161, *passim.,* especially 144–45.

64. *Federal Republican,* Jan 18, 1809.

65. Patterson to Nicholas, Dec. 1, 1808, and same to same May 11, 1808. Nicholas Mss.

66. Jefferson to William Branch Giles, Dec. 25, 1825. Ford (ed.), *Writings,* 10, pp. 353–54.

67. Jefferson to Thomas Mann Randolph, Feb. 7, 1809. Ibid., 9, p. 244.

68. Jefferson to General Henry Dearborn, July 16, 1810. Ibid., 9, p. 277. The two individuals referred to were Joseph Story and Ezekiel Bacon, both Massachusetts Republicans.

69. Nicholas to Jefferson, Oct. 20, 1808. Quoted in Adams, *History,* 4, p. 345.

70. Monroe to Nicholson, Sept. 24, 1808. Quoted in ibid., 4, p. 346.

71. *Federal Republican,* March 3, 1809.

72. For instance, Professor W. W. Jennings, in *The American Embargo, 1807–1809* (New York, 1921) refers to 39 New England newspapers as against 21 from all other sections (including two from Maryland) in his chapter entitled "Attitude of the United States Toward the Embargo." In the chapter "Growing Opposition to the Embargo Finally Forces Repeal" he uses 52 New England sources versus 23 from all other sections. Yet in 1807 New York alone exported more than all New England combined. The exports of Maryland, Virginia and the District of Columbia together totalled as much as New England. Even Professor Thomas Bailey, in his brief treatment of the subject in this *Diplomatic History* cites six New England sources as against two from other sections, although he points out that the "South and West, though probably even harder hit by losing the export market for their agricultural produce, complained the least" (p. 120). Cf., G. R. Taylor, "Agrarian Discontent in the Mississippi Valley Preceding the War of 1812," in the *Journal of Political Economy* Vol. 29 (1931).

73. *Annals,* 10th Congress, 2nd session, 354.

74. Nicholas to Jefferson, Dec. 12, 1809. Smith-Carter Mss. (copy).

75. Adams, *Gallatin,* p. 388.

76. Erskine to Canning, Nov. 5, 1808. Quoted in Adams, *History,* 4, pp. 384–85. Same to same, Dec. 4, 1808. Quoted in ibid., 4, pp. 387–88. Adams, *Gallatin,* p. 388.

77. Canning to Erskine, several despatches, January 23, 1809. Bernard Mayo, (ed.), *Instructions to British Ministers in the United States, 1791–1812, American Historical Association Annual Report for 1936,* 3 (Washington, 1941), pp. 261–267.

78. Smith-Erskine notes, April 17–19, 1809. *ASP FR,* 3, pp. 295–96.

79. Canning to Erskine, May 22 and 23, 1809. Mayo, *Instructions,* 270–76. Bradford Perkins, *Prologue to War: England and the United States, 1805–1812* (Berkeley, 1961), Chap. VI, especially pp. 211–13. William Pinkney to Robert Smith, June 23, 1809. *ASP FR,* 3, p. 203.

80. *Annals,* 11th Congress, 1st session, 608.

CHAPTER 7

1. Smith to George Clinton, May 9, 1809. Smith Mss.

2. Adams, *Gallatin,* p. 401. Gallatin to J. H. Nicholson, May 11, 1809. Nicholson Mss., Library of Congress. Raymond Walters, *Albert Gallatin: Jeffer-*

sonian Financier and Diplomat (New York, 1957), pp. 224–25. Smith to Gallatin, June 26, 1809. Adams, *Gallatin,* p. 402.

3. Gallatin to Smith, June 29, 1809. Adams, *Gallatin,* pp. 402–403.

4. Ibid., pp. 400–403.

5. Robert Smith to ____, March 12, 1811. Smith Mss. Duvall to S. Smith, June 26, 1809. Quoted in Tansill, "Robert Smith," *American Secretaries of State,* 3, p. 191.

6. James Boyd to James McHenry, Aug. 19, 1809. Quoted in Frank Cassell, "Samuel Smith: Merchant Politician, 1792–1812" (Unpublished Ph.D. dissertation, Northwestern University, 1968), p. 184.

7. Smith to Wilson Cary Nicholas, Jan. 13, 1810. Smith-Carter Mss.

8. *Annals,* 11th Congress, 1st session, 605.

9. Adams, *History,* 5, p. 197.

10. Robert Smith to Nicholas, June 11, 1810. Smith Mss.

11. Irving Brant, *James Madison: The President, 1809–1812* (Indianapolis, 1956), pp. 147–48 and note. Smith to Mrs. Mansfield (his daughter), Sept. 28, 1810. Smith-Carter Mss.

12. R. Smith, *Address to the People of Baltimore* (Baltimore, 1811).

13. *Annals,* 10th Congress, 2nd session, pp. 456–60, 615–72.

14. Smith to Madison, Aug. 8, 1810. Smith Mss.

15. *Annals,* 11th Congress, 3rd session, 243–68.

16. Richmond *Enquirer,* May 21, 1810.

17. James Madison, "Memorandum as to Robert Smith, Apl. 1811," *Letters and Other Writings . . . Published by Order of Congress* (Philadelphia, 1865), 2, p. 499. Cresson, *Monroe,* pp. 245–47. *National Intelligencer,* July 11, 1811.

18. Baltimore *American,* July 6, 1811. The reference to "his colleague . . . of eight years" refers to Robert Smith's tenure as Secretary of the Navy under Jefferson. The reference to the "few intriguers" obviously meant Samuel Smith and the "Invisibles."

19. Memorandum of Samuel Smith, May 16, 1811. Smith Mss. He concludes that his opposition to Madison was directly responsible for Robert Smith's dismissal.

20. For a more complete estimate of Robert Smith, see Tansill's sketch in *American Secretaries of State,* previously cited and George E. Davies, "Robert Smith and the Navy," *MHM,* 14 (1919), 305–22.

21. Madison, "Robert Smith," *Letters . . . of Madison,* 2, pp. 495–506.

22. Brant, *Madison: The President,* pp. 337, 341–43, 349, 364.

23. A. L. Burt, *The United States, Great Britain and British North America . . .* (New Haven, 1940), p. 275. Smith, *Address,* pp. 28–30. Perkins, *Prologue to War,* p. 213.

24. Brant, *Madison: The President,* pp. 270–71.

25. Ibid., pp. 280–87.

26. P. N. Nicholas to S. Smith, April 3, 1811. Smith Mss.

27. Attributed to Henry St. George Tucker by James Garnett in a letter to John Randolph, July 23, 1811. Quoted in Brant, *Madison: The President,* p. 305.

28. S. Smith to John S. Smith, March 24, 1811; John S. Smith to S. Smith, July 20, 1811. Smith Mss.

29. John Quincy Adams to S. Smith, July 7, 1809. Smith-Carter Mss. (copy). William Pinkney to John S. Smith, Nov. 11, 1811. Smith Mss. Adams, *History*, 4, p. 21.

30. Smith to Mrs. Mansfield, Oct. 25, 1811. Smith-Carter Mss. (copy).

31. Undated clipping, Baltimore *Sun*, Smith Mss. Smith to Mrs. Mansfield, June 14, 1811. Smith-Carter Mss. (copy).

32. Smith to Mrs. Mansfield, two undated letters, 1811. Smith-Carter Mss. (copies). Laura Smith to Mrs. Mansfield, Dec. 27, 1810; Smith to Mrs. Mansfield, Nov. 2, 1810. Smith-Carter Mss. Same to same, Nov. 6, 1811. Ibid. (copy).

33. *Democratic Press,* in the New York *Columbian,* Feb. 22, 1812. Quoted in Bernard Mayo, *Henry Clay, Spokesman for the New West* (Boston, 1937), p. 464.

34. Smith's Memorandum of March 31, 1812. Smith Mss. Perkins, *Prologue to War*, pp. 261–67. Norman Risjord, *The Old Republicans* (New York, 1935), pp. 120–27.

35. Mayo, *Clay,* 326ff. gives an excellent account of both frontier and eastern motives. See also Roger Brown, *The Republic in Peril* (New York, 1965), Chapter 6; and Reginald Horsman, *The Causes of the War of 1812* (Philadelphia, 1962), Chaps. 13 and 15.

36. Smith's Memo, March 31, 1811. Smith Mss.

37. S. Smith to Robert Smith, March 27, 1811. Smith Mss.

38. Smith to Mrs. Mansfield, Sept. 7, 1811. Smith-Carter Mss.

39. In 1810, during the period of the Non-Intercourse Act, Smith and Buchanan cleared over $200,000 despite the seizure of a number of their ships. Smith to Mrs. Mansfield, June 8, 1810. Smith-Carter Mss. (copy).

40. Scharf, *Maryland,* 3, pp. 3–24. Includes a number of documents, and accounts of the court proceedings. There were no convictions.

41. *Annals,* 12th Congress, 2nd session, 111.

42. Ibid., 12th Congress, 2nd session, 58–64.

43. Claude H. Van Tyne (ed.), *Letters of Daniel Webster* (New York, 1902), p. 36.

44. Smith had been appointed major general at the time of the Whiskey Rebellion in 1794. Scharf, *Maryland,* 2, p. 583.

CHAPTER 8

1. Adams, *History,* 8, p. 120.

2. Smith wrote to Governor Thomas Bowie on July 20, 1812, that the fort was in fair condition but that ammunition, guns, carriages and about $4,000 worth of repairs were necessary. Smith Mss.

3. State Council of Maryland to Smith, April 13; Wm. Pinkney to Smith March 29; Council to Smith, April 23, 1813. Ibid.

4. Smith to Armstrong, April 2, 1813. Ibid.

5. Scharf, *Maryland,* 3, pp. 41–44; pp. 48–51. Reports to Smith from

Walter Dorsey, April 12, 13; S. Ringgold, July 30; John Comigye, Aug. 7, 1813. Smith Mss.

6. Scharf, *Maryland*, 3, p. 99. Frederick M. Colston, "The Battle of North Point," *MHM*, 2 (1907), p. 112. *Niles' Weekly Register*, Hezekiah Niles, editor (Baltimore, 1811–1839), 4, p. 196 (May 22, 1813).

7. Ibid., 4, p. 166 (May 8, 1813); 4, p. 142 (May 1, 1813).

8. Smith to Gov. Levin Winder, March 12, 1813. Smith Mss. Scharf, *Maryland*, 3, p. 40.

9. *Niles' Register*, 4, p. 134 (April 24, 1813).

10. Gov. Winder to John Armstrong (Secretary of War), March 20 and May 26, 1813. Ibid., 4, p. 205.

11. Council to Smith, April 23 and 27, 1813. Smith Mss.

12. Scharf, *Maryland*, 3, pp. 44, 49. *Niles' Register*, 5, p. 286 (Sept. 3, 1813.

13. To William Jones, Aug. 27 and Sept. 1, 1813. Order Book, 3rd Division, Maryland Militia. Hereafter cited as O.B., 3rd Div. Smith Mss. *Niles' Register*, 4, p. 183 (May 15, 1813). Scharf, *Maryland*, 3, pp. 39n., 58.

14. Scharf, *Maryland*, 3, p. 918.

15. Smith to Generals Tobias Stansbury, C. Swearingen, and S. Ringgold, April 27, 1814; General Orders, Madison to Winder, forwarded to Smith, July 16, 1814, Smith to Army Hq., July 21, 1814; Smith to Armstrong, July 14 and 20, 1814. O.B., 3rd Div., Smith Mss.

16. Hulbert Footner, *Sailor of Fortune: The Life and Adventures of Commodore Joshua Barney, USN* (New York, 1940), Chap. 26.

17. The derisive poem titled "The Bladensburg Races" is quoted in Allen C. Clark, *Life and Letters of Dolly Madison* (Washington, 1914), pp. 177–84.

18. Neil Swanson, *The Perilous Fight* (New York, 1945), Chaps. VI and VIII.

19. Ibid., pp. 110–31, 134–47, *passim*. Cf., Footner, *Sailor of Fortune*, pp. 282–84.

20. General Orders, July 31, 1814; Rodgers to Smith, Aug. 8, 1814; Monroe to Smith, Aug. 2, 1814. O. B., 3rd Div., Smith Mss. Colston, "The Battle of North Point," *MHM*, 2, 113. Swanson, *The Perilous Fight*, p. 284. But Scharf says 12,000, *Maryland*, 3, p. 125.

21. Charles Oscar Paullin, *Commodore John Rodgers* (Cleveland, 1910), p. 289. See also reports of Perry, Porter and Rodgers to the Navy Department published in *Niles' Register*, 7, pp. 33–37 (Oct. 1, 1814).

22. Monroe to Smith, Sept. 2, 1814; Daniel Parker (Chief Clerk of the War Department) to Smith, ____, 1814; Winder to Smith, Aug. 26, 1814. Gov. Winder to Smith, Aug. 26, 1814. Smith Mss.

23. Resolution of the Committee of Safety, Aug. 25, 1814. Ibid. Gov. L. Winder to Gen. W. Winder, Aug. 27, 1814. Quoted in Ralph Robinson, "Controversy over the Command at Baltimore," *MHM*, 39 (1944), 181.

24. Daniel Parker to Smith ____, 1814. Parker added a note of his own: "I hope Colonel Monroe may not form your order of battle." Smith Mss. Monroe had taken over the War Department after Bladensburg in addition

to his duties as Secretary of State. Robinson, "Controversy over Command," *MHM*, 39, 183–84. Monroe to Smith, Sept. 2, 1814. Smith Mss.

25. Winder to Monroe, Sept. 4, 1814. Robinson, "Controversy over Command," *MHM*, 39, p. 187.

26. Rodgers' Report, Sept. 23, 1814. *Niles' Register*, 7, p. 156 (suppl.). Paullin, *Rodgers*, pp. 172, 290.

27. Smith to Gen. W. Winder, July 30, 1814; to Wadsworth, Aug. 4, 1814. O.B., 3rd Div., Smith Mss. Edmund Kimball Alden, "George Armistead," *DAB*, 1, 346. Scharf, *Maryland*, 3, p. 25. Swanson, *The Perilous Fight*, Chap. 5, *passim*, pp. 75–80. John Stricker, Jr., "John Stricker," *MHM*, 9 (1914) pp. 209–211. Swanson, *The Perilous Fight*, p. 296. Paullin, *Rodgers*, p. 286.

28. Smith's Orders, July 27 to Sept. 3, 1814, *passim*. O.B., 3rd Div., Smith Mss. Swanson, *The Perilous Fight*, p. 275. Captain James Piper to Brantz Mayer, April 17, 1854. Published uder the title, "The Defence of Baltimore," *MHM*, 7, (1912), 380.

29. Major W. B. Barney to Smith, Aug. 28—Sept. 7, 1814; Statement of Michael MacNamara, deserter from the 85th Regiment of Foot, Aug. 31, 1814; Capt. Gresham, "confidential agent," to Smith, Aug. 31, 1814. Smith Mss.

30. Patapsco River and the Approaches, under the direction of F. R. Hassler and A. D. Bache, Coastal Survey Office (Washington, 1859). James Kearny, Sketch of the military topography of Baltimore.... Made by Order of Br. Gen. Winder, 1814. Maryland Room, Enoch Pratt Library, Baltimore, Md.

31. Ralph Robinson, "New Light on Three Episodes of the British Invasion of Maryland in 1814," *MHM*, 37 (1942), pp. 287–89.

32. Smith to the Committee of Safety, Aug. 6, 1814; Babcock to Smith, Aug. 6, 1814. O.B., 3rd Div., Smith Mss. Order of the Committee of Safety, *Niles' Register*, 6, p. 448 (Aug. 27, 1814). Colston, "The Battle of North Point," *MHM*, 2, p. 112.

CHAPTER 9

1. Smith's Report to Monroe, Sept. 19, 1814. *Niles' Register*, 7, p. 27 (Sept. 24, 1814).

2. Stricker's Report to Smith, Sept. 15, 1814. Ibid., p. 127 (Oct. 2, 1814).

3. George Robert Gleig, *Narrative of the Campaigns of the British Army at Washington and New Orleans* (London, 1821), p. 174. Colston, "Battle of North Point," *MHM*, 2, 115.

4. Stricker's Report, *Niles' Register*, 7, p. 127 (Oct. 2, 1814). Gleig, *Narrative*, 180. Cockburn's Report to Cochrane, Sept. 15, 1814. *Niles' Register*, 7, p. 160 (suppl.).

5. The exception is Swanson, *The Perilous Fight*, pp. 425–29. Gleig, *Narrative*, p. 180. Adams, *History*, 7, pp. 170–71. Cockburn said the American line broke "soon." (Cockburn's Report, *Niles' Register*, 7, p. 160, suppl.) But if Stricker's report is accepted, the American line held about an hour and a half after the bombardment ceased and the British advance began. This

seems reasonable since Cockburn's Report says that the British finally halted because of approaching darkness, and the Americans made their camp for the night only about a mile from the scene of the battle. Allowing for possible errors and conflicts in reports, it seems probable that the British took about an hour for artillery preparation fire and disposing their forces for the assault. Since the reports are agreed that the opening fire was delivered about two or two thirty in the afternoon the Americans must have held the British in check for the rest of the afternoon. Any "pursuit" by the British could only have been half-hearted and token.

6. Smith's Report, *Niles' Register*, 7, p. 27 (Sept. 24, 1814).

7. Colston, "The Battle of North Point," *MHM*, 2, 118. Swanson, *The Perilous Fight*, p. 429. Adams says the British casualties totalled 319. *History*, 8, p. 170

8. Cockburn's Report, *Niles' Register*, 7, p. 160 (suppl.). Scharf, *Maryland*, 3, p. 101.

9. Swanson, *The Perilous Fight*, pp. 436–37.

10. Armistead's Report to the Secretary of War, Sept. 24, 1814. *Niles' Register*, 7, p. 40 (Oct. 1, 1814). Swanson, *The Perilous Fight*, pp. 460–62.

11. Swanson, *The Perilous Fight*, p. 464. Armistead's Report. *Niles' Register*, 7, p. 40 (Oct. 1, 1814).

12. Piper, "Defence of Baltimore," *MHM*, 7, p. 384. Armistead's Report. *Niles' Register*, 7, p. 40 (Oct. 1, 1814). William James, *The Naval History of Great Britain* (London, 1902), 6, p. 191.

13. Smith's Report. *Niles' Register*, 7, p. 27 (Sept. 24, 1814)

14. Stricker's Report. Ibid., p. 127 (Oct. 2, 1814). Smith's Report. Ibid., p. 27 (Sept. 24, 1814). Colston, "The Battle of North Point," *MHM*. 2, 119. Gleig, *Narrative*, pp. 187–88. Swanson, *The Perilous Fight*, p. 447.

15. Smith's Report, *Niles' Register*, 7, p. 27 (Sept. 24, 1814). Stricker's Report. Ibid., 7, p. 127 (Oct. 2, 1814). Gleig, *Narrative*, p. 188.

16. "Disastrous" is the word used by the British historian, James. *Naval History*, 6, p. 192. Ibid., p. 187. Benson J. Lossing, *Pictorial Field Book of the War of 1812* (New York, 1869), p. 954. Alfred T. Mahan, *Sea Power in its Relations to the War of 1812* (New York, 1905), p. 350. Swanson is the exception. *The Perilous Fight*, p. 463–66.

17. Gleig, *Narrative*, p. 188–89.

18. James, *Naval History*, 6, p. 191.

19. Diary of Lt. M. E. Bartgis, Maryland Room, Peabody Museum, Baltimore, Md.

20. James, *Naval History*, 6, p. 191–92. Armistead's Report, *Niles' Register*, 7, p. 40 (Oct. 1, 1814). Rodgers' Report, Ibid., 7, p. 156 (suppl.). [Anonymous, probably Robert Gleig], *A Subaltern in America* (London, 1817), p. 158. Gleig, *Narrative*, p. 193.

21. Smith's Report, *Niles' Register*, 7, p. 27 (Sept. 24, 1814).

22. Donnan (ed.) *Papers of James A. Bayard*, 2, p. 348. Henry Clay, *Life and Speeches*, edited by Greely and McElrath (New York, 1843), 1, p. 243.

23. The "Star-Spangled Banner" was published in the *Maryland Gazette*,

Oct. 3, 1814. See also Caleb Clark Magruder, "Dr. William Beanes, The Incidental Cause of the Star-Spangled Banner," *Records of the Columbia Historical Society* (Washington, D.C.), 22 (1919), 207–25. Swanson, *The Perilous Fight,* Chap. 27.

CHAPTER 10

1. Scharf, *Maryland,* 3, p. 142. Niles, *Register,* 9, p. 404 (Feb. 3, 1816). He received 2500 votes to 100 for his opponent, Petter Little.

2. *Annals,* 14th Congress, 1st session, 15.

3. Ibid., 13th Congress, 3rd session, 126, 214. Adams, *Memoirs,* 4, p. 36. *Annals,* 14th Congress, 1st session, 1074–1075.

4. *Annals,* 14th Congress, 1st session, 1073. Adams, *History,* 9, pp. 116–18. Ralph C. H. Catterall, *The Second Bank of the United States* (Chicago, 1903), pp. 16–21.

5. *Annals,* 14th Congress, 1st session, 16. Ibid., 14th Congress, 1st session, 16. Bruce, *Randolph,* 1, p. 427. C. M. Wiltse, *John C. Calhoun, Nationalist* (New York, 1944) 1, pp. 110–11.

6. *Annals,* 14th Congress, 1st session, 687. Adams, *History,* 9, pp. 112–13.

7. Sam Smith to Mrs. Mansfield, June 6, 1822. Same to same, May 3, 1823. Smith-Carter Mss. (copy). Correspondence between John Spear Smith and Robert Carter Nicholas July and Aug., 1822. Smith-Carter Mss.

8. Edward Stanwood, *American Tariff Controversies in the Nineteenth Century* (Boston and New York, 1904), 1, p. 139.

9. *Annals,* 14th Congress, 1st session, 842, 1870–71, 1351, 1313–314.

10. *National Intelligencer,* March 19, 1816. Crawford to Gallatin, May 10, 1816. Henry Adams (ed.), *Writings of Gallatin,* 1, p. 702. Wiltse, *Calhoun,* p. 115. John Bach McMaster, *History of the People of the United States* (New York, 1895), 4, pp. 363–64.

11. Richardson (ed.), *Messages and Papers,* 1, p. 567.

12. *Annals,* 14th Congress, 2nd session, 851–58, 881–83.

13. Ibid., 14th Congress, 2nd session, 915, 934. Richardson (ed.), *Messages and Papers,* 1, pp. 584–85.

14. George Morgan, *Life of James Monroe* (Boston, 1921), p. 365. Adams to J. S. Smith, Sept. 26, 1817. Smith-Carter Mss.

15. Monroe to Jefferson, Feb. 23, 1817. Hamilton (ed.), *Writings,* 6, pp. 2–4. Thomas Hart Clay, *Life of Henry Clay* (New York, 1910), p. 75.

16. *Annals,* 15th Congress, 1st session, 1406 ff, 1424–429, 1474, 1538, 1605–638.

17. John Mansfield to Smith, May 29, 1818. Smith-Carter Mss. (copy). Smith to Mrs. Mansfield, July 21, 1818. Ibid. (copy).

18. Catterall, *The Second Bank,* pp. 27–28.

19. *American State Papers, Finance,* 3, p. 353. James C. Fisher to Rufus King, January 11, 1819. *Life and Correspondence of Rufus King,* edited by Charles R. King (New York, 1894–1900), 6, p. 150. Catterall, *Second Bank,* pp. 30–38.

20. *Baltimore Losses and Conspiracy Cases. An Exhibit of Losses Sustained at the Office of Discount and Deposit, Baltimore* (Baltimore, 1823), pp. 97–99.

21. Ibid., pp. 91–92, 119, 129–30, 193–94. Smith's inactivity in company

affairs is indicated by a letter to Mrs. E. Thompson, June 12, 1815, apparently in reply to her request for a position for her nephew in the firm. Smith wrote that he had "persuaded Mr. Buchanan to receive him into our counting house." Smith Mss.

22. Smith to John Mansfield, July 29, 1818 and to Mrs. Mansfield, Aug. 8, 1818. Smith-Carter Mss. (copies). Catterall, *Second Bank*, p. 50. John Quincy Adams, *Memoirs*, 4, pp. 383–84.

23. Smith to John Purviance, May 10, 1819. Smith-Carter Mss. Undated copy of report of "Committee of the Bank." Smith Mss.

24. Smith to Mrs. Mansfield, June 6, 1822. Smith-Carter Mss. (copy). Didier, *Life and Letters of Madam Bonaparte*, p. 142. Smith to Mrs. Mansfield, Nov. 12, 1822. Smith-Carter Mss. (copy).

25. Deed of S. Smith to John Spear Smith, Sept. 27, 1820; Smith to Mrs. Mansfield, Nov. 12, 1822. Smith-Carter Mss. (copies). Hughes served as charge d'affairs for Sweden and Denmark under President Jackson but his mediocre ability kept him from attaining a high position in the diplomatic service.

26. Crawford to Smith, June 11, 1819. Smith Mss. Crawford observed that he was highly gratified at the "detachment and philosophical attitude" of Smith toward his losses. Smith to Mrs. Mansfield, Nov. 13, 1822. Smith-Carter Mss. (copy). Nicholas Biddle to Smith, June 25, 1834; Smith to Thomas Ellicott, Jan. 24, 1824. Smith Mss. Smith to Mrs. Mansfield, June 6, 1824. Smith-Carter Mss. (copy).

27. Crawford to Smith, June 11, 1819. Smith Mss. Crawford to Gallatin, Oct. 14, 1819. Adams, *Writings of Gallatin*, 2, p. 142. Smith to Mrs. Mansfield, Nov. 13, 1822. Smith-Carter Mss. (copy).

CHAPTER 11

1. Adams, *Diary*, 5, p. 57.

2. Ibid., 5, p. 20. For the facts of Crawford's career to this time, John E. D. Shipp, *Giant Days or the Life and Time of William H. Crawford* (American, 1909) and Ulrich B. Phillips, "William H. Crawford," *DAB*, 4, 527–29.

3. Quoted in Frederick Jackson Turner, *The Rise of the New West* (New York, 1909), p. 178. The preceding sketch of Adams is based on the excellent one by Turner, pp. 177–80.

4. Adam Hodgson, *Letters from North America* (London, 1824), 1, p. 81.

5. Smith to Mrs. Mansfield, April 28, 1825. Smith-Carter Mss. (copy).

6. Broadus Mitchell, "Stevenson Archer," *DAB*, 1, 342. Robert E. Moody, "John Chandler," ibid., 3, 613–14; Fletcher M. Green, "George Michael Troup," ibid., 18, 650.

7. *Annals*, 15th Congress, 2nd session, 1435–438, *passim*.

8. Ibid., 16th Congress, 1st session, 2, 1576–577. William Plumer, Jr., *The Missouri Compromises and the Presidential Election of 1824*, edited by Everett Somerville Brown (St. Louis, 1926), pp. 3–16, *passim*.

9. *Annals*, 16th Congress, 1st session, 1, 941–42.

10. William Plumer, Jr., *The Missouri Compromises*, p. 16.

11. Adams, *Diary,* 5, p. 4.

12. Turner, *The New West,* p. 193.

13. Plumer, *Missouri Compromises,* p. 16.

14. Carl Russell Fish, in *Civil Service and Patronage* (Cambridge, 1920), pp. 66–70, thinks Crawford was justified, and did not use the act to create a political machine. Adams (*Diary,* 5, p. 143) thought Crawford guilty of using patronage as a political weapon.

15. *Annals,* 16th Congress, 1st session, 2, 1615 ff.

16. Adams, *Diary,* 5, p. 58.

17. Ibid., 5, p. 304.

18. *National Intelligencer,* April 9, 1820.

19. Adams, *Diary,* 5, p. 121.

20. Crawford to Smith, July 19, 1820, Smith Mss.

21. *Annals,* 16th Congress, 2nd session, 437–38.

22. Ibid., 16th Congress, 2nd session, 903.

23. Plumer, *Missouri Compromise,* p. 43.

24. Ibid., p. 77.

25. Adams, *Diary,* 5, pp. 20–21.

26. Jackson to James Gadsden, Dec. 6, 1821. John Spencer Bassett, *Correspondence of Andrew Jackson* (Washington, 1929), 3, p. 140.

27. Adams, *Diary,* 5, pp. 20–21.

28. Ibid., p. 315.

29. *Annals,* 19th Congress, 1st session, 2. Ibid., 17th Congress, 1st session, 1625–632.

30. Adams, *Diary,* 5, p. 525.

31. Ibid., 5, p. 534.

32. Crawford to Gallatin, May 5, 1822. Adams, *Correspondence of Gallatin,* 2, pp. 242, 243.

33. William Penn Cresson, *James Monroe* (Chapel Hill, 1946), p. 457.

34. Marquis James, *The Life of Andrew Jackson* (New York, 1938), pp. 345–46.

Chapter 12

1. Smith to Mrs. Mansfield, Nov. 12, 1822. Smith-Carter Mss.

2. John Spear Smith to Robert Carter Nicholas, Aug. 12, 1822 and Sept. 16, 1822. Smith Mss.

3. Smith to Mrs. Mansfield, Nov. 12, 1822. Smith-Carter Mss.

4. Same to same, March 11, 1823. Ibid.

5. *Annals,* 17th Congress, 2nd session, 92–93.

6. Very few of Smith's letters were found but correspondence is indicated by letters from Crawford men, during entire period, 1820–1824, to Smith: e.g., Van Buren to Smith, Aug. 7, 1824; Josiah Randall to Smith, June 9, 1824; Jesse B. Thomas to Smith, June 3, 1823; Stevenson Archer to Smith, undated, 1823. Smith Mss.

7. Jefferson to Smith, May 3, 1823. Lipscomb and Bergh (eds.), *Writings of Jefferson,* 15, pp. 431–33.

8. *Washington Gazette,* Nov. 4, 1823.

9. *Baltimore American,* June 27, 1823.

10. *Gazette,* July 23, 1823.

11. Series in the *Gazette,* July 5, 15, Sept. 11, 12, and 13, 1823. A rough draft of an undated, unfinished article titled "To the editor from A Friend to Truth," written in Smith's hand is in the Smith Mss. In 1829 Virgil Maxey wrote to Calhoun, "You may recollect that . . . when Crawford, Gen. Smith's favorite, was in the field, I had occasion to answer some pieces written by Gen. Smith. . . ." April 9, 1829 in "Letters to John C. Calhoun," ed. J. Franklin Jameson, *American Historical Association Report for 1899,* 2, p. 795. The "chief" referred to was Secretary of War Calhoun.

12. *Gazette,* July 15, 1823.

13. Ibid., July 9, 1823.

14. Charles H. Ambler, *Thomas Ritchie, A Study in Politics in Virginia* (Richmond, 1913), pp. 85–92.

15. Martin Van Buren, "Autobiography," edited by John C. Fitzpatrick, *American Historical Association Report for 1918,* pp. 142–48. C. H. Rammelkampf, "Election of 1824 in New York," ibid., *Report for 1904,* 178–85. Van Buren to Smith, Aug. 7, 1824. Smith Mss.

16. Smith to Stevenson Archer, undated, 1823. Smith Mss.

17. Curtis Griswold Garrison, The National Election of 1824, unpublished dissertation presented to the faculty of the Johns Hopkins University for the Ph.D. requirement (1928), 15ff.

18. John Clark, *Considerations on the Principles of William H. Crawford* (Augusta, 1823), *passim.*

19. Crawford to Gallatin, Feb. 28, 1823. Adams, *Gallatin,* p. 585.

20. Crawford to Gallatin, May 26, 1823. Ibid., pp. 585–90.

21. *National Intelligencer,* Dec. 13, 1823.

22. *Gazette,* June 28, 1823. Smith to Mrs. Mansfield, July 25, 1823. Smith-Carter Mss. (copy). Joseph B. Cobb, *Leisure Labors* (New York, 1858), p. 212.

23. *Gazette,* Oct. 17, 1823, in which Crawford's health was reported as "in a fair way of being reestablished." But the paper did not report Crawford's return to the Treasury offices until April, 1824.

24. *Annals,* 18th Congress, 1st session, 591–614, *passim;* 702–10.

25. Ibid., 18th Congress, 1st session, 741–43.

26. Ibid., 17th Congress, 2nd session, 200, 227, 290. *Senate Journal,* 17th Congress, 144, 150.

27. *Annals,* 17th Congress, 1st session, 1, 556–70.

28. Ibid., 18th Congress, 1st session, 1, 149.

29. Ibid., 18th Congress, 1st session, 1, 218.

30. Ibid., 18th Congress, 1st session, 1, 225.

31. *Baltimore Patriot,* June 19, 1823. *Niles' Register,* 25, p. 225 (Dec. 13, 1823), p. 249 (Dec. 20, 1823). *Gazette,* Feb. 4, 1824. Madison refused to endorse any candidate, but he expressed a fear of the trend toward loose construction of the Constitution. Madison to Henry Lee, June 25, 1824. *Works.,* 3, p. 442.

32. Printed in *Niles' Register,* 25, p. 263 (Dec. 27, 1823), p. 384 (Feb. 14, 1824).

33. I can find no specific statement from Smith, but Edward Lloyd's letter, *Niles' Register,* 25, pp. 291–92 (Jan. 10, 1824) expresses this sentiment and indicates that it was the opinion shared by four pro-caucus Maryland Congressmen. Smith later expressed similar sentiments on the Senate floor. *Annals,* 18th Congress, 1st session, 80–84.

34. *National Intelligencer,* Feb. 16, 1824. *Niles' Register,* 25, pp. 388–93. (Feb. 21, 1824), p. 407 (Feb. 28, 1824).

35. *Baltimore Patriot,* Feb. 16, 1824.

36. Ibid., Feb. 21, 1824.

37. *Annals,* 18th Congress, 1st session, 1, 360–61, 395.

38. William Plumer, Jr. to William Plumer, April 20, 1824. *Missouri Compromises,* pp. 108–10.

39. Herman Halperin, "Pro-Jackson Sentiment in Pennsylvania," *Pennsylvania Magazine of History,* 50, 193–209. James, *Jackson,* pp. 364–91, *passim.*

40. Smith to his grandson, July 16, 1824. Smith-Carter Mss. (copy).

41. Ibid., Oct. 18, 1824.

42. Van Buren to Smith, Nov. 17, 1824. Smith Mss. Van Buren was here alluding to the coalition of Clay's supporters, led by Peter B. Porter, with the Adams men. Realizing that Clay had little chance of being elected, the coalition voted for Adams. When word of the intention of the Clay men became known, many Crawford men deserted and only four Crawford electors were chosen. Van Buren, "Autobiography," *American Historical Association Report for 1918,* 2, 145.

43. Cobb, *Leisure Labors,* p. 218.

44. Crawford to Smith, Nov. 13, 1824. Smith Mss. Smith to Mrs. Mansfield, Nov. 16, 1824. Smith-Carter Mss.

45. Smith to his gradson, Nov. 16, 1824. Ibid., (copy).

46. Gallatin to Walter Lowrie, Oct. 2, 1824. Adams, *Gallatin,* p. 604. See also Albert Ray Newsome, *The Presidential Election of 1824 in North Carolina* (Chapel Hill, 1939), pp. 106, 107. Cobb, *Leisure Labors,* p. 209. James, *Jackson,* p. 407.

47. *Niles' Register,* 27, p. 382 (Feb. 12, 1825).

48. Plumer to his father, April 1, 1824. Plumer, *Missouri Compromises,* p. 109.

49. Smith to Mrs. Mansfield, April 28, 1825. Smith-Carter Mss. (copy).

50. Smith to Crawford, Nov. 1, 1828. Smith Mss.

Chapter 13

1. The reason for the large gap between 40c and $2.50 was because the value of goods mostly manufactured in the U. S. mills sold at about $1.00 per yard. The gap was necessary to prevent fraudulent valuations which would place imported woolens in the lower brackets for purposes of escaping high duty.

2. *Register of Debates,* 3, 885.

3. Ibid., 4, part 1, 1274.

4. Frank W. Taussig, *The Tariff History of the United States* (New York, 1892), p. 101n.

5. Attributed to Smith by Webster, *Register of Debates,* 4, part 1, 756.

6. *Ibid.,* 4, part 1, 786.

7. Smith to Calhoun, July 5, 1828. Smith Mss.

8. Calhoun to Smith, July 28, 1828. Ibid.

9. *Register of Debates,* 5, 52.

10. Ibid., 6, part 1, 428.

11. Ibid., 8, part 1, 68.

12. Ibid., 8, part 1, 189.

13. *Debates in Congress,* 8, part 1, 298.

14. *Statutes at Large of South Carolina,* edited by Thomas Cooper and D. J. McCord (Columbia, 1836), 1, p. 329.

15. *Debates in Congress,* 9, part 1, 473–75.

16. Thomas H. Benton of Missouri afterwards asserted that an out-of-doors compromise was effected between the Clay and Calhoun wings and that Josiah Johnston, Senator from Louisiana, circulated the story that unless Calhoun agreed to the compromise, Jackson intended to arrest him for treason. The final compromise was that the manufacturing interests agreed to lower the duty if the Southerners would admit the constitutionality of the bill by voting for it. Whether it was true that Jackson intended to take such action or even that Johnston circulated such a story, Smith evidently believed, from the tone and words of his speech, that something of the sort had taken place. Thomas Hart Benton, *Thirty Years View* (New York, 1854), pp. 342–43.

17. F. Lee Benns, *The American Struggle for the West Indian Carrying Trade, 1815–1830* (Bloomington, Indiana, 1923), pp. 26–33.

18. Ibid., pp. 34–35.

19. *Annals,* 14th Congress, 1st session, 920.

20. *ASP, FR,* 4, pp. 381–82.

21. Ibid., 382.

22. Benns, *West Indian Trade,* pp. 65–67.

23. *Public Statutes at Large of the United States of America* (Boston, 1845), 3, pp. 602–604.

24. Petition of Jamaica Assembly for relief, printed in *Niles' Register,* 22, pp. 56–57 (March 23, 1822).

25. *Annals,* 17th Congress, 1st session, 2, 1305. Petition in *Niles' Register,* 22, p. 23 (March 9, 1823).

26. *ASP, FR,* 4, pp. 231–36.

27. Ibid., 214.

28. *Public Statutes,* 3, pp. 740–42.

29. Benton, *Thirty Years View,* 1, pp. 125–26.

30. *Register of Debates,* 3, 406.

31. Benns, *West Indian Trade,* p. 103.

32. *ASP FR,* 6, pp. 301–306.

33. Smith to Clay, July 24, 1825. Smith Mss.

34. Smith to Adams, Feb. 14, 1826. Ibid.

35. Smith to Clay, Feb. 2, 1826. Ibid.

36. Smith to Clay, Feb. 2, 1826; Clay to Smith, Nov. 10, 1825. Ibid.

37. *Register of Debates*, 2, part 1, 577, 589–90. *Niles' Register*, 32, p. 70 (March 24, 1827).

38. The British Ministry instructed the collector in Halifax not to close the port to American ships until specifically ordered to do so. Benns, *West Indian Trade*, p. 115.

39. *ASP, FR*, 6, pp. 262, 249, 333–334

40. *American Statesman and City Register* (Boston), Dec. 16, 1826. Quoted in Benns, *West Indian Trade*, p. 135.

41. Richardson, *Messages and Papers*, 2, p. 355.

42. *Register of Debates*, 3, 399–402.

43. Ibid., 3, 409–412.

44. Ibid., 3, 403–1501. The Act of 1818 prohibited trade between U.S. and British West Indian ports in British vessels; that of 1820 extended this to all British-American ports; that of 1823 opened the ports of the U.S. on a reciprocal basis for enumerated goods coming directly from the country where produced.

45. Ibid., 3, 1501–507, 1514–531.

46. *Richmond Enquirer*, March 20, 1827.

47. *ASP, FR*, 6, pp. 977–78.

48. McLane to Smith, May 13, 1829. Smith Mss. Same to same, Oct. 29, 1829. Ibid. Same to same, March 6, 1830. Ibid.

49. Benton, *Thirty Years View*, 1, p. 128.

50. *Senate Documents*, 21st Congress, 2nd session, 1, No. 20., 60–61.

51. Van Buren to Smith (undated). Smith Mss.

CHAPTER 14

1. Catterall, *Second Bank*, 182–85. Cf., John Spencer Basset's note in *Correspondence of Andrew Jackson*, 4, p. 97.

2. Catterall, *Second Bank*, pp. 190–200, *passim*.

3. Ibid., p. 200.

4. *Register of Debates*, 6, part 2, 103.

5. Samuel R. Gammon, Jr., *The Presidential Election of 1832* (Baltimore, 1922), p. 117.

6. Smith to Biddle, Dec. 7, 1831. Quoted in Catterall, *Second Bank*, p. 219n.

7. Smith to John Spear Smith, Dec. 24, 1831. Smith Mss. Catterall, *Second Bank*, pp. 217–19, *passim*.

8. Smith to Biddle, Jan 6, 1832. Catterall, *Second Bank*, p. 221.

9. *Register of Debates*, 8, part 1, 1042.

10. Smith to Jackson, June 17, 1832. Smith Mss.

11. Van Buren, *Autobiography*, p. 625.

12. Richardson, *Messages and Papers*, 2, p. 577.

13. *Niles' Register,* 48, pp. 415–16 (Aug. 25, 1835).

14. Scharf, *Chronicles,* pp. 497–98. *Niles' Register,* 56, pp. 129–30 (April 27, 1839).

Bibliography

PRIMARY SOURCES

Manuscripts

Baltimore Independent Cadets, Muster Roll. Maryland Historical Society, Baltimore.
Bartgis, M. E. Diary. Maryland Room, Enoch Pratt Library, Baltimore.
Nicholas, Wilson Cary. Library of Congress
Nicholas, Wilson Cary. University of Virginia
Nicholson, Joseph Hopper. Library of Congress.
Smith-Carter. Alderman Library, University of Virginia, Charlottesville, Va.
Smith and Company Letterbook. Maryland Historical Society, Baltimore.
Samuel Smith. Maryland Historical Society, Baltimore.
Robert Smith. Maryland Historical Society, Baltimore.
Samuel Smith. Library of Congress.
Otho Holland Williams. Maryland Historical Society, Baltimore

Newspapers

Annapolis *Maryland Gazette*.
Baltimore *American*.
Baltimore *Evening Post*.
Baltimore *Federal Gazette and Daily Advertiser*.
Baltimore *Federal Republican*.
Baltimore *Federal Republican and Commercial Gazette*
Baltimore *Patriot*.
Baltimore *Sun*.
New York *Columbian*.
Niles' Weekly Register. Edited by Hezekiah Niles.
Richmond *Enquirer*.
Washington, D. C. *Federalist*.
Washington, D. C. *Gazette*.
Washington, D. C. *National Intelligencer*.

Public Documents

American State Papers. Documents, Legislative and Executive of the Congress of the United States. 38 volumes. Washington, 1836–61.
Annals of Congress. Debates and Proceedings in the Congress of the United States, 1789–1824. 42 volumes. Washington, 1834–56.

Archives of Maryland: Journals and Corrspondence of the State Council of Maryland. Edited by W. H. Brown, C. C. Hall, B. C. Steiner and Raphael Semmes. 63 volumes. Baltimore, 1884–1946.

Congressional Globe, Containing Debates and Proceedings, 1833–1873. 109 volumes. Washington, 1834–73.

Debates on the Adoption of the Federal Constitution. Edited by Jonathan Elliot. 6 volumes. Philadelphia, 1901.

Journals of the American Congress from 1774 to 1778. 34 volumes. Washington, 1904–1937.

Maryland General Assembly Proceedings, 1791–1796. Annapolis, 1797.

Messages and Papers of the Presidents, 1789–1897. Compiled by J. D. Richardson. 10 volumes. Washington, 1897–1907.

The Parliamentary Debates, published under the supervision of Thomas Curzon Hansard. 1st series, volume X. 1808

Public Statutes at Large of the United States of America from the Organization of the Government in 1789 to March 3, 1845. 8 volumes. Boston, 1845–51.

Register of Debates in Congress, Comprising the Leading Debates and Incidents of the Second Session of the Eighteenth Congress to the First Session of the Twenty-Sixth Congress. 14 volumes. Washington, 1825–37.

Statutes at Large of South Carolina. Edited by Thomas Cooper and D. J. McCord. 10 volumes. Columbia, 1836–41.

Votes and Proceedings of the House of Delegates of the State of Maryland, 1790–96. Annapolis, 1797.

Writings of Contemporaries

Adams, John. *Works.* Edited by Charles Francis Adams. 10 volumes. Boston, 1856.

Adams, John Quincy. *Memoirs, Comprising Parts of His Diary from 1795 to 1848.* Edited by Charles Francis Adams. 12 volumes. Philadelphia, 1874–77.

Baltimore City Directory for 1832.

Baltimore Losses and Conspiracy Cases. An Exhibit of Losses Sustained at the Office of Discount and Deposit, Baltimore. Edited and printed by ___ Murphy. Baltimore, 1823.

Benton, Thomas Hart. *A Thirty Years' View.* New York, 1854.

Bayard, James A. *Correspondence.* Edited by Elizabeth Donnan. *American Historical Association Report for 1913,* Vol. 2. Washington, 1915.

Clark, John. *Considerations on the Principles of William H. Crawford.* Augusta, 1832.

Clay, Henry. *Life and Speeches.* Edited by Greely and McElrath. 2 volumes. New York, 1843.

Cobb, Jospeh B. *Leisure Labors.* New York, 1858

Correspondence of the American Revolution: Being Letters of Eminent Men to George Washington. Edited by Jared Sparks. 4. volumes. Washington, 1853.

Gallatin, Albert. *Writings.* Edited by Henry Adams. 3 volumes. Philadelphia, 1879.

Gleig, George Robert. *Narrative of the Campaigns of the Brisith Army at Washington and New Orleans.* London, 1821.

———. *A Subaltern in America*. [Probably Gleig]. London, 1817.

Graydon, Alexander, *Memoirs of His Own Time*. Philadelphia, 1846.

Hamilton, Alexander. *Works*. Edited by John C. Hamilton. 7 volumes. New York, 1851.

———. *Works*. Edited by Henry Cabot Lodge. 12 volumes. New York, 1904.

Hunter, Robert, Jr. *Quebec to Carolina in 1785–1786*. Edited by Louis B. Wright and Marion Tinling. San Marino, 1943.

Hodgson, Adam. *Letters from America*. London, 1824.

Jackson, Andrew. *Correspondence*. Edited by John Spencer Bassett. 7 volumes. Washington, 1926–35.

Jefferson, Thomas. *Writings*. Edited by Paul Leicester Ford. 10 volumes. New York, 1892–99.

———. *Writings*. Edited by Alfred A. Lipscomb and A. L. Bergh. 20 volumes. Washington, 1903.

King, Rufus. *Life and Correspondence of Rufus King*. Edited by Charles R. King. 10 volumes. New York, 1894–99.

Lee, Charles. "Papers." *Collections of the New York Historical Society*, Vols. 4–7. New York, 1871–74.

"Letters to John C. Calhoun." Edited by John Franklin Jameson. *American Historical Association Report for 1899*, Vol. 2. Washington, 1901.

Mayo, Bernard. *Instructions to British Ministers in the United States, 1791–1812*. *American Historical Association Report for 1936*, Vol. 3. Washington, 1941.

Madison, James. *Letters and Other Writings . . . Published by Order of Congress*. 4 volumes. Washington, 1865.

———. *Writings*. Edited by Gaillard Hunt. 9 volumes. New York, 1900–10.

Plumer, William. *Memorandum of the Proceedings of the United States Senate, 1803–1807*. Edited by Everett Somerville Brown. New York, 1923.

Plumer, William, Jr. *The Missouri Compromise and the Presidential Election of 1824*. Edited by Everett Somerville Brown. St. Louis, 1926.

St. Memin, Fevret de. *A Collection of Portraits*. London, 1862.

Smith, Robert. *Address to the People of Baltimore*. Baltimore, 1811.

Smith, Samuel. "The Defence of Fort Mifflin." *Maryland Historical Magazine*, Vol 5 (1910), 211–228. Letters from Smith to Washington during the defense of Fort Mifflin, Sept. 27 to Nov. 11, 1777.

———. "The Papers of General Smith." *Historical Magazine*, XVII (1870), 81–93. Submitted to the editor by John Spear Smith with the notation that it had been prepared "from General Smith's papers." The article itself is a biographical sketch.

Stephens, James. *War in Disguise: or, The Frauds of the Neutral Flags*. London, 1805.

Van Buren, Martin. "Autobiography." Edited by John C. Fitzpatrick. *American Historical Association Report for 1918*, Vol. 2. Washington, 1921.

Washington, George. *Writings*. Edited by John C. Fitzpatrick. 39 volumes. Washington, 1931–40.

———. *Writings.* Edited by Worthington C. Ford. 14 volumes. New York, 1889–93.
———. *Writings.* Edited by Jared Sparks. 10 volumes. Boston, 1839.
Webster, Daniel. *Letters.* Edited by Claude H. Van Tyne. Boston, 1902.

SECONDARY SOURCES

Books

Adams, Henry. *History of the United States During the Administrations of Thomas Jefferson and James Madison.* 9 volumes. New York, 1889–91.
———. *Life of Albert Gallatin.* New York, 1879. Rev. ed., 1943.
———. *John Randolph.* Boston, 1883.
Allen, Gardner W. *A Naval History of the Revolution.* 2 volumes. New York, 1913.
———. *Our Navy and the Barbary Corsairs.* Boston, 1905.
Ambler, Charles H. *Thomas Ritchie: A Study in the Politics of Virginia.* Richmond, 1913.
Anderson, Dice Robbins. *William Branch Giles: A Study in the Politics of Virginia and the Nation from 1790 to 1830.* Menasha, Wisconsin, 1914.
Bailey, Thomas A. *A Diplomatic History of the American People.* New York, 1947.
Baldwin, Leland. *The Whiskey Rebels.* Pittsburg, 1939.
Barker, Charles Albro. *Background of the Revolution in Maryland.* New Haven, 1940.
Bemis, Samuel Flagg. *Jay's Treaty: A Study in Commerce and Diplomacy.* New York, 1923.
———. Ed. *The American Secretaries of State and Their Diplomacy.* 10 volumes. New York, 1927–29. See individual entries under "Articles."
Benns, F. Lee. *The American Struggle for the West Indian Carrying Trade, 1815-1830.* Bloomington, Indiana, 1923.
Beveridge, Albert. *Life of John Marshall.* 4 volumes. Boston, 1916–1919.
Bowers, Claude. *Jefferson in Power.* Boston, 1936.
Brown, Roger. *The Republic in Peril: 1812.* New York, 1965.
Brant, Irving. *James Madison: Father of the Constitution, 1787–1800.* Indianapolis, 1950.
———. *James Madison: Secretary of State, 1801–1809.* Indianapolis, 1953.
———. *James Madison: The President, 1809–1812.* Indianapolis, 1956.
———. *James Madison: The Commander-in-Chief, 1812–1836.* Indianapolis, 1961.
Burt, A. L. *The United States, Great Britain and British North America.* New Haven, 1940.
Canby, Henry Seidel. *The Brandywine.* New York, 1941.
Cassell, Frank. *Samuel Smith: Merchant-Politician.* Unpublished Ph.D. dissertation, Northwestern University, 1968.

———. *Merchant Congressman in the New Republic: Samuel Smith of Baltimore, 1752–1839*. Madison, Wisc., 1971.

Catterall, Ralph C. H. *The Second Bank of the United States*. Chicago, 1903.

Chappelle, Howard I. *American Sailing Ships*. New York, 1935.

Channing, Edward. *History of the United States*. 6 volumes. New York, 1905–25.

Charles, Joseph. *Origins of the American Party System*. Williamsburg, 1951.

Clark, Allen C. *Life and Letters of Dolly Madison*. Washington, 1914.

Clay, Thomas Hart. *Life of Henry Clay*. New York, 1910

Cresson, William P. *Life of James Monroe*. New York, 1946

Crowl, Philip A. *Maryland During and After the Revolution*. Johns Hopkins *Studies in Historical and Political Science*. 61st series, 1943.

Davis, Matthew L. *Memoirs of Aaron Burr With Miscellaneous Selections from His Correspondence*. 2 volumes. New York, 1836–37.

Didier, Eugene L. *Life and Letters of Madame Bonaparte*. New York, 1879.

Fish, Carl Russell. *The Civil Service and the Patronage*. Cambridge, 1920.

Fisher, Sydney George. *The Struggle for American Independence*. 2 volumes. Philadelphia, 1908.

Footner, Hurlburt. *Sailor of Fortune: The Life and Adventures of Commodore Joshua Barney, USN*. New York, 1940.

Freeman, Douglas Southall. *George Washington: A Biography*. 7 volumes. New York, 1948–51.

Fuller, Herbert Bruce. *The Florida Purchase*. Cleveland, 1906.

Gammon, Samuel R. Jr. *The Presidential Election of 1832*. Baltimore, 1922.

Govan, Thomas P. *Nicholas Biddle: Nationalist and Public Banker*. Chicago, 1959.

Griswold, Curtis Garrison. The National Election of 1824. Unpublished Ph.D. dissertation, Johns Hopkins University, 1928.

Hildreth, Richard, *History of the United States, 1788–1821*. 6 volumes. New York, 1849–56.

Horsman, Reginald. *The Causes of the War of 1812*. Philadelphia, 1962.

Irwin, R. W. *The Diplomatic Relations of the United States with the Barbary Powers, 1776–1816*. Chapel Hill, 1931.

James, Marquis. *Life of Andrew Jackson*. New York, 1938.

James, William. *The Naval History of Great Britain*. 6 volumes. New edition, London, 1902.

Jensen, Merrill. *The New Nation: A History of the United States, 1781–1789*. New York, 1950.

———. *The Founding of the Nation*. New York, 1968.

Jennings, William W. *The American Embargo, 1807–1809*. New York, 1921.

Kennedy, John P. *At Home and Abroad*. New York, 1872.

Lossing, Benson J. *A Pictorial Field Book of the War of 1812*. New York, 1868.

Lynch, W. O. *Fifty Years of Party Warfare*. Indianapolis, 1931.

McLaughlin, J. Fairfax. *Matthew Lyon, the Hampden of Congress*. New York, 1900.

McMaster, John Bach. *A History of the People of the United States from the Revolution to the Civil War*. 8 volumes. New York, 1883–1913.

Mahan, Alfred T. *Sea Power in Its Relations to the War of 1812*. New York, 1905.

Malone, Dumas, and Allen Johnson. *The Dictionary of American Biography,* 21 volumes and supplements. New York, 1928–37.

Malone, Dumas. Vol. 1. *Jefferson and His Time*

———. Vol. 2. *Jefferson and The Rights of Man.* Boston, 1951.

———. Vol. 3. *Jefferson and the Ordeal of Liberty.* Boston, 1962.

———. Vol. 4. *Jefferson the President: First Term.* Boston, 1970.

Mayo, Bernard. *Henry Clay: Spokesman for the New West.* Boston, 1937.

Miller, John C. *Alexander Hamilton: Portrait in Paradox.* New York, 1959.

Morgan, George. *Life of James Monroe.* Boston, 1921.

Newsome, Albert Ray. *The Presidential Election of 1924 in North Carolina.* Chapel Hill, 1939.

Owens, Hamilton. *Baltimore on the Chesapeake.* New York, 1941.

Parmet, Herbert, and Hecht, Marie B. *Aaron Burr, Portrait of an Ambitious Man.* New York, 1967.

Parton, James. *Life and Times of Aaron Burr.* 2 volumes. New York, 1884.

Paullin, Charles O. *Commodore John Rodgers.* Cleveland, 1910.

Perkins, Bradford. *Prologue to War: England and the United States, 1805–1812.* Berkeley, 1961.

Peterson, Merrill. *Thomas Jefferson and The New Nation.* New York, 1970.

Pratt, Julius. *The Expansionists of 1812.* New York, 1925.

Randall, Henry Stephens. *Life of Thomas Jefferson.* 3 volumes. New York, 1871.

Risjord, Norman. *The Old Republicans: Southern Conservatives in the Age of Jefferson.* New York, 1965.

Rowland, Kate Mason. *Life of Charles Carroll of Carrollton.* 2 volumes, New York, 1898.

Rutter, Frank Roy. *The South American Trade of Baltimore.* Johns Hopkins *Studies in Historical and Political Science,* 15th series, 1897.

Schachner, Nathan. *Aaron Burr, A Biography.* New York, 1937.

———. *Alexander Hamilton.* New York, 1946.

Scharf, John Thomas. *Chronicles of Baltimore.* Baltimore, 1874.

———. *History of Maryland from Its Earliest Beginnings to the Present Day.* 3 volumes. Baltimore, 1879.

Schouler, James. *History of the United States under the Constitution.* 7 volumes. New York, 1880–1913.

Sears, Louis Martin. *Jefferson and the Embargo.* Durham, 1927.

Shipp, Joseph E. D. *Giant Days, or the Life and Time of William H. Crawford.* Americus, Ga., 1909.

Smith, Ellen Hart. *Charles Carroll of Carrollton.* Cambridge, 1943.

Steiner, Bernard C. *Life and Correspondence of James McHenry.* Cleveland, 1907.

Story, William. *Life of Joseph Story.* 2 volumes. Boston, 1851.

Sullivan, Katharine. *Maryland and France.* Philadelphia, 1936.

Swanson, Neil. *The Perilous Fight.* New York, 1945

Stanwood, Edward. *American Tariff Controversies in the Nineteenth Century.* 2 volumes. New York, 1904.

Tansill, Charles C. *The United States and Santo Domingo, 1798–1873.* Baltimore, 1938.

Taussig, Frank W. *The Tariff History of the United States.* New York, 1892.
Turner, Frederick Jackson. *The Rise of the New West.* New York, 1909.
Van Deusen, Glyndon G. *Life of Henry Clay.* Boston, 1937.
Van Tyne, Claude Halstead. *The American Revolution.* New York, 1905.
Walters, Raymond, *Albert Gallatin: Jeffersonian Financier.* New York, 1957.
Wandell, Samuel, and Meade Minnegerode. *Aaron Burr.* 2 volumes. New York, 1925.
Ward, Christopher. *The War of the Revolution.* 2 volumes. New York, 1952.
Whitaker, Arthur P. *The Mississippi Question, 1795–1803: A Study in Trade, Politics and Diplomacy.* New York, 1934.
Wiltse, Charles M. *John C. Calhoun: Nationalist, 1782–1828.* New York, 1944.
———. *John C. Calhoun: Nullifier, 1829–1839.* New York, 1949.
Zimmerman, J. F. *Impressment of American Seamen.* New York, 1925.

Articles

Abernethy, Thomas P. "George Nicholas." *Dictionary of American Biography,* Vol. 13, 482–83.
Alden, Edmund Kimball. "George Armistead." *Dictionary of American Biography,* Vol. 1, 346
Anderson, Dice Robbins. "The Insurgents of 1811." *American Historical Association Annual Report for 1911,* Vol. 1, 167–76.
Colston, Frederick M. "The Battle of North Point." *Maryland Historical Magazine,* Vol. 2 (1907), 111–25.
Corwin, Edward S. "Samuel Chase." *Dictionary of American Biography,* Vol. 4, 34–37.
Closen, Baron de. "French Troops in Maryland." *Maryland Historical Magazine,* Vol. 5 (1910), 229–32.
Davies, George E. "Robert Smith and the Navy." *Maryland Historical Magazine,* Vol. 14 (1919), 305–32.
Delaplaine, Edward S. "Luther Martin." *Dictionary of American Biography,* Vol. 12, 343–45.
Fowler, Lawrence Hall. "Montebello." *Architectural Review,* November, 1909, 146–49.
Govan, Thomas P. "The Rich, The Well-Born, and Alexander Hamilton." *Mississippi Valley Historical Review,* Vol. 36 (1950), 675–81.
Green, Fletcher M. "Robert Troup." *Dictionary of American Biography,* Vol. 18, 650–51.
Halperin, Herman. "Pro-Jackson Sentiment in Pennsylvania." *Pennsylvania Magazine of History,* Vol. 50 (1936), 193–209.
Hill, Charles. "James Madison." *The American Secretaries of State and their Diplomacy,* edited by Samuel Flagg Bemis, Vol. 3, 3–150.
Kenyon, Cecelia. "Alexander Hamilton: Rousseau of the Right." *Political Science Quarterly,* Vol. 63 (1958), 161–78.
Magruder, Caleb Clark. "Dr. William Beanes, The Incidental Cause of the Authorship of the Star-Spangled Banner." *Records of the Columbia Historical Society,* Vol. 22 (1919), 207–25.

Manning, W. R. "The Nootka Sound Controversey." *Annual Report of* the American Historical Society for 1904, 279–478.

Mitchell, Broadus. "Stevenson Archer." *Dictionary of American Biography,* Vol. 1, 342.

Moody, Robert E. "John Chandler." *Dictionary of American Biography,* Vol. 3, 613–14.

Phillips, Ulrich B. "William Harris Crawford." *Dictionary of American Biography,* Vol. 4, 527–29.

Piper, James. "The Defence of Baltimore." *Maryland Historical Magazine,* Vol. 7, 375–84.

Rammelkampf, C. H. "The Election of 1824 in New York." *American Historical Association Annual Report for 1918,* 178–85.

Robinson, Ralph. "Controversy over the Command at Baltimore." *Maryland Historical Magazine,* Vol. 39 (1944), 181–87.

––––––. "New Light on Three Episodes of the British Invasion of Maryland in 1814." *Maryland Historical Magazine,* Vol. 37 (1942), 287–89.

Steiner, Bernard C. "Maryland's Adoption of the Federal Constitution." *American Historical Review,* Vol. 5 (1899), 22–44.

––––––. "Maryland Politics in 1798 from the Correspondence of Dr. James McHenry, Secretary of War." *Publications of the Southern Historical Association,* Vol. 10 (1906), 101–106.

Stricker, John, Jr. "General John Stricker." *Maryland Historical Magazine,* Vol. 9 (1914), 209–18.

Tansill, Charles C. "Robert Smith." *The American Secretaries of State and Their Diplomacy,* edited by Samuel Flagg Bemis, Vol. 3, 151–200.

Taylor, George R. "Agrarian Discontent in the Mississippi Valley, Preceding the War of 1812." *Journal of Political Economy,* Vol. 29 (1931), 471–505.

Williams, Mary Wilhelmine. "Robert Smith." *Dictionary of American Biography,* Vol. 17, 337–38.

Index

DATE DUE
